The Battle for the Keys

Revelation 1:18 and Christ's Descent into the Underworld

PATERNOSTER BIBLICAL MONOGRAPHS

The Battle for the Keys

Revelation 1:18 and Christ's Descent into the Underworld

Justin W. Bass

WIPF & STOCK · Eugene, Oregon

Wipf and Stock Publishers
199 W 8th Ave, Suite 3
Eugene, OR 97401

The Battle for the Keys
Revelation 1:18 and Christ's Descent into the Underworld
By Bass, Justin
Copyright©2014 Paternoster
ISBN 13: 978-1-62564-839-6
Publication date 4/15/2014
Previously published by Paternoster, 2014

to Allison,
the love of my life

PATERNOSTER BIBLICAL MONOGRAPHS

Series Preface

One of the major objectives of Paternoster is to serve biblical scholarship by providing a channel for the publication of theses and other monographs of high quality at affordable prices. Paternoster stands within the broad evangelical tradition of Christianity. Our authors would describe themselves as Christians who recognise the authority of the Bible, maintain the centrality of the gospel message and assent to the classical creedal statements of the Christian belief. There is diversity within this constituency; advances in scholarship are possible only if there is freedom for frank debate on controversial issues and for the publication of new and sometimes provocative proposals. What is offered in this series is the best of writing by committed Christians who are concerned to develop well-founded biblical scholarship in a spirit of loyalty to the historic faith.

Series editors

I. Howard Marshall, Honorary Research Professor of New Testament, University of Aberdeen, Scotland, UK

Robert P. Gordon, Regius Professor of Hebrew, University of Cambridge, UK

Tremper Longmann III, Robert H. Gundry Professor and Chair of the Department of Biblical Studies, Westmont College, Santa Barbara, California, USA

Stanley E. Porter, President and Professor of New Testament, McMaster Divinity College, Hamilton, Ontario, Canada

CONTENTS

ACKNOWLEDGEMENTS

This book could not have been accomplished without the help of my professors, family and friends. I would like to specifically thank all my readers, Hall Harris III, Buist Fanning, Michael Svigel, Richard Taylor, for their penetrating insights and helpful criticism throughout this process. Dr. Hall Harris has been my advisor since I began the PhD program at Dallas Theological Seminary. I could not have completed this program successfully without his continuous, loving care and support. It has been such a blessing to have a supportive family and loving friends who have prayed for me throughout this process.

In addition, my wife Allison is truly a woman of excellence (Prov 31:10; Ruth 3:11) and is the reason I am the man I am. I am so thankful God gave her to me over thirteen years ago. It is impossible to describe how much she has supported, helped and loved me through these years at DTS in order that I could finish well. Lastly, my daughter Arianna was born two weeks after I finished the Comprehensive exams. She gave me great joy in the middle of the PhD program when many could run out of steam. I would like to thank my daughter Arianna for constantly bringing joy into my life

I entrust this work I have done to the hands of the Lord. May this book be used to exalt the Son to the glory of the Father.

Justin Bass
2013

ABBREVIATIONS

Primary Sources

Acts of Phil.	*Acts of Philip*
Acts Thom.	*Acts of Thomas*
Adv. Prax.	*Against Praxeas*
Aen.	*Aeneid*
Ag. Ap.	*Against Apion*
Ag.	*Agamemnon*
Aj.	*Ajax*
Alc.	*Alcestis*
An.	*The Soul*
Andr.	*Andromache*
Ant.	*Jewish Antiquities*
Antichr.	*De antichristo*
Apoc. Ab.	*Apocalypse of Abraham*
Apoc. Adam	*Apocalypse of Adam*
Apoc. Dan.	*Apocalypse of Daniel*
Apoc. El. (C)	*Coptic Apocalypse of Elijah*
Apoc. Mos.	*Apocalypse of Moses*
Apoc. Paul	*Apocalypse of Paul*
Apoc. Peter	*Apocalypse of Peter*
Apoc. Sedr.	*Apocalypse of Sedrach*
Apoc. Thom.	*Apocalypse of Thomas*
Apoc. Zeph.	*Apocalypse of Zephaniah*
(Apocr.) Ep. Tit.	*Aprocryphal Epistle of Titus*
Apocr. Ezek.	*Apocryphal Ezekiel*
1 Apol.	*First Apology*
As. Mos.	*Assumption of Moses*
[Ax.]	*Axiochus*
Bar	Baruch
Barn.	*Barnabus*
2 Bar.	*2 Baruch (Syriac Apocalypse)*
3 Bar.	*3 Baruch (Greek Apocalypse)*
4 Bar.	*4 Baruch (Paraleipomena Jeremiou)*
Bel	Bel and the Dragon
C. Ar.	*Orations against the Arians*
Cels.	*Against Celsus*
Cho.	*Libation-Bearers*
Civ.	*The City of God*
1–2 Clem.	*1–2 Clement*
Comm. Matt.	*Commentarium in evangelium Matthaei*
Comm. Jo.	*Commentarii in evangelium Joannis*
Comm. Rom.	*Commentarii in Romanos*

[Cons. Apoll.]	*Consolatio ad Apollonium*
Crat.	*Cratylus*
Cycl.	*Cyclops*
Dem. ev.	*Demonstration of the Gospel*
Dial.	*Dialogue with Trypho*
Diogn.	*Epistle of Diognetus*
El.	*Electra*
1 En.	*1 Enoch (Ethiopic Apocalypse)*
2 En.	*2 Enoch (Slavonic Apocalypse)*
3 En.	*3 Enoch (Hebrew Apocalypse)*
Epid.	*Demonstration of the Apostolic Preaching*
Ep. Apos.	*Epistle to the Apostles*
Ep. Epict.	*Letter to Epictetus*
Eum.	*Eumenides*
Eutrop.	*In Eutropium*
Exc.	*Excerpts from Theodotus*
Expl. Dan.	*Explanatio in Danielem*
Exp. Luc.	*Expositio Evangelii secundum Lucam*
4 Ezra	*4 Ezra*
5 Ezra	*5 Ezra*
Fid.	*De fide*
Fr. Luc.	*Fragmenta in Lucam*
Frm. of Papias	*Fragments* of Papias
Gen. imp.	*On the Literal Interpretation of Genesis: An Unfinished Book*
Gk. Apoc. Ezra	*Greek Apocalypse of Ezra*
Gorg.	*Gorgias*
Gos. Nic.	*Gospel of Nicodemus*
Gos. Pet.	*Gospel of Peter*
Gos. Truth	*Gospel of Truth*
Great Pow.	*Concept of Our Great Power*
Haer.	*Against Heresies*
Hec.	*Hecuba*
Hel. Syn. Pr.	*Hellenistic Synagogal Prayers*
Heracl.	*Children of Hercules*
Herc. fur.	*Madness of Hercules*
Herm. Sim.	*Shepherd of Hermas, Similtude(s)*
Herm. Vis.	*Shepherd of Hermas, Vision(s)*
Hipp.	*Hippolytus*
Hist. eccl.	*Ecclesiastical History*
Hist. Rech.	*History of the Rechabites*
Hom. Matt.	*Homiliae in Matthaeum*
Hom. Exod.	*Homiliae in Exodum*
Hom. Gen.	*Homiliae in Genesim*
Hom. Lev.	*Homiliae in Leviticum*
Hom. 1 Cor.	*Homiliae in epistulam i ad Corinthios*

Hom. 1 Reg.	*Homiliae in I Reges*
Ign. *Eph.*	Ignatius, *To the Ephesians*
Ign. *Magn.*	Ignatius, *To the Magnesians*
Ign. *Philad.*	Ignatius, *To the Philadelphians*
Ign. *Trall.*	Ignatius, *To the Trallians*
Il.	*Iliad*
Inst.	*The Divine Institutes*
Jdt	Judith
Jos. Asen.	*Joseph and Aseneth*
Jub.	*Jubilees*
J. W.	*Jewish War*
L.A.B.	*Liber antiquitatum biblicarum* (Pseudo-Philo)
L.A.E.	*Life of Adam and Eve*
Let. Aris.	*Letter of Aristeas*
Liv. Pro.	*Lives of the Prophets*
Luct.	*Funerals*
1–2 Macc	1–2 Maccabees
3 Macc.	*3 Maccabees*
4 Macc.	*4 Maccabees*
Mart. Ascen. Isa.	*Martyrdom and Ascension of Isaiah*
Men.	*Menippus, or Descent into Hades*
Odes Sol.	*Odes of Solomon*
Od.	*Odyssey*
Ol.	*Olympian Odes*
Paed.	*Christ the Educator*
Pan.	*Refutation of All Heresies*
Paraph. Shem.	*Paraphrase of Shem*
Phaed.	*Phaedo*
Philops.	*The Lover of Flies*
Pol. *Phil.*	Polycarp, *To the Philippians*
Praem.	*De Praemiis et Poenis*
Pr Man	Prayer of Manasseh
Princ.	*De principiis*
Ps.-Phoc	Pseudo Phocylides
Pss. Sol.	*Psalms of Solomon*
Pyr.	*Outlines of Pyrrhonism*
Ques. Bart.	*Questions of Bartholomew*
Ques. Ezra	*Questions of Ezra*
Res.	*The Resurrection of the Flesh*
Sacr.	*De sacrificiis Abelis et Caini*
Sg Three	Song of the Three Young Men
Sib. Or.	*Sibylline Oracles*
Sir	Sirach/Ecclesiasticus
Stat.	*Ad populum Antiochenum de statuis*
Strom.	*Miscellanies*
Sus	Susanna

Syn.	*On the Councils of Ariminum and Seleucia*
Syr. Men.	*Sentences of the Syriac Menander*
Teach. Silv.	*Teachings of Silvanus*
T. 12 Patr.	*Testaments of the Twelve Patriarchs*
T. Ab.	*Testament of Abraham*
T. Adam	*Testament of Adam*
T. Dan.	*Testament of Daniel*
T. Isaac	*Testament of Isaac*
T. Jac.	*Testament of Jacob*
T. Job	*Testament of Job*
T. Jos.	*Testament of Joseph*
T. Sol.	*Testament of Solomon*
Test.	*To Quirinius: Testimonies against the Jews*
Test. Truth	*Testimony of Truth*
Theog.	*Theogony*
Thes.	*Theseus*
Thom. Cont.	*Book of Thomas the Contender*
Tim.	*Timaeus*
Tob	Tobit
Trim. Prot.	*Trimorphic Protennoia*
Trin.	*The Trinity*
Tri. Trac.	*Tripartite Tractate*
Univ.	*De universo*
Ver. His.	*A True Story*
Wis	Wisdom of Solomon

Secondary Sources

AB	Anchor Bible
ABD	*Anchor Bible Dictionary*
ACNT	Augsburg Commentary on the New Testament
AER	*American Ecclesiastical Review*
AJP	*American Journal of Philology*
ANET	*Ancient Near Eastern Texts*
AR	*Andover Review*
AFR	*Archiv für Religionswissenschaft*
ATANT	*Abhandlungen zur Theologie des Alten und Neuen Testaments*
BDAG	Danker, F. W., W. Bauer, W. F. Arndt, and F. W. Gingrich. *Greek-English Lexicon of the New Testament and Other Early Christian Literature.* 3d ed. Chicago, 2000
BECNT	Baker Exegetical Commentary on the New Testament
BSac	*Bibliotheca sacra*
BNTC	Black's New Testament Commentaries

BST	Bible Speaks Today
BTCB	Brazos Theological Commentary on the Bible
CBQ	*Catholic Biblical Quarterly*
CCCS	Concordia Classic Commentary Series
CS	*Chicago Studies*
CurrTM	*Currents in Theology and Mission*
EDBT	*Evangelical Dictionary of Biblical Theology*
EDT	*Evangelical Dictionary of Theology*
ERE	*Encyclopedia of Religion and Ethics*
ETL	*Ephemerides theologicae lovanienses*
ExpTim	*Expository Times*
GRBS	*Greek-Roman and Byzantine Studies*
HNTC	Harper's New Testament Commentaries
IB	*Interpreter's Bible*
IBS	*Irish Bible Studies*
ICC	International Critical Commentary
ISBE	*International Standard Bible Encyclopedia*
JBL	*Journal of Biblical Literature*
JETS	*Journal of the Evangelical Theological Society*
JHI	*Journal of the History of Ideas*
MNTC	Moffat New Testament Commentary
NAC	New American Commentary
NCE	*New Catholic Encyclopedia*
NCBC	New Century Bible Commentary
NIBC	New International Biblical Commentary
NIDNTT	*New International Dictionary of New Testament Theology*
NIDOTTE	*New International Dictionary of Old Testament Theology and Exegesis*
NICNT	New International Commentary on the New Testament
NICOT	New International Commentary on the Old Testament
NIGTC	New International Greek Testament Commentary
NIVAC	New International Version Application Commentary
NKZ	*Neue kirchliche Zeitschrift*
NTC	New Testament Commentary
NTS	*New Testament Studies*
Nov Test	*Novum Testamentum*
PNTC	Pillar New Testament Commentary
RevExp	*Review and Expositor*
RL	*Religion in Life*
RTR	*Reformed Theological Review*
SJT	*Scottish Journal of Theology*
TDNT	*Theological Dictionary of the New Testament*
TDOT	*Theological Dictionary of the Old Testament*

THNTC	Two Horizons New Testament Commentary
TNTC	Tyndale New Testament Commentaries
TS	*Theological Studies*
TWOT	*Theological Word Book of the Old Testament*
USQR	*Union Seminary Quarterly Review*
VC	*Vigilae christianae*
WBC	Word Biblical Commentary
WLQ	*Wisconsin Lutheran Quarterly*
WTJ	*Westminster Theological Journal*
ZAW	*Zeitschrift für die alttestamentliche Wissenschaft*
ZCS	Zondervan Commentary Series
ZECNT	Zondervan Exegetical Commentary on the New Testament

CHAPTER 1

INTRODUCTION

St. Augustine forcefully asked in the fifth century, "Who, therefore, but an infidel will deny that Christ was in hell?"[1] Bishop Ussher said in the seventeenth century of the doctrine of Christ's descent that it has the "universal consent of Christians" and is acknowledged by all to be of "undoubted verity."[2] Yet, in the late twentieth century, theologian Wayne Grudem wrote an article entitled "Christ Did Not Descend into Hell."[3] What occurred that brought about such a radical change of beliefs concerning Christ's descent? According to Kelly, the first to deny the doctrine of the *Descensus* was Reginald Pecock (AD 1395–1460), Bishop of St. Asaph.[4] However, under closer examination this does not seem to be the case or at least cannot be proven definitively. Brockwell says of Bishop Pecock, "Doctor Pecock's criticism extended even to the Apostles' Creed and the Decalogue. . . . His own version of the Creed omitted the article of the descent into hell."[5]

Brockwell goes on to say that "We do, however, learn that Pecock made this deletion for historical, rather than theological reasons."[6] Therefore, I believe this is premature of Kelly to say Bishop Pecock outright denied the *Descensus* when he may have only believed it did not belong in the creed for historical reasons. Brockwell notes that we do not even have Pecock's discussion of the creed extant.[7] It seems highly unlikely that a Bishop of the fifteenth century would have placed himself in direct opposition to the fifteen centuries before

---

[1] *Ep.* 164.

[2] J. Ussher, "Limbus Patrum and Christ's Descent into Hell," in *Ussher's Works*, vol. 3 (London: Hodges and Smith, 1847), 604-605, 607.

[3] W.A. Grudem, "He Did Not Descend into Hell: A Plea for Following Scripture Instead of the Apostles' Creed," *JETS* 34 (March 1991): 103-13.

[4] J.N.D. Kelly, *Early Christian Creeds*, 3rd ed. (London: Longman, 1972), 5.

[5] W.C. Brockwell, *Bishop Reginald Pecock and the Lancastrian Church: Securing the Foundations of Cultural Authority*, Texts and Studies in Religion, vol. 25 (Queenston, Ontario: Edwin Mellen Press, 1985), 61.

[6] Brockwell, *Bishop Reginald Pecock*, 139, 203.

[7] Brockwell, *Bishop Reginald Pecock*, 61.

him in regards to this doctrine.[8] In short, it should not be said that Pecock was the first to deny this doctrine, but instead that he is the first to delete it from the Apostles' Creed for historical, not theological reasons. If Bishop Pecock was not the first to deny Christ's descent from Scripture, then the Reformer Martin Bucer (1491–1551) may have been (see below).

I would like to define from the outset what I mean by the phrases *Descensus ad inferos* and/or the doctrine of Christ's descent referenced throughout. I believe I am in line with the New Testament and the first few centuries of the church, when I define this doctrine as the belief that Jesus Christ, between his death and resurrection, by means of his soul, descended into the underworld in triumph for purposes that at least in the NT, are open for debate. In the second century, the threefold purpose of Christ's journey to the underworld are already defined as a preaching tour, releasing the saints of the Old Testament, and a triumphant defeat of Death and Hades. It is the third purpose that I believe is in the background of Revelation 1:18 and the primary thesis of this book. In short, the doctrine of the descent at minimum assumes that Christ descended into the underworld between his death and resurrection and should be understood this way when it is used throughout this book. Whether or not the threefold purpose of Christ's journey to the underworld can be found in the NT will depend on the exegesis and theological arguments of the NT passages discussed in this book.

In the Introduction of this book (Chapter 1), I will give a brief survey of Early Church Fathers from Ignatius to the Reformer Martin Bucer demonstrating that there was unanimous consent on the *Descensus* for the first fifteen centuries of church history. I will also briefly look at the Apostles' Creed and how the phrase *descendit ad inferna* was later added to it. Everyone who wrote on the subject of the *Descensus* (that we have extant) believed that between his death and resurrection, Christ descended in his soul to the spirits of the dead in the underworld. To be clear, beginning with Ignatius and moving into the middle ages, there were widely diverse beliefs on what Christ accomplished at his descent, but *that Christ descended in his soul to the underworld* there was "universal consent."[9]

I believe this ancient and widespread teaching on the *Descensus* is very important for the interpretation of the New Testament and specifically for Revelation 1:18. Many of the Apostolic Fathers and writers such as Ignatius, Polycarp, Hermas, Justin Martyr, Irenaeus, Melito and others wrote within the

---

8 Bishop Ussher did not believe Bishop Pecock denied the *Descensus* according to his quote above. Also, Cardinal Bellarmine (AD 1541–1621) a century or so after Pecock says, "All agree, that Christ did some manner of way descend into hell."

9 This is the very language used by Archbishop Parker in AD 1562 at a Synod on whether to delete the phrase *descendit ad inferna* from the Apostles' Creed. He said that the *Descensus* has the support of the "universal consent of the Fathers of both churches." J. Muenscher, "The Descent of Christ into Hell," *Bib Sac* 16 (1859): 330-31.

era of the book of Revelation (AD 96)[10] or one to two generations removed from that era. All of these writers understood the *Descensus* as the beginning of Christ's triumph and most make reference to Christ preaching to and releasing the righteous dead of the Old Testament. This creates a strong historical argument, since they are from the same cultural milieu as the audience (and author) of Revelation, that this is what the original readers of Revelation may have understood in Revelation 1:18 and other passages in the NT. On the other hand, this historical argument does not conclusively prove that the *Descensus* is taught in Revelation 1:18 or anywhere else in the NT. However, it does point to the fact that a similar descent tradition was known at the time of the writing of the book of Revelation. It further places a significant burden of proof on writers such as Martin Bucer so far removed from this worldview who would deny that this doctrine is found in Scripture (when everyone found it there before him!). What other Christian doctrine was universally believed by the church for fifteen centuries and now is rejected by Christians today?

Chapter 2 of this book will examine a survey of Death and Hades personified from the Greco-Roman world, the Old Testament, Second Temple Jewish Literature, and from the New Testament where Death and Hades meet their end. The main purpose of this chapter will be to show that throughout the ancient literature Death and Hades are personified frequently and this is the background of Revelation 1:18. Chapter 3 will deal with a survey of various key holders to the underworld in antiquity and what "keys" represent in the six NT passages where they are found (Matt 16:19; Luke 11:52; Rev 1:18; 3:7; 9:1; 20:1). I are exploring the significance of Death and Hades personified and the keys that Christ now possesses because the only time period where this transfer of the keys could have taken place was during Christ's descent between his death and resurrection.[11]

Other NT passages will be discussed, but Revelation 1:18 is our primary text to be exegetically and theologically analyzed for this monograph. Thus far, this text has been referenced in support of the *Descensus* by the ancient Fathers and recent NT commentators, but there is not one book, dissertation or ancient treatment on this verse. The most recent exhaustive treatments on the

---

[10] Irenaeus *Haer.* 5.30.3; Victorinus of Pettau *Apoc.* 10.11; Eusebius *His. Eccl.* 3.17–18 all attest to Revelation being written towards the latter reign of Domitian (AD 81–96). Most modern commentators on Revelation also favor the later date. See discussion and references in G.K. Beale, *The Book of Revelation: A Commentary on the Greek Text*, NIGTC, ed. I.H. Marshall and D.A. Hagner (Grand Rapids: Eerdmans, 1999), 4-27.

[11] Even though this language is metaphorical and symbolic, there is a reality behind it that is being communicated. Therefore, the two options for when this transfer of the keys took place is between Christ's death and resurrection or sometime after his resurrection. I will argue in this work that in light of Death and Hades being the referent (Rev 1:18), the *Descensus* is the primary background.

Descensus are from Kroll (1932),[12] Bieder (1949),[13] and MacCulloch (1930).[14] I hope to supplement and update these three works, especially in our focus on Revelation 1:18 as another passage in the NT teaching Christ's descent to the underworld and his activity there. In addition, there are many works that deal with various aspects of the *Descensus* such as important exegetical discussions on Ephesians 4:8-11[15] and 1 Peter 3:18-22,[16] in-depth studies on the afterlife and the underworld,[17] and even some works on the "keys" have been done.[18] This work, however, is the only work that brings all these ideas together to make a cumulative case not only for Christ's descent, but for the NT passages that should be used to support it. I also present a consistent theological picture of the underworld from the NT exploring the compartments Christ visited and so try to understand (according to the NT) the purpose for which he descended. I hope to make a unique contribution to scholarship in this area.

Chapter 4 will explore the various compartments in the underworld as discussed in the NT (Death, Hades, Paradise, Abraham's Bosom, Abyss, Tartarus, Gehenna, and the Lake of Fire). All of these words except for Abraham's Bosom, Tartarus, and Gehenna appear in the book of Revelation. Yet, it will be argued that Abraham's Bosom is a synonym for Paradise in Luke, Tartarus a synonym for Abyss, and Gehenna a synonym for the Lake of Fire. The NT presents Christ descending into all of these realms in the underworld except for Gehenna (Lake of Fire) and I will investigate these realms below. Chapter 5 will then exegetically explore four authors of the NT (Matthew, Luke, Paul, and Peter) who most fully discuss the *Descensus* in their writings. I will look at the history of interpretation of the relevant passages and

---

[12] J. Kroll, *Gott und Hölle: Der Mythos vom Descensuskampfe*, Studien der Bibliothek Warburg 20 (Leipzig-Berlin: B.G. Teubner, 1932).

[13] W. Bieder, *Die Vorstellung von der Höllenfahrt Jesu Christi: Beitrag zur Entstehungsgeschichte der Vorstellung vom sog. Descensus ad Inferos*, ATANT 19, ed. W. Eichrodt and O. Cullmann (Zürich: Zwingli-Verlag, 1949).

[14] J.A. MacCulloch, *The Harrowing of Hell: A Comparative Study of an Early Christian Doctrine* (Edinburgh: T. & T. Clark, 1930). For more recent treatments, brief but excellent, see references below from Bousset, Jeremias, Selwyn and Bauckham.

[15] W. Hall Harris III, *The Descent of Christ: Ephesians 4:7-11 and Traditional Hebrew Imagery*, Arbeiten zur Geschichte des antiken Judentums und des Urchristentums (Leiden: E.J. Brill, 1996; reprint, Grand Rapids: Baker, 1998).

[16] W.J. Dalton, *Christ's Proclamation to the Spirits: A Study of 1 Peter 3:18–4:6* (Rome: Pontifical Biblical Institute, 1965). B. Reicke, *The Disobedient Spirits and Christian Baptism* (Copenhagen: Ejnar Munksgaard, 1946).

[17] N.J. Tromp, *Primitive Conceptions of Death and the Nether World in the Old Testament* (Rome: Pontifical Biblical Institute, 1969). P.S. Johnston, *Shades of Sheol: Death and Afterlife in the Old Testament* (Downer's Grove, IL: InterVarsity Press, 2002).

[18] D.E. Aune, "The Apocalypse of John and Graeco-Roman Revelatory Magic," *NTS* 33 (October 1987): 481-501.

exegete each passage to see whether or not the *Descensus* is taught in all or none of them.

In Chapter 6, I hope to build on all I demonstrated in the previous chapters to argue historically, theologically and exegetically that the best way to understand Revelation 1:18 is in light of the *Descensus*. If Death and Hades are personified, as I will argue, then most commentators on Revelation 1:18 agree that the *Descensus* would be the primary point of the passage (see History of Interpretation in Chapter 6). Chapter 7 is the conclusion where I will restate the key historical, theological and Scriptural arguments for Christ's descent into the underworld and what he accomplished there according to various passages in the NT and especially Revelation 1:18.

The Apostles' Creed

The doctrine of Christ's descent into hell is known throughout the Christian world primarily because of the Apostles' Creed.[19] Penned in Latin, "the final form of the Apostles' Creed appears first, as is well known, in a work of the Frankish missionary Pirminius, who died in AD 758, and 'He descended into hell' is henceforward an article of the faith in the creed."[20] However, it will be shown that the phrase *descendit ad inferna*[21] has its origin in the second century of the church. Swete says, the words reflect an absolutely "primitive" belief and he dates the phrase to the end of the second century.[22] The first creedal appearance was in the Fourth Formula of Sirmium in AD 359 "... was crucified and died, and descended to the underworld (εἰς τὰ καταχθονìα) and regulated things there, Whom the gatekeepers of hell saw and shuddered."[23]

---

[19] Doehler says, "If Holy Scripture has been considered the 'Mighty Fortress' then the Apostles' Creed has heretofore served as the inner and most ancient wall around this 'Mighty Fortress.' G. Doehler, "The Descent into Hell," *The Springfielder* 39 (June 1975): 2.

[20] MacCulloch, *The Harrowing of Hell*, 72.

[21] In Latin, *inferos* is plural and means "lower" or "lower world" and *inferna* means "hellish/hell." Translating "underworld" instead of "hell" in the Apostles' Creed reflects what the Fathers believed and would have led to a lot less controversy on this phrase had it been translated this way instead of "hell." In Rufinus we have the earliest change from *inferos* to *inferna* which has led to such confusion about Christ's descending to the damned (Gehenna) instead of the underworld (Sheol/Hades) in general. M.F. Connell, "*Descensus Christi ad Inferos*: Christ's Descent to the Dead," *TS* 62 (2001): 266. "It is unfortunate that the Apostles' Creed, Article 3 and the Authorised Version create an unnecessary source of confusion by using 'hell' for *hades*" (italics his). J. Yates, "'He Descended into Hell': Creed, Article and Scripture," *Churchman* 102 (1988): 248 n. 19.

[22] H.B. Swete, *The Apostles' Creed: Its Relation to Primitive Christianity* (London: University Press, 1908), 61-62.

[23] Athanasius *Syn.* 1.8; Kelly, *Early Christian Creeds*, 378. It was the Athanasian Creed that first used the word ᾅδης instead καταχθονìα.

This is based on the LXX version of Job 38:17 πυλωροὶ δὲ ᾅδου ἰδόντες σε ἔπτηξαν "the gatekeepers of Hades, seeing you cowered in fear." Kelly adds that the doctrine of the *Descensus* also "figured very early in Eastern creed material."[24]

However, Rufinus (AD 400) says that the phrase *descendit ad inferna* "is not added in the Creed of the Roman Church, neither is it in that of the Oriental Churches. It seems to be implied, however, when it is said that 'He was buried.'"[25] Rufinus may be equating the *Descensus* with "he was buried" so as to do away with a literal descent in his soul to the underworld. This could not be further from the truth. Rufinus goes on to give Scriptural arguments for Christ's *Descensus* with Scriptures such as Psalms 16:10; 22:15; 30:3, 9; 69:2; Luke 8:20; and 1 Peter 3:18-20. This clearly proves that Rufinus does not think that the phrase "he was buried" means that Christ was merely buried and that his soul did not descend into the underworld. Rufinus is actually arguing the opposite because he is saying that the *Descensus* was always "implied" in the phrase "he was buried" and only later *descendit ad inferna* was added to expound what was already understood.[26]

In fact, those who composed the Nicene Creed (like Rufinus) understood the *Descensus* as implied by "he was buried" as the survey below will show. Athanasius, who was integral in composing the Nicene Creed, along with the others, believed in the literal descent of Christ in his soul to the underworld. The phrase "He was buried" always brought to mind the *Descensus* to the Christians from the beginning.[27] Pearson thinks the phrase may have been introduced to fight against the heresy Apollinarianism which denied Christ had a human soul.[28] At the Niceno-Constantinopolitan Council (AD 381), the

---

[24] J.N.D. Kelly, *Early Christian Creeds*, 3rd ed. (New York: Continuum, 2006), 379. The phrase is also found in the Council of Niké (AD 359), Council of Constantinople (AD 360), the Spanish Creeds and the Council of Toledo (AD 660). A.E. Burn, *An Introduction to the Creeds* (London: Methuen, 1899), 203. F.J. Badcock, *The History of the Creeds* (New York: Macmillan, 1938), 157.

[25] Rufinus *Symb.* 14.

[26] See 1 Cor 15:4 (ἐτάφη); Luke 16:23 (καὶ ἐτάφη καὶ ἐν τῷ ᾅδῃ); Acts 2:29 (ἐτάφη); Tertullian, *An.* 55 "Christ, who is God, yet being man too, died according to the Scriptures, *was buried, and went through the form of human death in Hades*; nor did He ascend into Heaven till He had gone down to the lower parts of the earth" (italics mine); Cyril of Jerusalem *Catech.* 4.11. E.C. Smyth, "Is the 'Descensus' in the Apostles' Creed an 'Interpolation' and Superfluous?," *AR* 2 (1889): 420. Contra W.G.T. Shedd, *Dogmatic Theology*, vol. 2 (New York: Charles Scribner's Sons, 1888), 604-5, 607.

[27] Smyth, "Is the 'Descensus' in the Apostles' Creed an 'Interpolation' and Superfluous?," 421. Doehler, "The Descent into Hell," 6-7.

[28] Kelly, *Early Christian Creeds*, 382-83. J. Pearson, *An Exposition of the Creed* (Oxford: Oxford University Press, 1857), 421. A.C. McGiffert, *The Apostles' Creed: Its Origin, Its Purpose, and Its Historical Interpretation* (New York: Charles Scribner's Sons, 1902), 193.

bishops "condemned those who denied that the Logos in His 'reasonable soul' had descended to Hades."[29]

However, Rufinus makes no mention of this heresy being the reason for why the phrase was added.[30] Whether the phrase *descendit ad inferna* was added to fight against Apollinarianism or not, it is clear from the Fathers' writings, beginning with Ignatius, that they all believed that Christ descended into the underworld between his death and resurrection.[31] The clause *descendit ad inferna* was more likely added to expound on "he was buried" and speak about what Christ accomplished in the underworld. Even if I am correct that the *Descensus* is implied in "he was buried," the phrase is still found in the creeds late, so the historical arguments for Christ's *Descensus* should not begin with the Apostles' Creed but with Ignatius of Antioch (AD 98–117).

Early Church Fathers

The Apostolic Fathers and many others in the early and late second century continually reference the *Descensus* and affirm the truth of this doctrine from the Scriptures. Even among modern scholars who deny that the doctrine of the *Descensus* is found in Scripture, there is virtual unanimity that from Ignatius to the medieval period, this doctrine was believed and affirmed by the church.[32]

---

[29] MacCulloch, *The Harrowing of Hell*, 71.

[30] Smyth, "Is the 'Descensus' in the Apostles' Creed an 'Interpolation' and Superfluous?," 421.

[31] Ign. *Magn.* 9.2; Pol. *Phil.* 1.2; Herm. *Sim.* 9:16:5-7; *Gos. Pet.* 10.39-42; *Ep. Apos.* 27; Justin Martyr *Dial.* 99; 72.4; Irenaeus *Haer.* 1.27.3; 5.31.2; 4.27.1-2; *Dem.* 83; Clement of Alexandria *Strom.* 6.6; *An.* 7; 55; Hippolytus *Antichr.* 45; *Frag. On Luc.* 23; *Antichr.* 26; Origen *Cels.* 2:43; Cyprian *Test.* 2.24-27; Eusebius *Hist. Eccl.* 1.13.20; Augustine *Haer.* 79; *Gos. Nic.* 17-26; *Odes of Sol.* 42:11-20.

[32] Selwyn says, "That Christ descended into Sheol or Hades is a well-attested belief in the Church of the second century." E.G. Selwyn, *The First Epistle of St. Peter: The Greek Text with Introduction, Notes, and Essays*, 2nd ed. (Grand Rapids: Baker Book House, 1981), 340. "Every major writer from the 'golden age of Eastern Christian literature' touches, in one way or another, on the theme of Christ's descent into Hades." Hieromonk Ilarion, *Christ the Conqueror of Hell: the Descent into Hades from an Orthodox Perspective* (Crestwood, NY: St. Vladimir's Seminary Press, 2009), 52. "The belief that Christ spent the interval between His expiry on the cross and His resurrection in the underworld was a commonplace of Christian teaching from the earliest times." Kelly, *Early Christian Creeds*, 379. "Indeed the descent into hell hath always been accepted . . . ." Kelly, *Early Christian Creeds*, 403. Huidekoper says, "In the second and third centuries, every branch division of Christians, so far as their records enable us to judge, believed that Christ preached to the departed; and this belief dates back to our earliest reliable sources of information in the former of these two centuries." F. Huidekoper, *The Belief of the First Three Centuries concerning Christ's Mission to the Underworld* (New York: David G. Francis, 1887), 49. Peel says, "From the second century on there was no more well-known and popular belief among early Christians than that pertaining to Christ's

7

Loofs adds the release of the Old Testament saints as something universally recognized by the early church,

> Thus the most primitive, or, at least, the earliest traceable, element in the conception of the *Descensus* would seem to be the belief that Christ, having descended into the underworld after His death, delivered the OT saints from that necessity of being confined in Hades which was thenceforward abrogated in the case of believers, and conveyed them to the Heaven which all believers have hereafter the right to enter.[33]

Ignatius of Antioch is only one generation removed from the apostles; therefore, his testimony is the earliest patristic reference to the *Descensus*. Ignatius says, "How can we possibly live without him, whom even the prophets, who were his disciples in the Spirit, were expecting as their teacher? Because of this he for whom they rightly waited raised them from the dead when he came."[34] A contemporary of Ignatius, Polycarp may allude to the descent when he says, ". . . our Lord Jesus Christ, who endured for our sins, facing even death, 'whom God raised up, having loosed the pangs of Hades.'"[35]

'Descensus ad Inferos.'" M.L. Peel, "The 'Descensus ad Inferos' in 'The Teachings of Silvanus'," *Numen* 26 (1979): 27.

[33] F. Loofs, "Descent to Hades (Christ's)," in *ERE*, ed. J. Hastings, vol. 4 (Edinburgh: T. & T. Clark, 1908–1921): 661.

[34] Ign. *Magn.* 9.2. That Christ descended to the OT saints and released them seems to be commonplace in Ignatius' thinking (cf. Ign. *Philad.* 5.2; 9.1; Ign. *Trall.* 9.1). Schoedel says of this passage, "'Came,' on the other hand, must refer to a descent of Christ into Hades; and 'raised them from the dead,' unusual as it may sound in this context, reflects the language of some descriptions of Christ's victory in the underworld." W.R. Schoedel, *Ignatius of Antioch*, Hermeneia, ed. H. Koester et al. (Philadelphia: Fortress Press, 1985), 124. For Daniélou, Ignatius reveals that the Descensus was common in Jewish Christianity at the end of the first century. J. Daniélou, *The Theology of Jewish Christianity*, trans. J.A. Baker (Philadelphia: Westminster Press, 1964), 237. Lightfoot comments, "Here our Lord is assumed to have visited (παρών) the souls of the patriarchs and prophets in Hades, to have taught them (ὡς διδάσκαλον) the truths of the Gospel, and to have raised them (ἤγειρεν) either to Paradise or to Heaven." Lake writes, "This is possibly a proleptic reference to final resurrection, but more probably to the belief, found in many documents of a later date, that Jesus by the descent into Hades set free, and took into Paradise, the righteous dead." *The Apostolic Fathers*, trans. K. Lake, Loeb Classical Library, ed. G.P. Goold (Cambridge, MA: Harvard University Press, 1912): 207. Cf. J. Wicks, "Christ's Saving Descent to the Dead: Early Witnesses from Ignatius of Antioch to Origen," *Pro Ecclesia* 17 (2008): 281-309. J. Lawson, *A Theological and Historical Introduction to the Apostolic Fathers* (New York: Macmillan, 1961): 127.

[35] Pol. *Phil.* 1.2. The vast majority and most reliable MSS of Acts 2:24 read τὰς ὠδῖνας τοῦ θανάτου and not τὰς ὠδῖνας τοῦ ᾄδου. Metzger argues that the substitution of Hades here is assimilation to Acts 2:27, 31. Bruce M. Metzger, *A Textual Commentary on the Greek New Testament* (New York: United Bible Societies, 1971): 259. If "pangs of death" is the original reading, then the fact that Polycarp

The first well known heretic of the church, Marcion (AD 85–160) is already at the beginning of the second century twisting the doctrine of Christ's descent. He is reported as saying, "that Cain, and those like him, and the Sodomites, and the Egyptians, and others like them, and, in fine, all the nations who walked in all sorts of abomination, were saved by the Lord, on His descending into Hades, and on their running unto Him, and that they welcomed Him into their kingdom."[36] In addition, the apocalyptic work attributed to Hermas (AD 140–154) speaks of the Apostles following Christ in his preaching in the underworld. He says,

> When these apostles and teachers who preached the name of the Son of God fell asleep in the power and faith of the Son of God, they preached (ἐκήρυξαν) also to those who had previously fallen asleep, and they themselves gave to them the seal of the preaching. Therefore they went down with them into the water, and came up again. But these went down alive and came up alive, whereas those who had previously fallen asleep went down dead and came up alive. So they were made alive through them, and came to full knowledge of the name of the Son of God.[37]

In light of the writings of Ignatius, Hermas, Irenaeus' presbyter (see below), and Marcion, it can be clearly seen that the teaching that Christ descended into the underworld (Hades) and released the OT saints waiting for him can be traced to the beginning of the second century.[38]

As we move later into the second century, the evidence for the descent of Christ gets stronger. The apocryphal *Gospel of Peter* (AD 150) speaks about ". . . a cross following them, and the heads of the two reaching to heaven, but that of him who was led of them by the hand over passing the heavens. And they heard a voice out of the heavens crying, 'Hast thou preached (ἐκήρυξεν) to

---

changed the text to have Christ released from the "pangs of Hades" and not merely "death" could reflect the descent motif.

[36] *Haer.* 1.27.3. On this passage attributed to Marcion, Bousset wrote, "We can trace the conception of the preaching in Hades back to the early second century." W. Bousset, *Kyrios Christos: A History of the Belief in Christ from the Beginnings of Christianity to Irenaeus*, trans. J.E. Steely (Nashville, TN: Abingdon Press, 1970): 61.

[37] Herm. *Sim.* 9:16:5-7. Also, quoted by Clement of Alexandria in reference to the *Descensus* in *Strom.* 2.9; 6.6; *Paed.* 2.9.

[38] "From the beginning of the second century a Hades proclamation of Christ was spoken of throughout the whole church." Leonhard Goppelt, *A Commentary on 1 Peter*, trans. John E. Alsup, ed. F. Hahn (Grand Rapids: Eerdmans, 1993): 261. For Marcion to already be able to pervert the teaching of the *Descensus* in the early second century strongly argues for its origins at the turn of the second century or earlier. Bousset wrote, "We can trace the conception of the preaching in Hades back to the early second century." Bousset, *Kyrios Christos: A History of the Belief in Christ from the Beginnings of Christianity to Irenaeus*: 61. "From the early second century on . . ." J.B. Green, *1 Peter*, THNTC, ed. J.B. Green and M. Turner (Grand Rapids: Eerdmans, 2007): 128.

them that sleep?, and from the cross there was heard the answer, 'Yea'."[39] *The Epistle of the Apostles*, dated about the same time, says, "And on that account I have descended and have spoken with Abraham and Isaac and Jacob, to your fathers the prophets, and have brought to them news that they may come from the rest which is below into heaven, and have given them the right hand of the baptism of life and forgiveness and pardon for all wickedness as to you, so from now on also to those who believe in me."[40]

Justin Martyr testifies that Jesus was in Hades after the crucifixion and quotes a fascinating verse he attributes to Jeremiah, "And again, from the sayings of the same Jeremiah these have been cut out: 'The Lord God remembered His dead people of Israel who lay in the graves; and He descended to preach to them His own salvation.'"[41] Murray argues that the Diatessaron witnesses to Tatian's traditional understanding of the *Descensus* because he uses "bars" for "gates" in Matt 16:18.[42] "Bars" become commonplace terminology among the Fathers to refer to Christ breaking the *bars* and destroying the gates of the underworld (see references below). Irenaeus (AD 180) is also a very early witness to the descent of Christ and the Scriptures used to support it. He says, "As I have heard from a certain presbyter, who had heard it from those who had seen the apostles, and from those who had been their disciples. . . ." referring to his source as someone who heard and seen the apostles. Irenaeus is claiming to have second hand apostolic testimony when he professes his belief in Christ's descent. He goes on to say,

> But the case was, that for three days He dwelt in the place where the dead were, as the prophet says concerning Him: "and the Lord remembered His dead saints who slept formerly in the land of sepulture; and He descended to them, to rescue and save them." And the Lord himself says, "As Jonas remained three days and three nights in the whale's belly, so shall the Son of man be in the heart of the earth." Then also the apostle says, "But when He ascended, what is it but that He also descended into the lower parts of the earth?" This, too, David says when prophesying of Him, "And thou hast delivered my soul from the nethermost hell;" and on his rising again the third day, He said to Mary, who was the first to see and to worship Him, "Touch Me not, for I have not yet ascended to the Father; but go to the disciples, and say unto them, I ascend unto My Father, and unto your

---

[39] *Gos. Pet.* 10.39-42. MacCulloch believes this is the earliest reference alluding to 1 Peter 3:19. MacCulloch, *The Harrowing of Hell*, 64. Cf. Reicke, *The Disobedient Spirits and Christian Baptism*, 17.

[40] *Ep. Apos.* 27.

[41] *Dial.* 99; 72.4. This verse is not found in the Old Testament but some have argued it could belong between Jeremiah 11:19 and 20. This verse is also cited by Irenaeus six times (*Haer.* 3.20.4 (attributing it to Isaiah); 4.22.1 (to Jeremiah); 4.27.2; 4.33.1 (no attribution), 12; 5.31.1 (no attribution); *Dem.* 78).

[42] Robert Murray, *Symbols of Church and Kingdom* (New Jersey: Gorgias Press, 2004): 231-32, 327.

Father." If, then, the Lord observed the law of the dead, that He might become the first-begotten from the dead, and tarried until the third day "in the lower parts of the earth. . . ."[43]

Lastly, Melito of Sardis (AD 169–190)[44] says: "'I,' he says, 'am the Christ, I am he who put down death, and triumphed over the enemy, and trod upon Hades, and bound the strong one and brought man safely home to the heights of the heavens; I,' he says, 'Christ.'"[45] Melito is the first to use the battle imagery for Christ's descent that will become commonplace throughout the Fathers and the medieval period. It is difficult to find a better Scripture than Revelation 1:18 for the background to Melito's belief that Christ conquered Death and Hades. Where else in the NT are Death and Hades personified and brought together in this way?

As we close the second century, Christ's descent is universally assumed, along with the preaching to and release of the OT saints; and the trampling of Death and Hades are referenced at least once.[46] I believe it is important to take a moment and realize the significance of how ancient and geographically widespread belief in the *Descensus* was since the close of the first century. If we apply the external canons of textual criticism to the doctrine of the *Descensus*, then we will discover that it is very ancient (Ignatius AD 98–117; Marcion; Irenaeus' presbyter), geographically widespread (Ignatius of Antioch, Polycarp of Smyrna, Melito of Sardis, Irenaeus of Lyons, Irenaeus' presbyter, Justin Martyr, Marcion of Pontus, etc.) and therefore, should be seen as truly bearing witness to the teaching of the autographs (the Apostles). Regardless of how imaginative the understanding of the *Descensus* becomes in the later centuries, the historical core of threefold purpose of Christ's descent: preaching, releasing the saints of the OT, and triumphant defeat of Death and Hades is one of the best attested Christian doctrines from the second century.

In the third century, Clement of Alexandria (AD 200) added something new to the doctrine of the *Descensus* that the Catholic Church would later declare as

---

[43] *Haer.* 5.31.2. Here Irenaeus is already quoting most of the key NT passages generally used to support the descent: Matt 12:40; John 20:17; Acts 2:27; Eph 4:9 (2x); Col 1:18; Rev 1:5. Irenaeus claims to have learned this doctrine from those who themselves knew the apostles! cf. *Haer.* 4.27.1-2; *Dem.* 83.

[44] C. Bonner, ed. *The Homily on the Passion by Melito Bishop of Sardis with Some Fragments of the Apocryphal Ezekiel*, Studies and Documents, ed. K. Lake and S. Lake, vol. 12 (Philadelphia: University of Pennsylvania Press, 1940), 3.

[45] *The Homily on the Passion,* 17.13-17 § 180; cf. 11.9-11 § 131 (italics in original).

[46] It should also be noted that the notorious passage 1 Peter 3:18-22 was not specifically used in support of the *Descensus* until Clement of Alexandria in the third century. Therefore, the doctrine of the descent of Christ arose at the end of the first century and the beginning of the second century independently of the passages in 1 Peter 3:18-22; 4:6.

heretical.[47] Clement is first to extend salvation (a second chance) to even noble unbelievers in Hades, but this is clearly his own conjecture. Clement writes,

> Wherefore the Lord preached the Gospel to those in Hades. Accordingly the Scripture says, Hades says to Destruction, We have not seen His form, but we have heard His voice. . . . Do not [the Scriptures] show that the Lord preached the Gospel to those that perished in the flood, or rather had been chained, and to those kept in ward and guard? It has been shown also, in the second book of the *Stromata*, that the apostles, following the Lord, preached the Gospel to those in Hades. For it was requisite, in my opinion, that as here, so also there, the best of the disciples should be imitators of the Master; so that He should bring to repentance those belonging to the Hebrews, and they the Gentiles; that is, those who had lived in righteousness according to the Law and Philosophy, who had ended life not perfectly, but sinfully.[48]

Tertullian (AD 220) discussed the *Descensus* extensively. He says,

> But what is that which is removed to Hades (*ad inferna*) after the separation of the body; which is there detained; which is reserved until the day of judgment; to which Christ also, on dying, descended? I imagine it is the souls of the patriarchs. . . . Inasmuch as we read that Christ in His Death spent three days in the heart of the earth, that is, in the secret inner recess which is hidden in the earth, and enclosed by the earth, and superimposed on the abysmal depths which lie still lower down. . . . With the same law of his being he fully complied, by

---

[47] Augustine *Haer.* 79, "Another heresy holds that, when Christ descended into hell, those who had not believed came to believe and were all delivered from there." Cf. Gregory the Great, *Ep.* 15. Boniface *Ep.* 57 (AD 745) and a synod at Rome condemned Irish missionary Clement for teaching that Christ released all detained in the underworld. He writes, "Hold ye nothing but what the true faith teaches through the Catholic Church: namely, that the Lord in descending into hell rescued from infernal durance those only whom while living in the flesh He preserved through His grace in faith and good conduct." The Council of Toledo (AD 625) ruled this as Canon, namely that Christ only rescued those who believed in him from the underworld. Bede the Venerable says, "The Catholic faith holds that when the Lord went down into the lower world and brought his own out from there, it was the faithful alone and not unbelievers whom he took with him to the heavenly kingdom." Bede, *The Commentary on the Seven Catholic Epistles of Bede the Venerable* (Kalamazoo, MI: Cistercian Publications, 1985): 104.

[48] *Strom.* 6.6; *Exc.* 18, "When the Saviour descended, he was seen by the angels (ὤφθη κατιών τοῖς ἀγγέλοις) and so they proclaimed him. But he was also seen by Abraham and the other righteous men who are in Paradise on his right hand. For he says, 'He rejoiced to see my day,' that is the advent in the flesh. Wherefore, the risen Lord preached (εὐηγγελίσατο) the good tidings to the righteous who are in Paradise, and moved them and translated them and they shall all 'live under his shadow.'" R.P. Casey, ed. *The Excerpta ex Theodoto of Clement of Alexandria*, Studies and Documents, ed. K. Lake and S. Lake (Cambridge, MA: Harvard University Press, 1934): 54-55.

remaining in Hades in the form and condition of a dead man; nor did he ascend into the heights of Heaven before descending into the lower parts of the earth, that he might there make the patriarchs and prophets partakers of Himself.[49]

Hippolytus (AD 170–235) is the first to say that John the Baptist was Christ's forerunner even in Hades. He says of John, "He also first preached to those in Hades, becoming a forerunner there when he was put to death by Herod, that there too he might intimate that the Saviour would descend to ransom the souls of the saints from the hand of death." He also speaks of Christ being "a soul among souls" and "preaching the Gospel to the souls of the saints."[50] Origen (AD 185–254) follows Clement of Alexandria that Christ converted souls of unbelievers in the underworld. The discussion between Origen and Celsus is this:

> Celsus says, "You will not, I suppose, say of him, that, after failing to gain over those who were in this world, he went to Hades to gain over those who were there." But whether he like it or not, we assert that not only while Jesus was in the body did he win over not a few persons merely, but so great a number, that a conspiracy was formed against Him on account of the multitude of His followers; but also, that when He became a soul, without the covering of the body, He dwelt among those souls which were without bodily covering, converting such of them as were willing to Himself, or those whom He saw, for reasons known to Him alone, to be better adapted to such a course.[51]

Augustine will follow Origen and indicate that all the Fathers affirm that Christ rescued Adam from the underworld even though it is not found explicitly in Scripture (see quote below). Moreover, Cyprian,[52] the *Teaching of Addai*, *Acts of Thomas* 10, and *Acts of Xantippe and Polyxena* 9 all expound on the *Descensus*.[53] Only Clement of Alexandria and Origen add more detail to the descent from the second century by arguing that even righteous pagans were converted through Christ's preaching in the underworld. However, this is restricted to these two Fathers and the church later declared this as heretical and maintained that only those who had believed (looked for) Christ while they were alive were released from Hades. Origen also sees Adam being released which is followed by most Fathers after him. The battle imagery of Christ destroying the gates of iron in Hades and defeating Death and Hades (first in Melito) begins to be expounded to a much greater degree with Tertullian,

---

[49] Tertullian *An.* 7; 55.

[50] Hippolytus *Antichr.* 45; *Frag. On Luc.* 23; *Antichr.* 26.

[51] Origen *Cels.* 2:43; cf. *Comm. Matt.* 35; *Comm. John* 5.37; 6.18; *Hom. Exod.* 6.6; *Hom. Lev.* 9.5(4); *Hom. 1 Reg.* 28.6. Origen is also the first to say that Christ rescued Adam from the depths of the underworld (*Hom. Gen.* 15.5) and that Christ conquered Satan in the underworld (*Comm. Rom.* 5.10.12).

[52] Cyprian *Test.* 2.24-27. This is the earliest direct reference to 1 Peter 4:6.

[53] Eusebius *Hist. Eccl.* 1.13.20.

Origen and the Gnostic *Acts of Thomas*, but is not fully developed until the fourth century.[54]

The best place to begin from the fourth century is the *Gospel of Nicodemus* (fourth century AD) and the vivid portrayal of Christ's harrowing of hell presented there. The Gospel of Nicodemus presents in one package just about everything said before about Christ's descent, but adds many imaginative details. For example, Adam was released, John the Baptist was Christ's forerunner in Hades, the OT saints are released, Christ crushes the gates of Hades, and defeats Satan.[55] While Christ's preaching and rescuing of the OT saints was the norm in the second and third century, his conquering Death and Hades and crushing its gates is the norm from the fourth century on. It must be asked again, what passage of the NT would best support the vanquishing of personified Death and Hades? Starting with Melito of Sardis, I believe Revelation 1:18 was in the background to this vivid imagery because it is the only passage in the NT where Death and Hades are brought together in this way. The best illustration of this from the fourth century is from the *Odes of Solomon*. It says,

> Sheol saw me and was shattered, and Death ejected me and many with me. I have been vinegar and bitterness to it, and I went down with it as far as its depth. Then the feet and the head it released, because it was not able to endure my face. And I made a congregation of living among his dead; and I spoke with them by living lips; in order that my word may not fail. And those who had died ran toward me; and they cried out and said, "Son of God, have pity on us. And deal with us according to your kindness, and bring us out from the chains of darkness. And open for us the door by which we may go forth to you, for we perceive that our death does not approach you. May we also be saved with you, because you are our Savior." Then I heard their voice, and placed their faith in my heart. And I placed my name upon their head, because they are free and they are mine.[56]

We can add to these witnesses Aphrahat (AD 270–345),[57] Ephrem the Syrian

---

[54] For Christ destroying the gates of Hades see *Sib. Or.* 2:225-229; 8:225-228; *Odes of Sol.* 17:6-16; 42:11-20; *Gos. Nic.* 21:3; *Apoc. Peter* 4:3; Eusebius, *Dem. Ev.* 8.1; *Teaching of Addai* (Thaddeus) cited in Eusebius *Hist. Eccl.* 1.13.20; *Ques. Bart.* 1:20; *Teach. Silv.* 110:19-24; *Acts Thom.* 10; Tertullian *Res.*, 44; Chrysostom *Hom. Matt.* 36; *Hom. 1 Cor.* 142; Hippolytus *Frag. On Luc.* 23; Lactantius *Inst.* 4, 12.15; Aphrahat *Pers.* 21.19; John Cassian *Inst. Coeb.* 3.3; Prudentius *Hymn* 9.69-84; Caesarius of Arles *Sermon* 118.5.

[55] *Gos. Nic.* 17-26 cf. *Ques. Bart.* 1.9-2.35.

[56] *Odes of Sol.* 42:11-20 cf. 17:6-16; 22:1; 24:5; *Ascen. Isa.* 4:21; 9:15-18; 10:8-11, 14, 19; 10:19-21; *T. Benj.* 9.3-5; *Sib. Or.* 1:377-378; 8:225-228, 310-314; *Gk. Apoc. Ezra* 7:1-3; *Apoc. Sedr.* 1:20-21; *Great Pow.* 41.32; *Paraph. Shem*, 36.24; *Teach. Silv.* 104.1-14; 110.19-30; *Testim. Truth* 32.24-33.8; *Trim. Prot.* 36.4; 41.6-7.

[57] Aphrahat *Demons.* 21.19.

(AD 306–373),[58] Hilary of Poiters (AD 300–368),[59] Athanasius (AD 293–373),[60] Cyril of Jerusalem (AD 313–386),[61] Basil the Great (AD 330–379),[62] Ambrose (AD 340–397),[63] he Apostolic Constitutions (AD 375–400),[64] and Gregory of Nazianzus (AD 329–389).[65] In these writers, Christ had not only preached to the OT saints and released them, but he found Adam in the lowest depths of hell, conquered Satan, and crushed the gates of iron guarded by Death and Hades (and Satan). Revelation 1:18 would be the best passage to support this plundering of Death and Hades through a victorious battle and is cited in reference to the *Descensus* by some of the Fathers (see chapter 6).

In the fifth century, Augustine (AD 354–430) discusses the *Descensus* most fully in response to a question from Evodius concerning 1 Peter 3:18-22. He says,

> It is established beyond question that the Lord, after He had been put to death in the flesh, "descended into hell;" for it is impossible to gainsay either that utterance of prophecy, "Thou wilt not leave my soul in hell." As to the first man, the father of mankind, it is agreed by almost the entire Church that the Lord loosed him from that prison; a tenet which must be believed to have been accepted not without reason,—from whatever source it was handed down to the Church,— although the authority of the canonical Scriptures cannot be brought forward as speaking expressly in its support . . . [66]

Jerome (AD 347–420) commenting on Daniel 3 says, "Our Lord Jesus Christ descended into the furnace of hell, wherein the souls both of sinners and of just men were held shut; that without any burning or hurt unto himself, he might free from the bonds of death those that were held shut up in that place."[67] John Chrysostom (AD 347–407) says, "For when this one was crucified, then were the dead raised up, then was that prison burst, and the gates of brass were broken, and the dead were loosed, and the keepers of hell-gate all cowered in fear."[68] In addition, Cyril of Alexandria (AD 376–444), Prudentius (AD 348–

[58] Ephrem the Syrian *Nis. Hymns* 55; *On our Lord* 1.2.

[59] Hilary of Poiters *Enarr. In* Pss. 53.14; 59; 118; 138; *Trinity* 3.15; 4.42; 10.34, 65-71; *Matth. Canon* 33.

[60] Athanasius *C. Ar.* 3.29; *Syn.* 1.8; *Ep. Epict.* 109.5.

[61] Cyril of Jerusalem *Catech.* 4.11; 12.15; 14.18-19.

[62] Basil the Great *Homily* 19.9 on Ps 48(49):15; *On the Holy Spirit* 14.32; 15.35.

[63] Ambrose *Fid.* 3.4, 14.

[64] P.F. Bradshaw, M.E. Johnson, and L.E. Phillips, *The Apostolic Tradition: A Commentary*, Hermeneia, ed. H. Koester and H.W. Attridge (Minneapolis, MN: Fortress Press, 2002): 4.8; 41.8.

[65] Gregory of Nazianzus *Orat. Easter* 45.24; *Theol. Orat.* 29.20.

[66] Augustine *Ep.* 164. cf. *Civ.* 20.15; *Gen. imp.* 12.33.

[67] Jerome *Expl. Dan.* 1; cf. *Hom.* 61 on Psalm 15 (16).

[68] John Chyrsostom *Hom. 1 Cor.* 24.7; cf. *Hom. Matt.* 2; 11; 36; *Stat.* 7.1; *Eutrop.* 2.13.

413),[69] John Cassian (AD 360–435),[70] and Leo the Great (AD 400–461)[71] continue illustrating and adding further creative details to the *Descensus*. In the fifth century, we see some of the greatest minds of church history; Augustine, Jerome, Chrysostom, wrestling with the *Descensus* doctrine, but all unanimously affirm it being taught in the NT, even if some deny it in certain passages (such as Augustine's original interpretation of 1 Peter 3:18-22).[72]

Like the previous centuries, the sixth and seventh centuries are filled with theological discussions of the *Descensus*. Gregory the Great (sixth century AD) strongly affirmed it and following Augustine, declared it heretical to teach that Christ released from hell those who did not believe in him (look for) while they lived.[73] Venantius Fortunatus (AD 530–600) included *descendit ad infernum* in his creeds.[74] Moreover, Caesarius of Arles (AD 470–542),[75] Maximus the Confessor (AD 580–662),[76] and John of Damascus (seventh century AD) all affirmed it. John of Damascus teaches,

> The soul when it was deified descended into Hades, in order that, just as the Sun of Righteousness rose for those upon the earth, so likewise He might bring light to those who sit under the earth in darkness and shadow of death. . . . And thus after He had freed those who had been bound for ages, straightway He rose again from the dead, showing us the way of resurrection.[77]

Throughout the middle ages, all the great teachers of that time unanimously affirmed the descent of Christ into the underworld. For example, Peter Abelard, Bernard of Clairvaux, Peter Lombard, Alain of Lille, Dante,[78] the Fourth

---

[69] Prudentius *Hymns* 3.195-200; 9.69-84; *Apotheosis* 635-636.

[70] John Cassian *Inst. Coeb.* 3.3; *Conf.* 14; *Incar.* 6.17; 7.1.

[71] Leo the Great *Pas. Serm.* 8.

[72] The significance of Augustine rejecting the traditional understanding of 1 Peter 3:18-22 and 4:5-6 as in reference to Christ's descent, but instead arguing that Christ preached through Noah should not go unnoticed. I believe this demonstrates that most of these commentators throughout church history were not just repeating what they had received from their predecessors, but were wrestling with the these passages themselves and are more concerned with the exegesis of the Old and New Testament texts than we give them credit for. Thomas Aquinas also rejects the *Descensus* being taught in 1 Peter 3:18-22 and 4:5-6. See *Summa.* 3.52.1-8.

[73] Gregory the Great *Ep.* 15.

[74] Badcock, *The History of the Creeds*, 99.

[75] Caesarius of Arles *Sermon* 118.5; 119.

[76] *Ques.* 57. *St. Maximus the Confessor's Questions and Doubts*, trans. D.D. Prassas (Dekalb, IL: Northern Illinois University Press, 2010): 75.

[77] John of Damascus *Exp. Orth. Faith* 3.29.

[78] R.V. Turner, "'Descendit ad Inferos': Medieval Views on Christ's Descent into Hell and the Salvation of the Ancient Just," *JHI* 27 (1966). Turner has extensive references to these writers' views on the *Descensus*.

Lateran Council (AD 1215) and of course, Thomas Aquinas[79] all understood the *Descensus* in the traditional sense. Furthermore, the founding Reformers such as Luther preached on the *Descensus*. The *Formula of Concord* (alluding to a famous sermon preached by Luther at the Castle of Torgau) says, "We believe simply that the entire person, God and human being, descended to Hell after his burial, conquered the devil, destroyed the power of Hell, and took from the devil all his power."[80]

In addition, Erasmus,[81] Henry the VIII,[82] Calvin, Zwingli,[83] Melanchthon,[84] Bullinger,[85] Peter Martyr,[86] the church of England[87] all affirmed and taught the *Descensus*. Calvin is the first to understand the phrase metaphorically for Christ experiencing (descending into) hell on the cross *before* his burial instead of after his burial, but Calvin is still affirming that the *Descensus* is taught in the Scriptures.[88] This view is untenable, however, because of the logical order of

---

[79] *Summa.* 3.52.1-8. Turner says that Aquinas' treatment of this doctrine is "the most exhaustive of all the medieval writers." Turner, 'Descendit ad Inferos': 187.

[80] Article 9.

[81] D.D. Wallace, "Puritan and Anglican: The Interpretation of Christ's Descent into Hell in Elizabethan Theology," *AFR* 69 (1978): 251-52.

[82] Wallace, "Puritan and Anglican": 256. Smith and Wallace list many other Protestant reformers who affirmed the traditional view of the descent such as Thomas Cranmer, Bernardino Ochino, Sebastian Castellio, John Ponet, Thomas Becon, Alexander Nowell, Thomas Cooper, Adam Hyll, Thomas Bilson, Richard Parkes, Mathias Flacius Illyricus. Wallace, "Puritan and Anglican: 256-57, 259, 270-71, 275, 277-78. C.I. Smith, "*Descendit ad Inferos–Again*," *JHI* 28 (1967): 87.

[83] J. Friedman, "Christ's Descent into Hell and Redemption through Evil: A Radical Reformation Perspective," *Archiv für Reformations-geschichte* 76 (1985): 219.

[84] Friedman, "Christ's Descent into Hell". Augsburg Confession (AD 1530) article 3, "The same Christ also descended into hell."

[85] Wallace, "Puritan and Anglican": 254.

[86] Wallace, "Puritan and Anglican": 254.

[87] E.H. Browne, "Of the Descent into Hell," in *An Exposition of the Thirty-Nine Articles: Historical and Doctrinal*, ed. J. Williams (New York: H. B. Durand, 1865): 84-103.

[88] Calvin, *Institutes*, 2.16.8-12. On how radical Calvin's position was at the time on the *Descensus* see M. Rakow, "Christ's Descent into Hell: Calvin's Interpretation," *RL* 43 (1974): 218-26. Many in the Reformed community have followed Calvin on his interpretation. G.C. Berkouwer, *The Work of Christ* (Grand Rapids: Eerdmans, 1965): 174-80. K. Barth, *Credo* (New York: Charles Scribner's Sons, 1962): 88-94. The Heidelberg Catechism Question 44 and the Westminster Larger Catechism Question 50 seem to follow Calvin. On the other hand, the descent of Christ was understood as Christ suffering in hell by a few commentators before Calvin, but in the literal hell (Gehenna) and not on the cross (which was completely unique to Calvin). Durand of Saint Pourcain (AD 1275–1334) was the first to teach that Christ underwent punishment at the descent. Wallace, "Puritan and Anglican": 251. Nicholas de Cusa (AD 1401–1464) also taught that Christ suffered in Hell at his descent. Wallace, "Puritan and Anglican": 251. They have been followed by Bishop

the Creed ("He suffered under Pontius Pilate, was crucified, died, and was buried. He descended into hell"). This understanding of Christ's descent seems to be sourced solely in Calvin's ingenuity.

Thus far it seems that Zwingli's Zurich colleague Leo Jud (AD 1482–1542) in a 1534 catechism and Martin Bucer (AD 1491–1551) were the first to argue that the *Descensus* meant merely that Christ descended to the grave (burial) and thus rejecting this doctrine of a literal descent after fifteen centuries of the church affirming it.[89] Richard Parkes said that never had a local descent of Christ to hell been denied "until this our last and worst age. . . ."[90] Plumptre rightly says, "We may be quite sure that no Jew or Greek in the apostolic age would ever have thought that the words 'He descended into Hades' meant only that the body of Christ had been laid in the grave, or that His soul had suffered with an exceeding sorrow in Gethsemane and on the cross."[91] I believe our survey of the Fathers from the second century onward has demonstrated this well. To equate the *Descensus* with Christ's burial was nothing more than a pre-Bultmannian attempt to demythologize the NT text because Bucer and those who followed him could no longer accept an underworld beneath the earth.[92] Smith summarizes the Reformers' views well when he says, "The

---

Latimer (AD 1549), J.S. Stone, *The Glory After the Passion: A Study of the Events in the Life of our Lord from His Descent into Hell to His Enthronement in Heaven* (New York: Longmans, Green, 1913), 51-52. the Lutheran Aepinus (AD 1553) J.J. van Oosterzee, *Christian Dogmatics*, trans. John Watson Watson and Maurice J. Evans, vol. 2 (New York: Charles Scribner's Sons, 1882), 2.560-61. More recently Hans Urs von Balthasar (1905–1988) argued this. A.L. Pitstick, *Light in Darkness: Hans Urs von Balthasar and the Catholic Doctrine of Christ's Descent into Hell* (Grand Rapids: Eerdmans, 2007), 90. Hans Urs von Balthasar, "The Descent into Hell," *CS* 23 (1984): 236. Yet, arguing that Christ suffered in hell at his descent goes against the first fifteen centuries of the church and even the Roman Catholic Church has stood firm in its creeds that Christ did not suffer at his descent, but instead was triumphant. See *Catechism of the Catholic Church* 624, 631-37. "He did not descend in order to suffer there. . . ." J.H. Rohling, "Descent of Christ into Hell," in *NCE*, ed. B.L. Marthaler, vol. 4 Com-Dyn (Washington, D.C.: Thomson and Gale, 2003): 685.

[89] Wallace, "Puritan and Anglican": 253-54. Smith, "*Descendit ad Inferos*–Again," 87. Beza (AD 1519–1605) also denied the descent by equating it to burial. B. Reicke, "Descent into Hell," in *The Oxford Companion to the Bible*, ed. B.M. Metzger and M.D. Coogan (Oxford: Oxford University Press, 1993), 40.

[90] Wallace, "Puritan and Anglican": 277.

[91] E.H. Plumptre, *The Spirits in Prison and Other Studies on the Life After Death* (New York: Thomas Wittaker, 1889): 102.

[92] For Bultmann said, "What sense does it make to confess today 'he descended into hell' or 'he ascended into heaven,' if the confessor no longer shares the underlying mythical word picture of a three-story world. . . . Thus, the stories of Christ's descent and ascent are finished, and so is the expectation of the Son of Man's coming on the clouds of heaven and of the faithful's being caught up to meet him in the air (1 Thess 4:15ff.)." R. Bultmann, *Theology of the New Testament*, trans. Kendrick Grobel, vol. 1 (New York: Charles Scribner's Sons, 1951): 4.

classical Protestant theologians interpreted the *Descensus* mystically, while representatives of different sectors of the Radical Reformation put forward the literal view through their desire for the salvation of the ancients."[93]

All in all, the historical argument for the doctrine of Christ's *Descensus* is one of the most primitive and most agreed upon teachings of the ancient church. We have found that from Ignatius on, the Fathers believed that Christ had released the OT saints from Hades and most of them also mention his preaching to them. In the late third and fourth century, the battle imagery receives vivid detail as Christ destroys the gates of Hades, defeats Satan, rescues Adam, and tramples on Death and Hades. I believe this imagery that began with Melito finds its source in Revelation 1:18, which is the only NT passage where a possible battle between Christ and personified Death and Hades can be found. Clement of Alexandria and Origen taught that the righteous pagans were converted through Christ's preaching, but the vast majority of the ancient Fathers reject this teaching as heretical.

The Scriptures the Fathers cited in support of the *Descensus* are most of the passages that will be discussed in this book (see chapters 5 and 6).[94] Sometimes their writings are fanciful and their imaginations go too far, but overall they are working with texts of Holy Scripture and the traditions they received from the Apostles or those who heard the Apostles. The doctrine of the *Descensus* is very ancient beginning in the early second century, geographically widespread, and is unanimously assumed and taught by the church for fifteen centuries. I believe this weighty historical argument should be considered when the *Descensus* is a possible interpretation of various passages in the NT. Given the Fathers' understanding of these passages from Ignatius to Aquinas, would those in the first century who first read Matthew 12:40; 27:52-53; Acts 2:25-27; Ephesians 4:8-10; 1 Peter 3:18-22; 4:5-6; and Revelation 1:18 not understood them in light of the *Descensus*?

---

[93] Smith, "*Descendit ad Inferos*–Again," 88.

[94] The most popular NT passages used to support the *Descensus* throughout the Fathers were Matthew 12:40; 27:52-53; Acts 2:25-27; Eph 4:8-10; 1 Pet 3:18-22; 4:5-6, but Rev 1:18 does receive some treatment by the Fathers in reference to Christ's descent.

CHAPTER 2

A SURVEY OF DEATH AND HADES PERSONIFIED

Death and Hades in the Greco Roman World

Jesus said, "I am the Living One; I was dead, and behold I am alive for ever and ever! And I hold the keys of death and Hades (τοῦ θανάτου καὶ τοῦ ᾅδου)" (Rev 1:18). In this chapter, I will explore the background to Revelation 1:18 by looking at various passages where Death and Hades are personified in the Greco-Roman literature, the OT, Second Temple Literature, and in a few other relevant texts in the NT. From exploring these texts, we will come to a better understanding of the background and imagery behind Christ taking away the keys from Death and Hades. The background to Hades begins in the ancient Greek world.

The original, literal meaning of ᾅδης seems to be "invisible, unseen."[1] Bietenhard explains, "The etymology of the word *Hades* is uncertain. It either comes from *idein* (to see) with the negative prefix, a-, and so would mean the invisible; or it is connected with *aianes*, and would have meant originally gloomy, gruesome."[2] In fact, the god of the underworld was most likely given the name Hades because it is an unseen (invisible) realm.

Beginning in Homer, Hades is personified as the god of the underworld and is the brother of Zeus.[3] Moreover, the underworld is predominantly personified as the god Hades.[4] Hades is "horrible" and "the most hated of all the gods."[5]

---

[1] Plato, *Phaed.* 80d; *Gorg.* 493b; J.N. Bremmer, *The Rise and Fall of the Afterlife: The 1995 Read-Tuckwell Lectures at the University of Bristol* (New York: Routledge, 2002): 4.

[2] H. Bietenhard, "Hell, Abyss, Hades, Gehenna, Lower Regions," in *NIDNTT*, ed. Colin Brown (Grand Rapids: Zondervan, 1976, 1986): 206. In Homer, a helmet which makes the person invisible is called a "helmet of Hades" (*Il.* 5.845).

[3] *Il.*, 15.187-93. W. Burkert, *Greek Religion*, trans. J. Raffan (Cambridge, MA: Harvard University Press, 1985): 196.

[4] *Il.*, 15.188. He is known as "Hades, that is Lord of the dead below" and described as the ". . . imperious Hades, whose heart knows no mercy in his subterranean dwelling,

Hades was worshiped in a temple near Elis in Greece.[6] He is also pictured as the judge of the dead.[7] Hades is simultaneously portrayed not only as the god of the underworld, but also the very realm of the underworld that houses the souls of the dead.[8] The dead are frequently referred to as entering the house of Hades (εἰν Ἀΐδαο δόμοισι).[9] There is a river or lake that is the boundary between the dead and the living and a ferryman takes the dead across to pass through the gates of Hades.[10] In Greek mythology, even Death is personified as a demon or monster from the underworld who is the "sacrificer of the dead."[11] It is clear that the Greeks sometimes personified Hades as a god of the underworld and simultaneously understood Hades as the abode or realm of the dead. I believe this Greek portrayal of Hades as ruler over the dead and realm of the dead find clear parallels in the OT and especially in Revelation.[12] This understanding of Death and Hades would have most certainly been in the minds of the Christians who first read the book of Revelation in the churches of Ephesus, Sardis, Pergamum and others. Let us look at the true origins of these figures according to the Hebrew Scriptures.

Death and Hades (Sheol) in the Old Testament

In the OT, Hades is used more than a hundred times in the LXX and almost always to translate the Hebrew word שְׁאוֹל.[13] The author of Revelation seems to be using the Septuagint in his allusions to the OT because of the way he

---

and the rumbling Earthshaker" (*Il.*, 23.244; *Theog.* 767, 774; cf. *Theog.* 455, 850; *Od.* 4.834).

[5]   *Il.* 8.368; 9.158.

[6]   Strabo 8.3.14; Pausanias 6.25.2.

[7]   Aeschylus, *Eum.* 273.

[8]   Soph. *Aj.* 635; Eur. *Alc.* 25, 73, 436-37, 457, 626; *El.* 142-43; *Herc. fur.* 610, 619; *Heracl.* 218, 912-13, 949; *Hipp.* 895; *Andr.* 414; Ap. Rhod. 2.609; 3.810.

[9]   *Il.*, 10.483; 11.263, 445; 15.251; 20.336; 21.48; 22.52, 213, 425, 482; 23.19, 71, 74, 103, 179; 24.246; *Od.* 14.208; 20.208.

[10]   Burkert, *Greek Religion*, 197.

[11]   Eur. *Alc.* 27-28.

[12]   "The sea gave up the dead that were in it, and death and Hades gave up the dead that were in them, and each person was judged according to what he had done. Then death and Hades were thrown into the lake of fire" (Rev 20:13-14).

[13]   Sheol is used sixty-six times in the MT. Sixty times שְׁאוֹל is translated ᾅδης except for 2 Sam 22:6; Isa 28:15 (though here Death and Hades have been switched); Prov 23:14 it is θάνατος, Ezek 32:21 uses βόθρος, and it is untranslated in Isa 7:11 (conjectural emendation); Job 24:19. It is surprising that Sheol is used so seldom in the OT when the root of the Hebrew word מָוֶת "to die/death" is used exactly a thousand times. P.S. Johnston, *Shades of Sheol: Death and Afterlife in the Old Testament* (Downer's Grove, IL: InterVarsity Press, 2002), 72.

21

translates certain passages.[14] I believe Death and Hades for the author of Revelation[15] find their primary background in the OT and this is also where they are both personified together and individually. Unlike Hades, we do not know what the word Sheol meant originally.[16] Regardless of its etymology, like Hades in the Greco-Roman world, Sheol is the common destiny of all; both the righteous and the wicked.[17] According to the OT and the rest of Second Temple literature, everyone went to Sheol unless God miraculously intervened.[18] Others living in the ancient near east had this same understanding of the afterlife. In the most ancient Sumerian myths, "The netherworld is the 'land of no return,' guarded by seven walls, each with a gate and a gatekeeper whose role is to let only the dead enter and to let no one leave."[19] Bauckham goes on to say, "Ancient Israel shared the conviction of the Mesopotamian peoples that 'he who goes down to Sheol [the underworld] does not come up.' No exceptions were known: There is no Old Testament instance of a true descent to and return from the underworld by a living human being."[20]

In fact, Enoch and Elijah are the only exceptions who can be found to have gone to Heaven (and remain there) instead of Sheol/Hades before the NT

---

[14] See ποιμανεῖ in Rev 2:8-9; 19:15 and ποιμανεῖς in LXX Ps 2:9 against the MT Ps 2:9.

[15] Rev 1:18; 6:8; 20:13, 14.

[16] Merrill says bluntly, "All attempts to recover its etymology have failed." E.H. Merrill, "שְׁאוֹל," in *NIDOTTE*, ed. W.A. VanGemeren, vol. 4 (Grand Rapids: Zondervan, 1997): 6. Heidel says, "The etymology of this word is still obscure, despite the numerous efforts that have been made to determine its root and to discover its basic meaning." A. Heidel, *The Gilgamesh Epic and OT Parallels*, 2nd ed. (Chicago, IL: University of Chicago Press, 1949): 173.

[17] One of the primary arguments of this book that I hope to establish from this chapter is that everyone, righteous and wicked, descended to the underworld at death and so Christ, as fully man, experienced the law of the dead and descended to the underworld. Bauckham says, "Since the commonest Jewish view in the New Testament times was that all the dead descend to Sheol (Hades), Jesus' descent to Hades was simply the corollary of his death, just as it was implied in his resurrection 'from the dead.'" R. Bauckham, *The Fate of the Dead: Studies on the Jewish and Christian Apocalypses*, Supplements to Novum Testamentum, ed. C.K. Barrett, J.K. Elliott, and M.J.J. Menken, vol. 93 (Leiden: Brill, 1998): 38.

[18] Ps 89:47-48; 1 Sam 2:6; 2 Sam 12:23; Job 7:9; 10:21-22; 16:22; Eccl 9:10; Jonah 2:7; Wis 2:1, 5; 16:13; Sir 38:21; 2 Macc 6:23-24; *4 Ezra* 5:45-49; *1 En.* 22; 51:1; 102:5; 103:7; *2 Bar.* 21:23; 23:4-5; *Sib. Or.* Book 1:80-85; *T. Ab.* 8:9; 19:7; Ps.-Phoc. 110-113; *Syr. Men.* 34-37, 127, 470-473.

[19] Bauckham, *The Fate of the Dead*, 10. Tromp says, "Everybody returns to the nether world, but nobody returns from it." N.J. Tromp, *Primitive Conceptions of Death and the Nether World in the Old Testament* (Rome: Pontifical Biblical Institute, 1969), 189.

[20] Bauckham, *The Fate of the Dead*, 16.

times.[21] Jewish and Christian writings after the time of Jesus begin to speak of the OT saints in heaven such as Abraham, Isaac, and Jacob,[22] Job's children,[23] and the souls of the righteous go to the third heaven.[24] Heidel argues for the OT saints being taken to heaven at their death, but besides Enoch and Elijah he cannot produce one example of someone specifically said to have been taken to heaven from the OT or ancient Jewish literature. He argues primarily from Psalm 49 and 73, but this is the great hope of the faithful Israelite and there is no evidence that it had been fulfilled. Johnston commenting on these particular Psalms says, "These Psalms give no elaboration of how, when or where this communion will take place."[25] Heidel goes so far as to say that it was an evil spirit instead of the real Samuel in 1 Samuel 28 so as to not have Samuel coming from Sheol![26] The account recorded by the Jewish historian Josephus[27] does not agree with Heidel's view. Josephus believes that the real Samuel did come up from Hades to pronounce judgment on Saul. As a primary source from the first century, Josephus' opinion carries much more weight than Heidel's opinion. Rosenberg argues that going to Sheol represents an "evil death" and even says that being "gathered to the fathers" is never parallel with Sheol.[28] On the other hand, Harris says, "One problem with *sheol* is that both good men (Jacob, Gen 37:35) and bad men (Korah, Dathan, etc., Num 16:30) go there."[29]

I agree with Harris against Heidel and others since the account in Genesis not only testifies that Jacob will go to Sheol (Gen 37:35; 42:38; 44:29, 31), but being "gathered to one's fathers" is parallel with Sheol (Gen 49:29). If being "gathered to one's fathers" and "sleeping with your fathers" is parallel with Sheol then it is clear that the vast majority of the righteous went to Sheol.[30]

---

[21] Gen 5:21-24; 2 Kgs 2:9-12; 1 Macc 2:58; *1 En.* 9.3; *2 En.* 1.1; *(Apocr.) Ep. Tit.*; *T. Isaac* 3:16; *Hel. Syn. Pr.* 16.8; *Ques. Ezra* 40; *Ant.* 9.28.

[22] Abraham, Isaac, and Jacob (*3 En.* 44.7); Abraham (*T. Ab.* B7:16; *T. Isaac* 6:1) and Isaac (*T. Isaac* 2:5-8).

[23] *T. Job* 39:11-13; 47:2-4. Charlesworth argues for Christian redaction here. *The Old Testament Pseudepigrapha.* vol. 2, ed. J.H. Charlesworth (Garden City, NY: Doubleday, 1983–85): 859.

[24] *Apoc. Paul* 11.

[25] Johnston, *Shades of Sheol*, 217.

[26] Heidel, *The Gilgamesh Epic and OT Parallels*, 189-90.

[27] *Ant.* 6.332.

[28] R. Rosenberg, "The Concept of Biblical Sheol within the Context of ANE Beliefs" (Ph.D. diss., Harvard University Press, 1980): 178-252.

[29] R. Harris, "שׁאוֹל," in *TWOT*, ed. G.L. Archer and B.K. Waltke (Chicago, IL: Moody, 1999): 892.

[30] Gen 15:15; 25:8; 35:29; 47:30; 49:29, 33; Num 31:2; Deut 32:50 (2x); 1 Kgs 1:21; 2:2, 10; 11:21, 43 (2x); 14:31; 15:8, 24; 16:6, 28; 22:40, 51; 2 Kgs 8:24; 10:35; 13:9, 13; 14:16, 22, 29; 15:7, 22, 38; 16:20; 20:21; 21:18; 22:20; 24:6; 1 Chr 17:11; 2 Chr 9:31; 16:13; 21:1; 26:2, 23; 27:9; 28:27; 32:33; 33:20; 34:28; 36:8; Jer 28:16; Dan 6:29; cf. Jdt 16:22; Sir 47:23.

This could not be just another way of saying they were buried because Abraham (Gen 25:8-9), Jacob (Gen 47:30), Moses (Deut 31:16), David (1 Kgs 2:10; 8:1; 11:21), Ahaz (2 Chr 28:27), and Manasseh (2 Kgs 21:18) were not literally buried with their ancestors, but were still said to "lie with their fathers." Moreover, Abel spoke after death (Gen 4:10), Rachel gave up her "soul" (Gen 35:18), David hoped to go to his child in Sheol (2 Sam 12:23), the "soul" of the widow's son returned presumably from Sheol (1 Kgs 17:21), righteous Hezekiah expected to pass through the gates of Sheol at death (Isa. 38:9-20), the righteous martyrs went to Hades (2 Macc 6:23), and I believe the strongest evidence for this view is that the real spirit of righteous Samuel came from Sheol, not heaven (1 Sam 28:11-19).[31]

Yet as Harris says, the wicked dead also go to Sheol at death such as Korah and his rebels (Num 16:30, 33), wicked kings (Isa 14:9-11; 29:4; Ezek 26:19-21; 31:14-18; 32:18-32) and the wicked in general (Ps 48:15-16 (49:14-15)); Prov 21:16; Lam 3:6). However, the righteous hoped that God would rescue their souls out of Hades,[32] they are at peace in death (Isa 57:1-2), and hope to be united with their bodies for a physical resurrection (Ezek 37:12-14; Isa 26:19; Dan 12:2). These spirits dwelling in the underworld are called רְפָאִים "shades" eight times in the OT.[33] Other words used synonymously with Sheol are שַׁחַת "pit," בּוֹר "dungeon," מָוֶת "death," and אֶרֶץ "earth." שַׁחַת means literally "pit" but parallels Sheol (Ps 16:10), בּוֹר (Ps 7:15), and Death (Job 33:22) and so is used for the underworld.[34] בּוֹר is pictured as a dungeon (Exod 12:29; Jer 37:16) and the entrance to Sheol (Isa 14:15; Ezek 32:21, 23) and the dead sink down into it (Isa 38:18; Ezek 26:20; Ps 28:1).[35] In short, Sheol is the realm of the dead in the OT and all go there (except Enoch and Elijah), but the righteous have the hope that God would one day rescue them out of there.[36]

---

[31] See 1 Sam 15:35; 25:1; 28:3; LXX 1 Chr 10:13; Sir 46:20; *Ant.* 6.332, "She not knowing who Samuel was, called him out of Hades." Also, *Ant.* 6.334 speaks of the "soul of Samuel" and *Ant.* 6.336 says Saul would be in Hades. This was also the Rabbinic view, K.A.D. Smelik, "The Witch at Endor: 1 Samuel 28 in Rabbinic and Christian Exegesis till 800 AD," *VC* 33 (1979): 162-65, 173. Smelik cites Justin Martyr, Origen, Ambrose, Augustine, and many others in order to demonstrate that the view that this was the real Samuel was the most ancient and widespread view among the Rabbis and Christians.

[32] Pss 15 (16):9-11; 16 (17):15; 29 (30):4; 48:15-16 (49:14-15); 106 (107):8-22; Isa 25:8; 42:7; 45:1-3; Hos 13:14; Zech 9:11-12.

[33] Isa 14:9; 26:14, 19; Ps 88:11; Prov 2:18; 9:18; 21:16; Job 26:5; cf. 4Q548; 1QH 20.25. See M. L. Brown, "רְפָאִים," in *NIDOTT*, ed. W.A. VanGemeren, vol. 3 (Grand Rapids: Zondervan, 1997).

[34] E.H. Merrill, "שַׁחַת," in *NIDOTTE*, ed. W.A. VanGemeren, vol. 4 (Grand Rapids: Zondervan, 1997): 93-94.

[35] בּוֹר (*lakkos*) is parallel with Hades in LXX Ps 30:3; Ezek 32:21; Isa 14:15; Pss 27 (28):1; 142 (143):7; Zech 9:11-12.

[36] Pss 15 (16):9-11; 16 (17):15; 29 (30):4; 48:15-16 (49:14-15); 106 (107):8-22; Isa 25:8; 42:7; 45:1-3; Hos 13:14; Zech 9:11-12.

Death in the OT is usually a state of being dead or the body absent of the soul/spirit. Death can also represent the realm of the dead when it is used synonymously with Sheol.[37] Death entered the world as a result of God's penalty for sin (Gen 2:17; 3:3, 4; cf. Rom 5:12). Death is also personified throughout the OT.[38] Many see this personified figure as Mot, the Canaanite god from Ugaritic texts with very similar characteristics to Death in the OT.[39] To illustrate, Death uses waves of the sea against his victims (2 Sam 22:5-6), cords and snares (Pss 17:5-6 [18:4-5]; 114:3 [116:3]; Prov 13:14; 14:27; 21:6), ascends through windows (Jer 9:21), kills (Job 18:13; Jer 18:21), terrorizes (Ps 54:5 [55:4]), consumes (Job 15:21), is never satisfied (Hab 2:5), crushes (Job 30:23), speaks (Job 28:22), shepherds (Ps 48:15 [49:14]), is the enemy of man (Cant 8:6), has weapons (Ps 7:13), is sent by God (Isa 9:7; Hab 3:13), meets people (Prov 24:8; Dan 2:9), can be called upon (Job 17:14; Prov 18:6), makes covenants (Isa 28:15, 18), has a soul (Jonah 2:5), has an angel/messenger (LXX Prov 16:14), gives no praise to God (Isa 38:18), and the Lord will swallow up death forever (Isa 25:8; Hos 13:14). Death sometimes is even presented like a city with gates (i.e. the gates of death).[40]

Similarly, Sheol/Hades is predominantly the realm of the underworld,[41] but also can be personified as a being that unleashes terror. Sheol/Hades is personified throughout the OT as seizing his victims (Job 24:19), never being satisfied (Prov 27:20; Hab 2:5), an irresistible power (Cant 8:6), terrorizes with weapons (Pss 17 [18]:6; 114:3 [116:3]), has a house (Job 17:13; 30:23), has a hand (Pss 48:15-16 [49:14-15]; 88 [89]):49; Hos 13:14), has a belly (Jonah 2:3), has a mouth to feed on his victims (Isa 5:13), can be embittered (LXX Isa 14:9), can make a covenant (Isa 28:15), is naked before God (Job 26:6), and

---

37 Judg 5:18; 1 Sam 20:3; 2 Kgs 20:1; 1 Chr 21:12, 14; 2 Chr 32:24; Job 3:21, 23; 5:20; 12:22 24:17 (2x); 28:3; 33:22, 24, 30; 38:17; Pss 6:6; 9:14 (13); 12:4 (13:3); 15 (16):10; 21:16 (22:15); 22 (23):4; 32 (33):19; 43:20 (44:19); 54:16 (55:15); 55:14 (56:13); 67:21 (68:20); 87:7 (88:6); 88:49 (89:48); 106 (107):10, 14, 18, 26; 114:8 (116:8); 117 (118):18; Prov 2:18; 5:5; 7:27; 8:36; 10:2; 11:19; 12:28; 18:21; 23:4; 11; Isa 9:1; 38:1; 39:1; 53:8, 12; Ezek 31:14; Hosea 13:14; Amos 4:10; 5:8.

38 U. Cassuto, *Biblical and Oriental Studies*, trans. Israel Abrahams, vol. 2, Bible and Ancient Oriental Texts (Jerusalem: Magnes Press, 1975), 172-74. Mot was the "king of the netherworld" according to the Ugaritic texts.

39 J. Day, *Yahweh and the Gods and Goddesses of Canaan*, Journal for the Study of the Old Testament: Supplement Series 265 (Sheffield: Sheffield Academic Press, 2000), 185-225.

40 Job 38:17; Pss 9:14 (13); 23 (24):7, 9; 106 (107):16, 18; Isa 45:1-2; *T. Isaac* 4:10; 4Q184.

41 Gen 37:35; 42:38; 44:29, 31; Num 16:30, 33; Deut 32:22; 1 Sam 2:6; 1 Kgs 2:6, 9; Job 7:9; 11:8; 14:13; 17:13, 16; 21:13; 30:23; 33:22; Pss 6:6; 9:18; 48 (49):15b; 54:16 (55:16); 85 (86):13; 87:4 (88:3); 93:17 (94:17); 113:25 (115:17); 138 (139):8; Prov 1:12; 2:18; 5:5; 7:27; 9:18; 14:12; 15:11, 24; 16:25; 29:4; 30:16; Eccl 9:10; Isa 14:11, 15, 19; 38:10, 18 (2x); 57:9; Ezek 31:15-17, 16, 17; 32:27; Amos 9:2.

God will rescue souls from Hades.[42] Furthermore, Yahweh's burning wrath reaches to Sheol (Deut 32:22) and it is the place reserved for the wicked that the righteous must escape (Prov 2:18-19; 5:5; 7:27; 9:18; 15:24; 21:16). On the other hand, Yahweh can dwell in Sheol (Ps 139:8), it lies completely open to him (Prov 15:11; Job 26:6), and he has the power over who goes there and who gets out (Ps 138 [139:8]; Amos 9:2; 1 Sam 2:6; Hos 13:14). Similar to Death, Sheol is also presented as a city with impenetrable gates.[43] In LXX Job 38:17, gatekeepers of Hades are presented as cowering with fear before the true God. John may be alluding to this passage in Revelation 1:18 and may have understood personified Death and Hades as the gatekeepers holding the keys.

Most important for the background to Revelation, Death and Hades appear together frequently in the OT.[44] When they appear together they are usually personified and seem to be inseparable brothers as they are consistently paired together in Revelation (1:18; 6:8; 20:13, 14). Interestingly, Abaddon and Hades also appear together not infrequently in the OT (Job 26:6; 28:21 [22][45]; Pss 87 [88]:12; Prov 15:11; 27:20). Revelation presents Abaddon (Apollyon)[46] as the angel who is king over the abyss in the underworld (Rev 9:11), but John sees him as a demon from the underworld and not equivalent to Death and Hades. Even though Death and Hades are found in the Greek literature, it is the OT where they are paired together numerous times, frequently wreaking havoc on mankind. Therefore, the OT should be seen as Revelation's primary source text for personifying Death and Hades and presenting them as lords of the

---

[42] Pss 15 (16):9-11; 16 (17):15; 29 (30):4; 48:15-16 (49:14-15); 106 (107):8-22; Isa 25:8; 42:7; 45:1-3; Hos 13:14; Zech 9:11-12.

[43] Isa 38:10; Jonah 2:3, 7; cf. Matt 16:18; Wis 16:13; *Pss. Sol.* 16:2; *3 Macc.* 5:51; 6:31; *Apoc. Zeph.* 5:1-6; 1QH 11.16-19; 11Q11 3-4; *Sib. Or.* 2:225-229; 8:217-229; *Il.*, 5.646; 9.312; *Od.* 14.156; Virgil *Aen.* 6.551; Euripides *Hippol.* 56-57; *Hec.* 1; Aeschylus, *Ag.* 1291; Diogenes Laertius 8.34-35; Theocritus 2.33-34; Pseudo-Plato *[Ax.]* 371B. Heaven is also pictured as a city with gates (Gen 28:17; Pss 23 (24):7, 9; 86 (87):2; 99 (100):4; 117 (118):19, 20; Prov 14:19; cf. Rev 22:14; *Apoc. Zeph.* 3.6-10; *T. Levi* 5:1; 18:10; *T. Ab.* 10:15; 11:1-12; *Mart. Ascen. Isa.* 10:24-28; *L.A.E.* 31:2-3; 37:1; 40:2; 19:1; *4 Bar.* 9:5; *Apoc. Paul* 19; 20; 21; *Apoc. Thom.*

[44] 1 Sam 2:6; Job 17:13-14; 33:22; 38:17; Pss 6:6; 17 (18):5, 6; 48:15 (49:14); 54 (55):16; 88 (89):49; 114:3 (116:3); Prov 2:18; 5:5; 7:27; Cant 8:6; Isa 28:15, 18; Hosea 13:14; Hab 2:5. It should be noticed that מָוֶת "death" and קֶבֶר "grave" or θάνατος "death" and τάφος "grave" never appear together nor are they ever personified in the OT, NT, or in ancient literature. This demonstrates that the ancient writers did not see Sheol or Hades as the "grave," but as a distinct realm where the souls of the dead dwell.

[45] *Tg.* Job 28:22 has "Abaddon and the angel of death say. . . ." Cf. Rev 9:11.

[46] Domitian believed himself to be an incarnation of Apollo. Beasley-Murray concludes, "John's last word about the fifth trumpet was a master stroke of irony: the destructive host of hell had as its king the emperor of Rome!" G.R. Beasley-Murray, *The Book of Revelation*, NCBC, ed. M. Black (Grand Rapids: Eerdmans, 1981), 162-63.

underworld (Rev 20:13-14). Whether a Jew or a Greek, if they heard that Christ holds the keys of Death and Hades; battle imagery would have filled their minds. Most would not see Death and Hades kindly giving away their authority over the realm of the dead, but they must have been taken forcefully. They would have understood that the two great terrors of the Greek world and the Jewish world have been defeated by Christ. More on this battle imagery may be found in chapter 6.

Death and Hades in Second Temple Literature

The Second Temple literature follows the OT quite literally with Death and Hades appearing together frequently and being presented as either a realm or being personified. The book of Wisdom makes clear that God did not create death (Wis 1:13) and it was through the Devil's envy that death entered into the world (Wis 2:24; cf. *Sib. Or.* 1:40). Death can be seen as a realm or state of being[47] or personified. To illustrate, Death can be summoned by mankind to make a covenant (Wis 1:16), Death is summoned by God to take Abraham (*T. Ab.* 8:9-12; 16-20), Death decrees (Sir 41:2-3), has a hand (Song of the Three Jews 1:88), and can marry (*Sib. Or.* 3.480). Hades, on the other hand, is usually presented as the realm of the souls of the dead in this period.[48] Hades can still be seen as personified as making decrees (Sir 14:12), swallowing up sinners (*1 En.* 56.8; *Apoc. Ab.* 31:3-4), oppressive (*1 En.* 63.11), destructive (*Sib. Or.* 3.393), a dragon that feeds on the wicked (*3 Bar.* 4:6), and must be tamed (*Apoc. Ab.* 10:11). In Josephus, Hades can be referred to either as a person or a place.[49]

Death and Hades also appear together as personified beings during this time.[50] Similar to the OT, Hades throughout the Second Temple period remains

[47] *Pss. Sol.* 7:4; 16:2; Tob 4:10; 12:9; Jdt 11:11; 14:5; Wis 1:12, 13; 2:24; Sir 11:14; 14:12; 17:28; 28:6, 21; 41:1; 48:5; *4 Ezra* 8:53.

[48] Sir 14:16; 17:27; 21:10; 28:21; 41:4; 48:5; 51:5, 6; Tob 3:10; 4:19; 13:2; Wis 1:13; 2:1; 16:13; 17:13; Bar 2:17; 3:11, 19; Song of the Three Jews 1:88; 2 Macc 6:23; *3 Macc.* 4:8; 6:31; Add Esth 13:13; *Pss. Sol.* 4:13; 14:9; 15:10; 16:2; *1 En.* 51.1; 102.4-5, 11; 103.7; *Ant.* 6.332-336; *J. W.* 3.375; *3 En.* 44:2; *Sib. Or.* Book 1:80-85; 1:233; 303, 306; 2:196-199; 3:393, 458; 5:178; 8:105, 159, 199; 11:138; 12:77, 146; 14:184; *4 Ezra* 4:7-8, 36, 41; 8:53; *3 Macc.* 5:42, 51; *3 Bar.* 4:3, 6; 5:3; *Apoc. Dan.* 9:1-3; *Frag.* 1: 22; *Apoc. Zeph.* B:1-7; 6:11-17; 7:9; 9:2; *T. Job* 43:7; *T. Ab.* 8:9-10; 19:7; *T. Adam* 3:3; *Jub.* 5:14; 7:29; 24:31; Ps.-Phoc. 110-113; *Syr. Men.* 34-37, 68-69, 371-376, 470-473; Pss 152:2, 6; 153:3; 4QM 14.15-16; 1QH 4.13; 11.9, 16-19; 14.17; 17.4; 18.33-34; 4Q184 § 10; 11Q11 4.8-9.

[49] *Ant.* 6.332; 18.14-15; *J.W.* 2.156; 3.375; Hades is personified only in *J.W.* 1.596 as "the avenger in the invisible world."

[50] *Pss. Sol.* 16:2; Wis 1:13-16; 16:13; Sir 14:12; 17:27-28; 28:21; 41:1-4; 48:5; 51:6; Sg Three 1:88; *4 Ezra* 8:53; *T. Ab.* 8:9; 19:7; *Syr. Men.* 68-69; *Odes of Sol.* 15:9; 29:4; 42:11-20; *L.A.B.* 3:10; 1QH 17.4; 4Q184; cf. *1 Clem.* 51.4. Hades and Abaddon are

the place where all the dead go.[51] On the other hand, the theology of the underworld has been significantly developed from the OT with both Hades (dwelling for the wicked) and Paradise (dwelling for the righteous) in the underworld or in some other location.[52] Josephus[53] reports that the Pharisees taught that the righteous received rewards and the wicked received punishment in the underworld (Hades). As in the OT, only God can open the gates of Hades (Sheol) (1 Sam 2:6; Wis 16:13; 2 *Enoch* 42:1; *Ap. Pet.* 4:3.). In short, the intertestamental theology of the underworld added numerous compartments such as Paradise (for the righteous), Hades (for the wicked), and the Abyss (for disobedient angels). Hades especially came to be seen more as the place of the wicked and a place of eternal punishment in fire (Sir 21:9-10). As was shown above, there is not any evidence that before Christ the souls of humans went anywhere but to the underworld in hope that God would rescue them.

The End of Death and Hades in the New Testament

The NT uses numerous words to describe different compartments in the underworld, but Hades is predominant being used a total of ten times.[54] A brief survey of the use of Hades will reveal this. First, Matt 11:23/Luke 10:15 use Hades similar to the OT as the lowest place in the cosmos in contrast to heaven as the highest. Second, Revelation uses Hades four times (always paired with death) and the two of them are personified agents of evil that Christ will (has) overcome (Rev 1:18; 6:8; 20:13, 14). However, Hades as a city with gates and souls dwelling within is still clearly present in Revelation as well (Rev 20:13). Third, Matthew specifically mentions the "gates of Hades" not being able to overcome the church (Matt 16:18) (see discussion in chapter 3). Fourth, Luke uses Hades twice as much as the others and two of those times are in the section where Peter quotes Psalm 16:8-11.

The other time in Luke is significant because in the parable of the rich man and Lazarus, Hades and Abraham's bosom (Paradise) are both placed in the underworld.[55] Hades is the place of punishment and Abraham's bosom

---

also paired together a few times (*Pss. Sol.* 14:9; 1QH 11.16, 19; 18.33-34; 11Q11 3.7-8).

[51] 2 Macc 6:23-24; 1 *En.* 22; 51:1; 102:5; 103:7; *2 Bar.* 23:4-5.

[52] *1 En.* 22; *2 Bar.* 30:1-5; *Apoc. Ab.* 21.3-6; *4 Ezra* 4:7-8, 35, 41-43; 7:32, 36-38, 80, 85, 95, 101, 121; *Ps. Sol.* 14:6; 15:11; cf. Luke 16:19-31.

[53] *Ant.* 18.14-15. However, Josephus himself testifies a belief that souls of the righteous have a place in heaven at death while the wicked go to the darkest places of Hades (*J. W.* 3.374-375). It should be noted that Josephus is writing after the death of Christ.

[54] Matthew (2); Luke (2); Acts (2); Revelation (4). In 1 Cor 15:55, the reading ᾅδη (see Metzger) is an assimilation to LXX Hos 13:14. Metzger also rightly notes that Paul never uses ᾅδης. B.M. Metzger, *A Textual Commentary on the Greek New Testament*, 2nd ed. (Stuttgart: United Bible Societies, 1994): 503.

[55] Luke 16:19-31 cf. *1 En.* 22; *4 Ezra* 7:32, 36-38; *Ant.* 18.14-15.

(Paradise) is a place of peace and rest. In the passage quoted by Peter it speaks of Christ's "soul" being left (temporarily) in Hades twice (Acts 2:27, 31) and then being resurrected out of Hades (Acts 2:31-32). Luke, therefore, must have seen the compartment Paradise located in the underworld because Christ said to the thief on the cross "today" you will be with me in Paradise (Luke 23:43). Yet Peter says that Christ's soul was in Hades for the interval between his death and resurrection (Acts 2:27, 31). If Paradise is equated with Abraham's bosom this makes the argument even stronger that Luke envisioned two compartments in the underworld: a place of torment for the wicked and Abraham's bosom/Paradise as the dwelling place of the righteous dead. We will explore the different compartments of the underworld further in Chapter 4 of this book.

Qάνατος ("Death") is found about a hundred and twenty times in the NT. Moreover, Death is personified throughout the NT,[56] but Hades is only personified in Revelation (1:18; 6:8; 20:13, 14). These are also the only four places in the NT where Death and Hades appear together. The author of Revelation is the only writer of the NT who continues to portray Death and Hades as a duo of terror against mankind as has been shown to be somewhat normative in the OT and the Second Temple Literature.

Νεκρός ("dead") is another word used in the NT that is relevant to our discussion. Jesus is consistently (43x) described as being "raised from the dead" or "the realm of the dead."[57] Νεκρός is always plural when speaking of Christ being resurrected from the underworld which should then be translated "realm of the dead" or "the dead ones (spirits)."[58] In the OT, νεκρῶν is sometimes synonymous with Sheol/Hades.[59] In addition, according to Paul, Christ rising "from the dead" (ἐκ νεκρῶν) is parallel to him rising out of the abyss (Rom 10:7; cf. Luke 16:30-31). Bauckham says, "The basic image of

---

[56] Rom 5:14, 17; 6:9; 1 Cor 15:26, 54-55; 2 Tim 1:10; Heb 2:14; Rev 1:18; 6:8; 9:6; 20:14.

[57] Matt 14:2 (John the Baptist); 17:9; 27:64; 28:7; Mark 6:14 (John the Baptist); 9:9, 10; Luke 9:7 (John the Baptist); 16:30, 31; 24:46; John 2:22; 12:1 (Lazarus), 9 (Lazarus), 17 (Lazarus); 20:9; 21:14; Acts 3:15; 4:2, 10; 10:41; 13:30, 34; 17:3, 31, 32; Rom 1:4; 4:24; 6:4, 9; 7:4; 8:11 (2x); 10:7, 9; 1 Cor 15:12, 20, 21; Gal 1:1; Eph 1:20; 5:14; Col 1:18; 2:12; 1 Thess 1:10; 2 Tim 2:8; Heb 13:20; 1 Pet 1:3, 21; Rev 1:5. This is also the word consistently used to speak of the general resurrection of the dead when the souls will be reunited with their physical bodies (Matt 22:31-32; Mark 12:25, 26, 27; Luke 20:35, 37, 38; John 5:21, 25; Acts 23:6; 24:21; Rom 4:17; 6:13; 11:15; 1 Cor 15:12, 13, 15, 16, 29 (2x), 32, 35, 42, 52; 2 Cor 1:9; Phil 3:11; 1 Thess 4:16; Heb 6:2; 11:19).

[58] "The νεκροί are often the dead in the underworld of whom Christ is the πρωτότοκος." R. Bultmann, "νεκρός," in *TDNT*, ed. G. Kittel, G. Friedrich, and G. Bromiley, vol. 4 (Grand Rapids: Eerdmans, 1964–1976): 4:893. W. Bales, "The Descent of Christ in Ephesians 4:9," *CBQ* 72 (2010): 88.

[59] LXX Deut 18:11; Pss 87:11 (88:5); 113:25; Lam 3:6; Ezek 32:18; Eccl 9:3, 5, 10; Isa 26:14, 19; cf. Bar 3:11; 2 Macc 12:41.

resurrection is that *the place of the dead will give back the dead.*"[60] So every time Christ is spoken of as being raised from the dead, the original readers would not have thought of him coming back from just the state of death, but that he came back from the realm of the dead, namely Hades. This should also give understanding to Jesus being hailed as the Judge or Lord of the living ones and the dead ones (νεκρῶν) (Acts 10:42; Rom 14:9; 2 Tim 4:1; 1 Pet 4:5). Jesus is the Lord of both realms: the realm of the living and the realm of the dead. Why? The reason is that Jesus was the firstborn from the νεκρῶν because he was the first to return from Hades as its conqueror (Col 1:18; Rev 1:5, 18).

Death and Hades' reign of terror meet their end in the book of Revelation (20:13-14). Not only are they forced to give back the souls of the dead by the glorified Christ and the holder of the keys (1:18; 20:13), but they themselves will be thrown into the lake of fire. John says there will be no more "death" (Rev 21:4) and if there is no more death, there is no more need for a realm of the dead (Hades). This survey has revealed the consistent use of Death and Hades as personified beings not just in the Greco-Roman world but also in the Jewish world especially when they are paired together. A key interpretive issue in Revelation 1:18 is whether or not Death and Hades are personified (as they clearly are in Revelation 6:8 and 20:14). The burden of proof is on those who would not see personification in Rev 1:18 because the Greco-Roman and Jewish background argues strongly for it. The next chapter will further demonstrate this with an in-depth study of "keys" and "keyholders" in the ancient world that is in the background to Revelation 1:18.

---

[60] Bauckham, *The Fate of the Dead*, 277.

CHAPTER 3

THE BATTLE FOR THE KEYS TO THE UNDERWORLD

What would the first century Christian in the church of Sardis or Ephesus have understood when he heard that Christ is now the possessor of the keys to the underworld (Rev 1:18)? This chapter will demonstrate that many gods, goddesses, and angels are said to be the key holders to the underworld and therefore, Revelation 1:18 may be one of the strongest polemics in Revelation against the false religions of the Greco-Roman world. Six passages in the NT mention key or keys[1] and I will analyze the meaning of "keys" in each one. The word κλείς occurs only five times in the Septuagint and four out of the five are speaking of literal keys.[2] Only in Isaiah 22:22 are the "keys" used in a metaphorical sense, as Eliakim's authority and power over the kingdom of David. In the other passages, Bel and the Dragon 11 speaks of the priests of Baal telling the king to "shut the door" (ἀπονκλεισον τh;ν θυνραν). In Job 31:22, the word would better be translated "socket" or "connecting bone." Judges 3:25 speaks of the servants of Eglon becoming embarrassed because he was taking too long to relieve himself. Finally, they open the door with a "key" and find him assassinated by Ehud. First Chronicles 9:27 speaks of the time of Ezra when four chief Levites had charge over the gates of the temple in Jerusalem. They spent the night there "and were over the chambers and over the treasuries in the house of God" (1 Chr 9:26). Every morning they would open the gates since they had charge over the "keys" (1 Chr 9:27). In the NT, every time a "key" or "keys" are mentioned, they are used in a metaphorical sense.[3] Keys are also predominantly used metaphorically in the texts of ancient

---

[1] Matt 16:19; Luke 11:52; Rev 1:18; 3:7; 9:1; 20:1.

[2] Judg 3:25; Isa 22:22; 1 Chr 9:27 (3x for Hebrew word מַפְתֵּחַ); Job 31:22 ("socket" translating the Hebrew word שֶׁכֶם); Bel 11 (OG "bolts" with no Hebrew equivalent). On the literal use of keys in the ancient world cf. *1 Clem.* 43:3; Livy 24.23.1; 24.37.8-9.

[3] "Keys of the kingdom of heaven" (Matt 16:19); "Key of knowledge" (Luke 11:52); "Keys of Death and Hades" (Rev 1:18); "Key of David" (3:7); "Key of the abyss" (9:1; 20:1). The Fathers generally interpreted "keys" metaphorically as the authority

Greece, Rome, and Egypt as possessed by a god or goddess of the underworld as the brief survey below will demonstrate.

A Brief Survey of Key Holders to the Underworld

Keys had a very important place in the ancient Jewish and Greco-Roman world. The Jewish, Roman, and Greek writers wanted to present their gods as the one who holds the keys to the underworld. The imagery used to describe both the underworld and heaven is consistent in the ancient world. The underworld was presented as protected by strong and impenetrable gates that required keys to enter.[4] Therefore, we have numerous angels, gods, and goddesses who are said to possess the keys to these gates. One of the earliest references comes from fifth century BC writer Pindar who says to his goddess Dike, "Kindly Goddess of Peace, daughter of Justice, that makest cities great; thou that holdest the master-keys (ἔξοισα κλαῖδας) of councils and of wars. . . ."[5] This is a clearly figurative use of the keys for councils and wars. In addition, Pausanias presents the god Ploutos (god of wealth), who is often together with Hades, holding the key that he just used to lock up the god Hades.[6]

Another predominant figure in the ancient Greco-Roman world who is said in multiple places to have the keys of the underworld is the goddess Hekate (also known as Persephone, Artemis, and Diana). In fact, Aune argues that Jesus holding the keys to Death and Hades is a polemic against the Hellenistic conceptions of the goddess Hekate. Hekate was the primary figure in the ancient Greco-Roman world to be associated with having the keys to Hades.[7] To illustrate, the Greek writer Hesiod gives her origin:

> Perses brought her to his great house, to be his dear wife. There she conceived and bore Hekate, whom Zeus honored above all others; he gave her dazzling gifts, a

---

and power of bishops as they succeeded one another. See Robert Murray, *Symbols of Church and Kingdom* (New Jersey: Gorgias Press, 2004): 182-87.

[4] Job 38:17; Pss 9:14 (13); 23 (24):7, 9; 106 (107):16, 18; Isa 38:10; 45:1-2; Jonah 2:3, 7; Matt 16:18; Wis 16:13; *Pss. Sol.* 16:2; *3 Macc.* 5:51; 6:31; *Apoc. Zeph.* 5:1-6; *T. Isaac* 4:10; 1QH 11.16-19; 11Q11 3-4; 4Q184; *Sib. Or.* 2:225-229; 8:217-229; *Il.*, 5.646; 9.312; *Od.* 14.156; Virgil *Aen.* 6.551; Euripides *Hippol.* 56-57; *Hec.* 1; Aeschylus, *Agam.* 1291; Diogenes Laertius 8.34-35; Theocritus 2.33-34; Pseudo-Plato *[Ax.]* 371B.

[5] 8.4 in Pindar, *The Odes of Pindar*, Loeb Classical Library, ed. T.E. Page (Cambridge, MA: Harvard University Press, 1915): 260-61.

[6] Pausanias 5.20.3; cf. Hom *Il.* 8.367. Pseudo-Plato speaks of ". . . a dwelling beneath the earth where Pluto's palace is not inferior to Zeus' court. . . . The entrance to the way to Pluto's palace is protected with iron bolts and keys" (Pseudo-Plato *[Ax.]* 371B).

[7] D.E. Aune, "The Apocalypse of John and Graeco-Roman Revelatory Magic," *NTS* 33 (October 1987): 484-89.

share of the earth and a share of the barren sea. She was given a place of honor in the starry sky, and among the deathless gods her rank is high. For even now, when a mortal propitiates the gods and, following custom, sacrifices well-chosen victims, he invokes Hekate, and if she receives his prayers with favor, then honor goes to him with great ease, and he is given blessings, because she has power . . . and her domain extends over land and sky and sea, and she can greatly aid a man if this is her wish [8]

Hekate also known as Artemis in magic papyri texts, "Mother of all things, for you frequent Olympos, and the broad and boundless chasm you traverse. Beginning and end are you, and you alone rule all. For all things are from you, and in you do all things, Eternal one, come to their end. . . . And you hold in Your hands a golden scepter."[9] She is given multiple titles here that are exclusively used for God and Christ in Revelation. Hekate is the "beginning and end" (cf. Rev 21:6; 22:13), she alone rules all and holds a golden scepter (cf. Rev 1:5; 2:27; 12:5; 19:15), and all things come from her and in her are all things (cf. Rev 4:11). In the *Orphic Hymns* (AD 200), Hekate is described as "the queen and mistress of the whole world" and is given the title "keybearer." Lastly, it is said of Persephone, with whom Hekate is often identified, "you command the gates of Hades in the bowels of the earth."[10] The parallels between Hekate and the book of Revelation are staggering, but I agree with Beale that "a more general polemic could be intended, not merely against Hekate, but all the pagan gods popularly thought of as rulers of the underworld."[11]

The Egyptian deity Anubis is also called the "key-holder" and "guardian" of the "eternal bars" of the underworld and is commanded to "send up to me the phantoms of the dead." In the most striking parallel, Anubis has this power because he is described as the one who τῷ τὰς κλεῖδας ἔχοντι τῶν κατά Ἅιδους "holds the keys of Hades."[12] Aeacus is another god that is said to be the

---

[8] *Theog.* 410-20, 427-29. Hesiod, *Theogony*, trans. A.N. Athanassakis (London: Johns Hopkins University Press, 1983): 23-24.

[9] PGM 4.2836-37. *The Greek Magical Papyri in Translation*, ed. H.D. Betz (London: University of Chicago Press, 1986): 91.

[10] 1.1-7 § 6-7; 29.4. *The Orphic Hymns*, trans. A.N. Athanassakis, Society of Biblical Literature Texts and Translations Graeco-Roman Religion Series, ed. H.D. Betz and E.N. O'Neil (Atlanta, GA: Scholars Press, 1977): 41.

[11] G.K. Beale, *The Book of Revelation: A Commentary on the Greek Text*, NIGTC, ed. I.H. Marshall and D.A. Hagner (Grand Rapids: Eerdmans, 1999), 215. Thomas says further, "It is difficult to see, however, that John as one so deeply imbued with OT revelation could have looked primarily to Hellenistic magic as a source of his terminology." R.L. Thomas, *Revelation 1–7: An Exegetical Commentary* (Chicago, IL: Moody Press, 1995): 112.

[12] PGM 4.1466; 4.341-42. *The Greek Magical Papyri in Translation*, 66, 44; G.H.R. Horsley, *New Documents Illustrating Early Christianity: A Review of the Greek Inscriptions and Papyri Published in 1976*, vol. 1 (North Ryde, N.S.W: Ancient

"keeper of the gate of Hades."[13] It is said of Aeacus, "Even after his death Aeacus is honoured in the abode of Pluto, and keeps the keys of Hades."[14] In addition, Zeus, the goddess Quiet, and Proteus are all said to hold the keys to the underworld.[15] These many gods and goddesses are given the power and authority of the keys of the underworld, but there can only be one true key-bearer.

When we move into the Jewish literature before and after the time of the NT, angels are predominantly said to possess the keys. The angels 'Anapi'el YHWH,[16] Metatron,[17] Iaoel,[18] Eremiel/Uriel,[19] and the archangel Michael[20] are all said to possess the keys to either the underworld or the kingdom of heaven. Instead of having the keys to the levels of Heaven, other angels are said to have the keys to Hades. 2 *Enoch* portrays the gates of Hades as very large and guarded by snakelike creatures. Enoch says, "And I saw the guardians of the keys of hell, standing by the very large doors, their faces like those of very large snakes, their eyes like extinguished lamps, and their teeth naked down to their breasts" (2 *En.* 42.1). The *Apocalypse of Zephaniah* has striking parallels with the first vision of Revelation (1:12-18). Zephaniah says,

> Then I arose and stood, and I saw a great angel standing before me with his face shining like the rays of the sun in its glory since his face is like that which is perfected in its glory. And he was girded as if a golden girdle were upon his breast. His feet were like bronze which is melted in a fire. And when I saw him, I rejoiced, for I thought that the Lord Almighty had come to visit me. I fell upon my

---

History Documentary Research Center, Macquarie University, 1981), 33-35. Horsley notes that Moulton and Milligan must not have been aware of this text on Anubis because they say, "We can supply no good parallel to the figurative use of κλείς in the NT. . . ." J.H. Moulton and G. Milligan, *The Vocabulary of the Greek Testament: Illustrated from the Papyri and Other Non-Literary Sources* (1930; reprint, Grand Rapids: Eerdmans, 1980): 345.

[13] Lucian *Dial. Mor.* 6[20].1. Lucian, *Dialogues of the Dead*, trans. M.D. Macleod, Loeb Classical Library, ed. T.E. Page, vol. 7 (Cambridge, MA: Harvard University Press, 1961): 25.

[14] Apollodorus 3.12.6. Apollodorus, *The Library*, Loeb Classical Library, ed. T.E. Page (Cambridge, MA: Harvard University Press, 1921): 57.

[15] For more references see D.E. Aune, *Revelation 1-5*, WBC, ed. D.A. Hubbard, G.W. Barker, and R.P. Martin, vol. 52A (Dallas, TX: Word, 1997): 104-5.

[16] *3 En.* 18.18.

[17] *3 En.* 48C.3.

[18] *Apoc. Abr.* 10.11.

[19] *4 Ezra* 4:36; *1 En.* 20:8 cf. *Sib. Or.* 2:225-229; *2 Bar.* 55:3; 63:6.

[20] *3 Bar.* 11.1-2. Baruch says, "And taking me from this, the angel led me to the fifth heaven. And the gate was closed. And I said, 'Lord, will the gate be opened so that we can enter?' And the angel said to me, 'We are not able to enter until Michael the holder of the keys of the kingdom of heaven (ὁ κλειδοῦχος τῆς βασιλείας τῶν οὐρανῶν) comes.'"

face, and I worshiped him. He said to me, "Take heed. Don't worship me. I am not the Lord Almighty, but I am the great angel, Eremiel, who is over the abyss and Hades, the one in which all the souls are imprisoned from the end of the flood, which came upon the earth, until this day."[21]

Clearly, Eremiel has replaced Christ in this vision, Christ has replaced Eremiel if Revelation was written after the *Apocalypse of Zephaniah*, or they are both using a common source.[22] Either way, Christ is presented as deity in Revelation because he accepts worship from John (1:17) (in contrast to Eremiel), and he is the one who has the keys of Death, Hades (Rev 1:12-18), and the abyss (Rev 9:1).

In the Rabbinic literature[23] angels once again have the authority over the keys, but keys are also given to righteous men. However, the Rabbis are consistent that the keys ultimately belong to God, and yet some say that God loans them for a time to his righteous emissaries. "There are four keys in the hands of the Master of the universe and that are not handed over into the hand of any dignitary: the key of life, of graves, of food, and of rain."[24] Despite this, God is said to have entrusted these keys to his righteous emissaries: Elijah received the key to rain, Elisha received the key to the womb, and Elisha and Ezekiel were given the key to the resurrection.[25] Elijah is also said to receive all three keys, "Elijah prayed that the keys of resurrection might be given him, but was answered, three keys have not been entrusted to an agent: of birth, rain, and resurrection."[26] The NT alludes to Elijah's key because Jesus says, "I assure

---

[21] *Apoc. Zeph.* 6:11-15.

[22] Charlesworth dates the *Apocalypse of Zephaniah* sometime from 100 BC to AD 175. He favors a pre-AD 70 date which would put the work before the book of Revelation. *The Old Testament Pseudepigrapha*. vol. 2, ed. J.H. Charlesworth (Garden City, NY: Doubleday, 1983–85): 500-501.

[23] The Rabinnic literature cited throughout the rest of this chapter is generally late, dating three to four centuries after the NT era. However, the traditions contained within them may go back to the first century or earlier.

[24] *Targ. Ps.-Jon.* on Deut 28:12. E.G. Clarke, ed. *Targum Pseudo-Jonathan: Deuteronomy*, The Aramaic Bible, ed. K. Cathcart, M. Maher, and M. McNamara, vol. 5B (Collegeville, MN: Liturgical Press, 1998): 75. M. Ginsburger, ed. *Pseudo-Jonathan: (Thargum Jonathan ben Usiël zum Pentateuch), Nach der Londoner Handschrift (Brit. Mus. add. 27031)* (Berlin: Calvary, 1903): 347.

[25] *Midr. Ps.* 78:5. *The Midrash on Psalms*, trans. W.G. Braude, Yale Judaica Series, ed. L. Nemoy, vol. 13 (London: Yale University Press, 1959): 25-26. *Midr.* Dt. 7:6. *Deuteronomy*, trans. J. Rabbinowitz, Midrash Rabbah, ed. H. Freedman and M. Simon (New York: Soncino Press, 1983), 137-38. *b. Ta'an* 2a, b. "Tractate Taanith," in *Hebrew-English Edition of the Babylonian Talmud*, ed. I. Epstein (New York: Soncino Press, 1969). In this section, God is said to have the key to open the graves and Ezekiel 37:13 is quoted.

[26] *b.* Sanh. 113a. "Tractate Sanhedrin," in *Hebrew-English Edition of the Babylonian Talmud*, ed. I. Epstein, trans. Jacob Shachter and H. Freedman (New York: Soncino Press, 1969).

you that there were many widows in Israel in Elijah's time, when the sky was shut (ἐκλείσθη) for three and a half years" (Luke 4:25).

In Revelation, the two witnesses "have power to shut up the sky (ἔχουσιν τὴν ἐξουσίαν κλεῖσαι τὸν οὐρανόν) so that it will not rain during the time they are prophesying" (Rev 11:6). This verse could just as easily read, they 'have *the key of heaven* so that it will not rain during the time they are prophesying.' While the Rabbis freely speak of righteous men having keys, some forbid angels from possessing them. For they say, "Four keys there are which are given into the hand of the Lord, the master of all worlds, and he does not hand over them either to angel or to Seraph: the key of rain and the key of provision and the key of the sepulchers and the key of barrenness."[27] In contrast to the Rabbis, the author of the book of Revelation freely gives the full authority and power of the keys to someone other than God the Father, the Lord Jesus Christ.

An Exegetical Analysis of "Keys" in the New Testament

Let us now turn to the six passages that speak of "keys" in the NT. I will only briefly reference Revelation 1:18 because this passage will be discussed extensively in chapter 6. First, the passage in Matthew 16:19 where Jesus gives the "keys to the kingdom of heaven"[28] to Peter should be seen in conjunction with Revelation 1:18 and 3:7. Cullman sees the clear allusion to Eliakim in Matthew 16:19, for he says, "Just as in Isaiah 22:22 the Lord lays the keys of the house of David on the shoulders of his servant Eliakim, so Jesus commits to Peter the keys of his house, the Kingdom of Heaven, and thereby installs him as administrator of the house."[29] Jeremias says, "Materially, then, the keys of the kingdom of God are not different from the key of David."[30] Just before this bestowal of the keys, Jesus says, "And I tell you that you are Peter, and on this rock I will build my church, and the gates of Hades will not overcome it (πύλαι ᾅδου οὐ κατισχύσουσιν αὐτῆς)" (Matt 16:18). The promise that the gates of

---

[27] *Targ. Neof.* Gen 30:22. M. McNamara, ed. *Targum Neofiti I: Genesis*, The Aramaic Bible, ed. K. Cathhart, M. Maher, and M. McNamara, vol. 1A (Collegeville, MN: Liturgical Press, 1992): 148-49. A.D. Macho, ed. *Neophyti 1: Tomo 1 Genesis*, trans. A.D. Macho, Textos Y Estudios, ed. F.P. Castro, vol. 1 (Madrid: Consejo Superior de Investigaciones Científicas, 1968): 194-95. Others present angels with the keys to Gehenna. R. 'Aqiba says, "In that hour the Holy One, blessed be He, takes the keys of *gehinnom* and gives them to Michael and Gabriel before the eyes of all the righteous, and says to them: Go and open the gates of *gehinnom*. . . . Forthwith Michael and Gabriel go and open the 40,000 gates of *gehinnom*." J. Jeremias, "κλείς," in *TDNT*, ed. G. Kittel, G. Freidrich, and G. Bromiley, vol. 3 (Grand Rapids: Eerdmans, 1964–1976): 3.746. cf. *b. Chag.* 15b.

[28] cf. *3 Bar.* 11.1-2 above.

[29] O. Cullmann, *Peter: Disciple, Apostle, Martyr*, trans. F.V. Filson (Philadelphia: Westminster Press, 1953): 203.

[30] Jeremias, "κλείς," 3.749.

Hades will not overcome the new people of God seems to parallel the implied promise that Death and Hades will not overcome the church in Revelation 1:18. They are just different metaphors that illustrate the same reality. If the gates of Hades cannot prevail over/contain the people of God then all who are in Christ will either be released from Hades or never go there. The phrase πύλαι ᾅδου "the gates of Hades" is only found here in the NT (Matt 16:18), but that Hades was guarded by impenetrable gates was well known in the ancient world.[31] Jesus promises that "the gates of Hades will not prevail against/contain" (Matt 16:18) the new eschatological community. The Greek word κατισχύσουσιν can mean "overcome, prevail over, contain" and I will argue for this meaning.[32]

Many commentators of this passage have argued that the "gates of Hades" should not be seen as a city with impenetrable gates enclosing the new people of God, but instead as "powers" that are fighting against the church.[33] Jeremias argues that in the LXX κατισχύω is always active ("to vanquish") when followed by the genitive.[34] The release of the demonic hosts to unleash hell (literally) on the earth in Revelation have been seen as an appropriate parallel to these powers that are attacking the church (Rev 6:8; 9:1-12; 20:3, 7-10; cf. Luke 10:17). This view is very attractive because it pictures Christ as the "Cosmic rock" that stands firm against the most vicious attacks of Satan and the world and the church will follow in this victory (Isa 28:15-18; Matt 7:24-27; 8:23-27; 14:22-24).

However, the greatest weakness of this view is that the phrase "gates of Hades" never means powers that attack in the ancient world, but consistently

---

[31] LXX Isa 38:10; Jonah 2:3, 7; Wis 16:13; *Pss. Sol.* 16:2; *Apoc. Zeph.* 5:1-6; *3 Macc.* 5:51; 6:31; *Il.*, 5.646; 9.312; *Od.* 14.156; Virgil *Aen.* 6.551; Euripides *Hippol.* 56-57; *Hec.* 1; Aeschylus, *Agam.* 1291; Diogenes Laertius 8.34-35; Theocritus 2.33-34; Pseudo-Plato *[Ax.]* 371B; 1QH 3:16-18; 6:22-24; cf. Job 38:17; Pss 9:13; 107:18.

[32] Cf. LXX Exod 17:11; Deut 1:38; 1 Kgs 19:8; OG Dan 11:5; J. Jeremias, "πύλη," in *TDNT*, ed. G. Kittel, G. Freidrich, and G. Bromiley, vol. 6 (Grand Rapids: Eerdmans, 1964–76): 6.927. W. Bousset, *Kyrios Christos: A History of the Belief in Christ from the Beginnings of Christianity to Irenaeus*, trans. J.E. Steely (Nashville, TN: Abingdon Press, 1970): 65. T.R. McLay, *The Use of the Septuagint in New Testament Research* (Grand Rapids: Eerdmans, 2003): 162-63. W.D. Davies and D.C. Allison Jr., *A Critical and Exegetical Commentary on the Gospel According to Saint Matthew*, vol. 3, ICC, ed. J.A. Emerton, C.E.B. Cranfield, and G.N. Stanton (Edinburgh: T. & T. Clark, 1991): 2.630-32.

[33] C.L. Blomberg, *Matthew*, NAC, ed. D.S. Dockery (Nashville, TN: Broadman Press, 1992): 253. G. Bornkamm, *Jesus of Nazareth* (New York: Harper, 1960): 187. Jeremias, "πύλη," 6.924-28. Davies and Allison, *A Critical and Exegetical Commentary on the Gospel According to Saint Matthew*: 2.632-33. W.F. Albright and C.S. Mann, *Matthew*, AB, ed. W.F. Albright and D.N. Freedman, vol. 26 (Garden City, NY: Doubleday, 1971): 196. R.E. Brown, K.P. Donfried, and J. Reumann, eds., *Peter in the New Testament: A Collaborative Assessment by Protestant and Roman Catholic Scholars* (New York: Geoffrey Chapman, 1973): 90.

[34] *T. Dan.* 5.2; *T. Jos.* 6.7; *T. Reub.* 4.11. Jeremias, "πύλη," 6.926.

refers to the gates of the underworld that one passes through in death.[35] Referring to the ancient literature on the gates of Hades, Lewis says, "In all of these cases gates are means of entry and exit. In none of them do they equal militant powers."[36] Moreover, Plummer says, "If aggressiveness were the prominent idea, we should hardly have the metaphor of a building with gates. Gates keep people in and keep people out, and are necessary for the strength of a citadel, but they do not fight."[37] A striking parallel passage from Homer says, "In no wise methinks shall thy coming from Lycia prove a defense to the men of Troy, though thou be never so strong, but thou shalt be vanquished by my hand and pass the gates of Hades."[38] If this is a good representative of the background and meaning of "gates of Hades" then Jesus is promising that his community would not pass through the gates of Hades like Patroclus, but enters instead into the kingdom of heaven (Matt 16:19).

I do not believe that the *Descensus* is the primary point of Jesus' promise here, but neither can it simply mean that the state or realm of death will not stop Christ's church.[39] For this promise to be true throughout the ages it is a logical necessity for the new community to not be enclosed in the gates of Hades.[40]

Jesus is promising that the impenetrable gates of Hades will not enclose him (Matt 12:40) or his new community (Matt 27:52-53). The fact that "The tombs broke open and the bodies of many holy people who had died were raised to life" (Matt 27:52) proved to the Matthean community that the "gates of Hades" would not prevail against those who are in Christ. Brown says, "the expression 'gates of Hades/Sheol/death' denotes the one way entrance to the realm of the dead from which there is no return."[41] He goes on to say,

It makes good sense to see the underlying imagery of Matt 16:18 as involving

---

[35] Isa 38:10; Wis 16:13; 3 Macc. 5:51; *Pss. Sol.* 16:3. In all these passages, the "gates of Hades" are seen as the real entrance to the underworld that one must pass at death. Only God is able to rescue them once they have passed through the "gates of Hades."

[36] J.P. Lewis, "'The Gates of Hell Shall Not Prevail against It' (Matt 16:18): A Study of the History of Interpretation," *JETS* 38 (1995): 350.

[37] A. Plummer, *An Exegetical Commentary on the Gospel according to St. Matthew* (Grand Rapids: Baker, 1982): 230.

[38] *Il.* 5.646.

[39] Contra C.S. Keener, *Revelation*, NIVAC, ed. T. Muck (Grand Rapids: Zondervan, 2000): 428. D.A. Hagner, *Matthew 14–28*, WBC, ed. D.A. Hubbard, R.P. Martin, and J.D.W. Watts, vol. 33B (Dallas, TX: Word, 1995): 472. R.T. France, *The Gospel of Matthew*, NICNT, ed. N.B. Stonehouse, F.F. Bruce, and G.D. Fee (Grand Rapids: Eerdmans, 2007), 624. Lewis, "'The Gates of Hell Shall Not Prevail against It'," 366-67.

[40] Bousset argues for the *Descensus* as the primary point of the passage. Bousset, *Kyrios Christos*, 65. Cf. McLay, *The Use of the Septuagint in New Testament Research*, 159-70.

[41] C. Brown, "The Gates of Hell and the Church," in *Church, Word, and Spirit*, ed. J.E. Bradley and R.A. Muller (Grand Rapids: Eerdmans, 1987): 21-22.

someone approaching and passing through the gates of Hades/Sheol. However, the gates will not prevail in the sense that they will not be able to keep the one who passes through them or put an end to his mission and cause. On the other hand, it would seem anachronistic to read into the text an implied crusade to liberate the dead in Hades.[42]

Therefore, Brown argues that the language of Matthew 16:18 may imply the liberation of Christ's community from Hades, but since he believes the *Descensus* was not taught until later, it is anachronistic to speak of it here! What if Matthew had this in mind when he wrote it since that is what the phrase "gates of Hades" probably implies according to Brown?[43] Why couldn't Matthew have originally taught the *Descensus* as a theological motif throughout his Gospel (Matt 12:39-41; 16:4, 17-19; 27:52-53)? In Revelation, this promise becomes even clearer because Christ possesses the keys of Death and Hades (Rev 1:18) and therefore, can release his community from the gates of Hades.

The keys to the kingdom of heaven that Christ gives on loan to Peter are also metaphorical for gaining access into salvation in the present in order to pass through the gates of the New Jerusalem later (Rev 21:25; 22:14). Peter uses the keys to unlock the gates of the kingdom of heaven to the Jews in Acts 2, the Samaritans in Acts 8, and the Gentiles in Acts 10.[44] Jesus had scolded the Pharisees because they "shut the kingdom of heaven in men's faces. You yourselves do not enter, nor will you let those enter who are trying to" (Matt 23:13).[45] In contrast, Peter as the chief representative of Christ will open the

---

[42] Brown, "The Gates of Hell and the Church," 35.

[43] It should also be noted that the texts that are used from Matthew to argue that the *Descensus* motif is behind the Gospel are all special material unique to Matthew (Matt 12:40; 16:4, 17-19 (Σίμων Βαριωνᾶ, πύλαι ᾅδου); 27:52-53). See McLay, *The Use of the Septuagint in New Testament Research*, 159-70.

[44] "On arriving there, they gathered the church together and reported all that God had done through them and how he had opened the door of faith to the Gentiles" (ὅτι ἤνοιξεν τοῖς ἔθνεσιν θύραν πίστεως) (Acts 14:27). One needs a metaphorical key to open this metaphorical door of salvation to the Gentiles.

[45] The Lucan parallel to Matt 23:13 (Luke 11:52) is the only other reference to a "key" in the NT (outside of Matthew and Revelation). Jesus says, "Woe to you experts in the law, because you have taken away the key to knowledge (τὴν κλεῖδα τῆς γνώσεως). You yourselves have not entered, and you have hindered those who were entering" (Luke 11:52). This is a different use of "key" than in Revelation and Matthew because it has nothing to do with the underworld. Collins says, "In Jewish tradition, the key of David refers to the authority of the teachers of the law." R.F. Collins, "Keys of the Kingdom of Heaven," in *ABD*, ed. D.N. Freedman (New York: Doubleday, 1992): 31. The Rabbinic literature interprets the keys similarly. *b.* Shab., 31a, b: "Rabbah b. R. Huna said: 'Every man who possesses learning without the fear of Heaven is like the treasurer who is entrusted with the inner keys but not with the outer: how is he to enter?" "Tractate Shabbath," in *Hebrew-English Edition of the Babylonian Talmud*, ed. I. Epstein (New York: Soncino Press, 1972). Cf. Luke 24:32,

kingdom of heaven for men because he has the keys/authority to let them in or shut them out.[46] Lewis sums up the primary point of this passage well, "All are agreed that the ongoing permanency of the Church is promised."[47] However, I believe the ongoing permanence of God's people goes beyond this world and Jesus' promise guarantees that all of his new community will not be enclosed within the "gates of Hades," but will pass through the gates to the kingdom of heaven in this life (Matt 12:28) and the next (Matt 25:34, 46).

The other references to "keys" in the NT all appear in Revelation. Christ's declaration about himself to the church of Philadelphia as ὁ ἔχων τὴν κλεῖν Δαυίδ "the one who has the key of David" (Rev 3:7) should be seen as parallel to Revelation 1:18.[48] Christ not only has the "keys belonging to Death and Hades," but he also has the "key of David." Christ is presented in Revelation as the "Root and offspring of David" (Rev 5:5; 22:16) and therefore has the keys to the "Eternal palace of God,"[49] the messianic kingdom, which in Revelation is called the New Jerusalem (Rev 21-22). It is no coincidence that the New Jerusalem is surrounded by gates (Rev 21:12-13, 15, 21, 25; 22:16) and the wicked are "outside" not able to get in (Rev 22:15). Christ not only holds the keys to the gates of Death and Hades, but also the keys to the gates of the New Jerusalem. He goes on to say, "I know your deeds. See, I have placed before you an open door that no one can shut" (Rev 3:8). The open door here could be further opportunities for missions and evangelism (1 Cor 16:9; 2 Cor 2:12; Col

---

45; *Gos. Thom.* 39. Many of the Fathers carried on this tradition by interpreting "keys" primarily as the means to unlock the Scriptures. Andrew of Caesarea on Rev 3:7, "His kingdom is called *the key of David*, for it is the symbol of authority. The key is also the Holy Spirit, (the key) of both the book of Psalms and every prophecy, through which the *treasures of knowledge* are opened. On the one hand, he receives the first according to his humanity, and on the other hand he possesses the second according to the beginninglessness of his divinity. Since in some manuscripts instead of *David*, *Hades* is written, (this would mean that) through the key of Hades, the authority over life and death has been confirmed in Christ. He is holy and true, as absolute Holiness and self-existent Truth." Nicholas of Lyra on Rev 3:7 "'Who has the key of David,' That is, the power to open the understanding of the Scriptures (Lk 24:33, 'And he opened to them the sense of the Scriptures')." *Nicholas of Lyra's Apocalypse Commentary*, trans. P.D.W. Krey (Kalamazoo, MI: Medieval Institute Publications, 1997): 58.

[46] Yet, all the disciples seem to have this authority according to Matt 18:18 and John 20:22-23, not just Peter.

[47] Lewis, "'The Gates of Hell Shall Not Prevail against It' (Matt 16:18): A Study of the History of Interpretation," 356.

[48] Some MSS replace Δαυίδ ("David") here with αδου ("Hades"; e.g., 104* 218 459 620 2050 2067*) or with του θανατου και του αδου ("death and Hades"; e.g., 1893). Armenian reads τοῦ παραδείσου. This demonstrates that the Christian scribes from very early saw a clear parallel between Revelation 1:18 and 3:7.

[49] Jeremias, "κλείς," 3.748.

4:3; Acts 14:27)[50] or entrance to the messianic kingdom (New Jerusalem) (Rev 2:7; 3:12; 21:12-15, 21, 25; 22:14).[51] This may allude to the door to heaven (Rev 4:1) or the gates of the New Jerusalem. I believe because of the messianic overtones from Isaiah 22:22 and the book of Revelation in general (Rev 5:5; 22:16); this should be seen as an open door leading into the gates of the eternal city of God.

In addition, the "key of David" is alluding to the story in Isaiah about Eliakim replacing the worthless steward Shebna. For Christ quotes Isaiah 22:22 almost verbatim when he says, ὁ ἀνοίγων καὶ οὐδεὶς κλείσει καὶ κλείων καὶ οὐδεὶς ἀνοίγει "One who opens and no one can shut, and One who shuts and no one can open" (see Rev 3:7). Christ has the authority to lock up and release those in Hades and to open and shut out whom he chooses from the New Jerusalem. The Targum of Isaiah 22:22 says, "And I will place the key *of the sanctuary and the authority* of the house of David *in his hand*; and he will open, and none shall shut; and he will shut, and none shall open."[52] According to Watts, Isaiah 22:20-24 contains the "fullest description of this position of honor and authority that exists in Scripture."[53]

[50] I. Boxall, *The Revelation of Saint John*, BNTC, ed. M.D. Hooker (London: Hendrickson Publishers, 2006): 72. W.M. Ramsay, *The Letters to the Seven Churches*, ed. M.W. Wilson (Peabody, MA: Hendrickson, 1994): 296; H.B. Swete, *Commentary on Revelation* (Grand Rapids: Kregel, 1977; reprint, London: Macmillan, 1911): 53-54. C.J. Hemer, *The Letters to the Seven Churches of Asia in Their Local Setting*, Journal for the Study of the New Testament: Supplement Series 11, ed. D. Hill (Sheffield: JSOT Press, 1986): 162. R.H. Charles, *A Critical and Exegetical Commentary on the Revelation of St. John*, vol. 1, ICC, ed. J.A. Emerton, C.E.B. Cranfield, and G.N. Stanton (Edinburgh: T. & T. Clark, 1966): 1.87. J.F. Walvoord, *The Revelation of Jesus Christ* (Chicago, IL: Moody Press, 1966), 85. G.B. Caird, *A Commentary on the Revelation of St. John the Divine* (New York: Harper and Row, 1966): 51-53.

[51] G.R. Beasley-Murray, *The Book of Revelation*, NCBC, ed. M. Black (Grand Rapids: William B. Eerdmans Publishing Company, 1981): 100. Beale, *The Book of Revelation*, 285. G.R. Osborne, *Revelation*, BECNT, ed. M. Silva (Grand Rapids: Baker Academic, 2002): 187-88. Thomas, *Revelation 1–7*, 278. G.E. Ladd, *A Commentary on the Revelation of John* (Grand Rapids: Eerdmans, 1972): 59. R.H. Mounce, *The Book of Revelation*, NICNT, ed. G.D. Fee (Grand Rapids: Eerdmans, 1977): 101. I.T. Beckwith, *The Apocalypse of John: Studies in Introduction with a Critical and Exegetical Commentary* (New York: Macmillan Company, 1919): 480. H. Kraft, *Die Offenbarung des Johannes* (Tübingen: Mohr-Siebeck, 1974): 81. E. Lohse, *Die Offenbarung des Johannes* (Göttingen: Vandenhoeck and Ruprecht, 1976): 33. Keener, *Revelation*, 150.

[52] B.D. Chilton, ed. *The Isaiah Targum*, The Aramaic Bible, ed. K. Cathcart, M. Maher, and M. McNamara, vol. 11 (Wilmington, DE: Michael Glazier, 1987): 44.

[53] J.D.W. Watts, *Isaiah 1–33*, WBC, ed. D.A. Hubbard, G.W. Barker, and J.D.W. Watts, vol. 24 (New York: Word, 1985): 289. Rabbinic interpretation of Isaiah 22:22 became figurative for opening and closing the teaching of Torah. For example, the rabbis say of Gabriel, with allusion to Is. 22:22, that he was called "Sigaron .

Furthermore, Eliakim is called "my servant" (22:20), "father to the inhabitants of Jerusalem" (22:21), he will become a "throne of glory" (22:23), and the key of the house of David is to be "on his shoulder."[54] In the time of Ezra, four Levites and the chief porters had keys to gates to the temple (1 Chr 9:27). They also had charge "over the chambers and over the treasuries in the house of God" (1 Chr 9:26). This gives us great insight to what the keys were used for at the time of Eliakim. Although Eliakim had great authority as holder of the keys to Davidic kingdom, he was still subject to the king as can be seen in 2 Kings 18:18 and Isaiah 36:3. On the other hand, since Christ is both King and Priest, he has complete authority over the eschatological city of God and is the true Lord of the key of David. Von Rad argues, "The almost Messianic full powers of the unworthy Shebna pass over, solemnly renewed, to Eliakim. Yet he too will fail. Thus, the office of 'the key of David' remained unprovided for until finally it could be laid down at the feet of Christ (Rev. 3:7)."[55] The faithful Christians in the church of Philadelphia would find great comfort that though they were put out of the synagogues, Christ would bring them into the eternal city of God.

The "keys" appear two more times in Revelation and in both cases it is in reference to the key to the shaft of the abyss. According to Revelation (9:1-2), there is a shaft that must be opened by a key in order to enter the abyss.[56] This is the most literal use of the word "key" in the NT, but still should be seen metaphorically explaining the authority of exit and entry to the abyss in the underworld. On the other hand, the abyss must be a real place that exists somewhere in some kind of reality because Satan is a real being and he will be locked up in the abyss for a thousand years (Rev 20:1, 3). God is spoken of as

---

. . because when he concludes a matter, none can reopen it" (*b. Sanh.*, 44b). "Tractate Sanhedrin." "'Out of them shall come forth the corner-stone.' This refers to King David, for it says, The stone which the builders rejected is become the chief corner stone (Ps. CXVIII, 22). 'Out of them the stake'—this refers to the High Priest, for it says, And I will fasten him as a peg in a sure place (Isa. XXII, 23)." *Midr. Rab.* Exod. 37.1. *Exodus*, trans. S.M. Lehrman, Midrash Rabbah, ed. H. Freedman and Maurice Simon (New York: Soncino Press, 1983): 442. Cf. 2 *Bar.* 10:18.

[54] There are striking similarities here to the messianic king that is foretold in Isaiah 9:6-7. "For to us a child is born, to us a son is given, *and the government will be on his shoulders.* And he will be called Wonderful Counselor, Mighty God, *Everlasting Father*, Prince of Peace. Of the increase of his government and peace there will be no end. *He will reign on David's throne and over his kingdom. . . .*" (Isa 9:6-7).

[55] G. von Rad, *Old Testament Theology: The Theology of Israel's Prophetic Traditions*, trans. D.M.G. Stalker, vol. 2 (London: Westminster John Knox Press, 1960,1965): 373. For a full discussion on Eliakim and parallels with Rev 3:7 see Beale, *The Book of Revelation: A Commentary on the Greek Text*, 284.

[56] Aune argues that the definite article here (τοῦ φρέατος) means that the shaft of the abyss was well known to the readers. D.E. Aune, *Revelation 6–16*, WBC, ed. D.A. Hubbard, B.M. Metzger, and G.W. Barker, vol. 52B (Nashville, TN: Thomas Nelson, 1998): 2:525.

having "the key to the abyss" in the Prayer of Manasseh. Manasseh prays, "O Lord Almighty, God of our ancestors, of Abraham and Isaac and Jacob and of their righteous offspring; you who made heaven and earth with all their order; who shackled the sea (ὁ κλείσας τὴν ἄ]βυσσον) by your word of command, who confined the deep and sealed it with your terrible and glorious name" (Pr Man 1:1-3).

In Revelation, the key of the Abyss is both times in the hands of an angel (9:1-2; 20:1-3). The first angel is called a "star" and said to have "fallen" and the key was "given" to him; most likely by Christ but possibly by God the Father (9:1-2). The second angel is seen καταβαίνοντα "descending" with a great chain and locks Satan in the abyss (20:1-3). One angel releases evil and the other restrains evil for a thousand years. Stars usually refer to angels in the OT and apocalyptic literature.[57] It seems that the first angel is evil[58] because he is a πεπτωκότα "fallen" angel and ἐδόθη αὐτῷ "it was given to him" is usually in reference to evil agents in Revelation.[59] This fallen angel could be Satan[60] or some other demon like Abaddon who is the king of the demons in the abyss (Rev 9:11). If this fallen angel is Satan this would be the only clear reference to Satan himself possessing a key to the underworld (cf. Heb 2:14). The second angel is most assuredly a good angel who seizes Satan with a great chain; maybe even Michael the archangel (cf. Rev 12:7-9). The chain here is bigger than the one used to bind Samson (Judg 16:6) and the one used for Legion (Mark 5:4) because Satan is a mighty and ferocious enemy (Rev 12:12). All in all, the key given to both of these angels is not theirs, but belongs to Christ. If

---

[57] Judg 5:20; Job 38:7; *1 En.* 88:1; *T. Sol.* 8:2-11; 18:1-42.

[58] Commentators who argue for an evil, fallen angel: G.B. Caird, *The Revelation of Saint John*, BNTC, ed. Henry Chadwick (Peabody, MA: Hendrickson Publishers, 1966): 118. Beale argues that in the OT, Jewish writings and the NT a "falling star" is always an evil angel. Beale, *The Book of Revelation*, 491-92. Boxall, *The Revelation of Saint John*, 142, 279. J.A. Seiss, *The Apocalypse: Lectures on the Book of Revelation*, ZCS (Grand Rapids: Zondervan, 1950): 205. Commentators who argue for a good angel: Oecumenius, *Apoc.* 1.29, Andrew of Caesarea *Apoc.* Rev 9:1. Osborne, *Revelation*, 362. Ladd, *A Commentary on the Revelation of John*, 129. Mounce, *The Book of Revelation*, 185. Keener, *Revelation*, 266. Aune, *Revelation 6–16*, 2.525. Charles, *A Critical and Exegetical Commentary on the Revelation of St. John*, 1.238-39. S.S. Smalley, *The Revelation to John: A Commentary on the Greek Text of the Apocalypse* (Downers Grove, IL: InterVarsity Press, 2005): 225.

[59] ἐδόθη occurs 21 times in Revelation and is used twice as much in reference to evil agents than in reference to good agents: evil agents (Rev 6:2, 4 (2x), 8; 9:1, 3, 5; 11:2; 13:5 (2x), 7 (2x), 14, 15 (14x)) and good agents (Rev 6:11; 7:2; 8:3; 11:1; 16:8; 19:8; 20:4 (7x)).

[60] See Isa 14:12; Luke 10:17-19; Rev 12:9, 13; *1 En.* 86:1; *Apoc. El. (C)* 4.11-12; Mart. *Asc. Isa* 4:2; Tyconius, *Com. Apoc.* 9.1; Walvoord, *The Revelation of Jesus Christ*, 159. Swete, *Commentary on Revelation*, 114-15. M. Wilcock, *I Saw Heaven Opened: The Message of Revelation*, BST, ed. J.R.W. Stott (Downers Grove, IL: InterVarsity Press, 1975): 97.

43

Christ has the keys of Death and Hades, he most certainly also has the key to the abyss as well as every other region of the cosmos (cf. Rom 10:6-7; Matt 28:18-20).

After surveying the diverse key holders from the Greco-Roman, Egyptian and Jewish world we gain a much better understanding to Christ's divine claim to be the true key holder of the underworld. The six passages in the NT that reference keys are all metaphorical, but point to the same reality. Christ will ensure that the gates of Hades will not contain his church, but will release them and grant them access (the keys) to the kingdom of heaven (Matt 16:18-19; 27:52-53). Similarly, the believers of the seven churches in Revelation can rest assured that no god or goddess or demon or Roman emperor holds their destiny in his or her hands, but only the Lord Jesus Christ (Rev 1:18; 3:7; 9:1; 20:1). Revelation 21:25 makes it clear that the exercise of the power of the keys have been forever transformed, because the gates to God's eternal city have been flung wide open and will never be closed. Jesus Christ is the Lord of the keys and will grant access to the New Jerusalem for all who trust in him (Rev 2:7; 3:12; 21:12-15, 21, 25; 22:14). He also chooses who goes into Hades and who ultimately is thrown into the Lake of Fire (Rev 20:10, 13-14; cf. Matt 25:41).

CHAPTER 4

COMPARTMENTALIZATION OF THE UNDERWORLD

I will now explore the numerous compartments of the underworld and argue that there is a consistent theological picture of the afterlife from the NT. It shall be further revealed that one or more of these compartments are mentioned throughout the NT as having been visited by Christ at his descent between his death and resurrection. The NT terms for these compartments include Death, Hades, Paradise, Abraham's bosom, the Abyss, Tartarus, Gehenna, and the Lake of Fire.[1] All of these words except for Abraham's bosom, Tartarus, and Gehenna appear in the book of Revelation.[2] Yet, it will be argued that Abraham's bosom is a synonym for Paradise, Tartarus a synonym for the Abyss, and Gehenna a synonym for the Lake of Fire.

Compartmentalization of the underworld in *seed form* may be found in Isaiah 26:19-20, "But your dead will live; their bodies will rise. You who dwell in the dust, wake up and shout for joy. Your dew is like the dew of the morning; the earth will give birth to her dead. Go, my people, enter your rooms and shut the doors behind you; hide yourselves for a little while until his wrath has passed by." Wachter comments, "the statement 'the earth will give birth to the shades' (*npl* hiphil) means that the dead will emerge from the underworld, an element of hope transcending the old understanding of Sheol."[3] God tells his people, presumably who are dead (οἱ νεκροί 26:19), to "enter into your rooms or chambers" (εἴσελθε εἰς τὰ ταμίειά σου).[4] Therefore, the souls of the dead (רְפָאִים) are pictured as dwelling in rooms in the underworld waiting for the

---

[1] Gehenna and the Lake of Fire are not compartments of the underworld and were not visited by Christ at his descent, but this realm is the final destiny of all the wicked (men and angels) and must be discussed to receive a full picture of the NT teaching on the afterlife.

[2] All of these compartments except for Tartarus and the Lake of Fire appear in Luke-Acts.

[3] L. Wächter, "שְׁאוֹל," in *TDOT*, ed. G.J. Botterweck, H. Ringgren, and Heinz-Josef Fabry, trans. Douglas W. Stott, vol. 14 (Grand Rapids: Eerdmans, 2004): 243-44.

[4] Same word for "room" (ταμεῖον) is also used for compartments of the underworld in Prov 7:27; *1 En.* 22; *1 Clem.* 50:4.

general resurrection when their souls will be reunited to their bodies.[5] This passage along with the general view in the OT that both the righteous and the wicked descend into Sheol (see Chapter 2) furthered the understanding of a compartmentalized view of the underworld. This became much more fully developed in the Jewish intertestamental literature. For example, Bauckham says, "There can be little doubt that both *2 Bar.* and *4 Ezra* imply that the chambers are in Sheol. So the phrase 'the chambers of souls' is another equivalent to Sheol, the place of the dead, at least with reference to the righteous dead."[6]

Moreover, *1 En.* 22 is the clearest and earliest development of chambers in the underworld as different holding places for disobedient angels, the wicked, and the righteous. Josephus confirms that this is the view of the Pharisees in the NT era and before when he says, "They also believe that souls have an immortal vigor in them, and that under the earth there will be rewards or punishments."[7] Jesus, in the parable of the rich man and Lazarus, may be affirming this view of compartments in the underworld where both the righteous and wicked dwell (Luke 16:19-31). MacCulloch thinks he is. For he writes, "The current popular Jewish doctrine of the life after death was probably represented by the parable of Dives and Lazarus. All souls passed to an intermediate state, or place of waiting, called Hades (Sheol), in which there were two divisions—one for the righteous (Abraham's bosom), and one for the

---

[5] Most scholars both ancient and modern agree that Isaiah 26:19 is speaking of the bodily resurrection of the dead. "Dust" is used in both Isaiah 26:19 and Daniel 12:2 which are two of the key passages in the OT cited to support the resurrection of the dead (cf. Job 21:26; Ps 22:15 [21:16]; 22:30 [21:29]). *b.* Sanhedrin 90b-91a cites Isa 26:19 in support of resurrection. Blenkinsopp says on Isa 26:19, "the LXX translator and 1QIsa scribe have changed the following injunction addressed to the dead to future tense, presumably as an affirmation of their belief in the resurrection of the dead." J. Blenkinsopp, *Isaiah 1–39: A New Translation with Introduction and Commentary*, AB, ed. W.F. Albright and D.N. Freedman, vol. 19 (New York: Doubleday, 2000): 370. Cf. Irenaeus *Haer.* 5.34.1; Tertullian *Res.* 31; Augustine *Civ.* 20.21; Cyril of Jerusalem *Catech.* 18.15-16; J. Jeremias, "ᾅδης," in *TDNT*, ed. G. Kittel, G. Freidrich, and G. Bromiley, vol. 1 (Grand Rapids: William B. Eerdmans Publishing Company, 1964–76): 1:147. P.S. Johnston, *Shades of Sheol: Death and Afterlife in the Old Testament* (Downer's Grove, IL: InterVarsity Press, 2002): 225. R. Martin-Achard, *From Death to Life: A Study of the Development of the Doctrine of the Resurrection in the Old Testament* (Edinburgh: Oliver and Boyd, 1960): 137. G.F. Hasel, "Resurrection in the Theology of Old Testament Apocalyptic," *ZAW* 92 (1980): 272-76. B.S. Childs, *Isaiah* (Louisville, KY: Westminster/John Knox Press, 2001): 191-92. E.J. Young, *The Book of Isaiah*, NICOT, ed. R.K. Harrison (Grand Rapids: Eerdmans, 1969), 226-27.

[6] R. Bauckham, *The Climax of Prophecy: Studies on the Book of Revelation* (Edinburgh: T. & T. Clark, 1993): 65.

[7] *Ant.* 18.14-15.

wicked."[8] Bauckham argues similarly, "The common view in the early period, which still survives in Virgil, is that the place of happiness after death is also in the underworld."[9]

It is virtually agreed among the Jewish literature that when someone dies their soul is separated from their body.[10] If the spirit/soul departs the body at death, where did it go? As demonstrated in Chapter 2, there is no evidence before the NT era that the souls of men and women went to heaven, but instead all descended into one of these compartments in the underworld. I will now discuss the background and exegetical and theological contribution of each of these compartments to the *Descensus* and demonstrate that many of them are synonymous terms illustrating the same reality.

Paradise/Abraham's Bosom

Jesus promised the criminal crucified next to him, "I tell you the truth, today you will be with me in paradise (ἐν τῷ παραδείσῳ)" (Luke 23:43). Ambrose said, long ago concerning this promise, "More abundant is the favor shown than the request made."[11] The unnamed criminal hoped that Jesus would remember him at the end of the age when the kingdom comes, but Jesus went extraordinarily above and beyond his request and promised to bring him into

---

[8] J.A. MacCulloch, *The Harrowing of Hell: A Comparative Study of an Early Christian Doctrine* (Edinburgh: T. & T. Clark, 1930): 312.

[9] R. Bauckham, *The Fate of the Dead: Studies on the Jewish and Christian Apocalypses*, Supplements to Novum Testamentum, ed. C.K. Barrett, J.K. Elliott, and M.J.J. Menken, vol. 93 (Leiden: Brill, 1998): 29. For Jewish and Greco-Roman writers arguing for good and bad compartments in the underworld see Aristophanes, *Frogs* 145-48; Luke 16:23; Wis 2:1; *1 En.* 22; 51; *4 Ezra* 4:7-8, 35, 41-43; 7:32, 36-38, 80, 85, 95, 101, 121; *2 Bar.* 4:7-8; 21:23; 23:4; 30:1-5; *Ps. Sol.* 14:1-10; 15:11; 16:2; *Ant.* 18.14-15; *J.W.* 2, 163; 3, 375; *Midr. Eccl.* 7.14, 3 § 197; *Discourse to the Greeks Concerning Hades* 1-3; Irenaeus *Haer.* 5.5.1; Hippolytus, *Univ.* 1; Augustine, *Civ.* 20.15, *Liv. Pro.* 1:8; 2:4, 19; *Apoc. Paul* 11; E.G. Selwyn, *The First Epistle of St. Peter: The Greek Text with Introduction, Notes, and Essays*, 2nd ed. (Grand Rapids: Baker, 1981): 322. T.R. McLay, *The Use of the Septuagint in New Testament Research* (Grand Rapids: Eerdmans, 2003), 163. MacCulloch, *The Harrowing of Hell*, 278. M.D. Goulder, *Luke: A New Paradigm*, Journal for the Study of the New Testament: Supplement Series 20, ed. S.E. Porter (Sheffield: Sheffield Academic Press, 1989, 1994): 636. J.H. Charlesworth, "Paradise," in *ABD*, ed. D.N. Freedman, vol. 5 (New York: Doubleday, 1992): 154. E.H. Merrill, "מָוֶת," in *NIDOTTE*, ed. W.A. VanGemeren, vol. 2 (Grand Rapids: Zondervan, 1997): 888.

[10] Gen 35:18; 1 Kgs 17:21; Pss 104:29; 146:4; Eccl. 12:7; Jonah 4:3; Matt 10:28; *T. Abr.* A20:12-14; B7:16; *T. Isaac* 2:1; *T. Jac.* 4:1; *T. Job* 4:9; 52:10; Bar 2:17; Ps-Philo, *L.A.B.* 23:13; *Apoc. Paul* 14; *Apoc. Mos.* 32-42; *Ant.* 8.326; 9.119; *J.W.* 6.309; 7.354-355; *4 Ezra* 7:78, 88-89, 100; *Strom.* 6:15; *An.* 7. "Death consists in the separation of body and soul, or body and spirit." A. Heidel, *The Gilgamesh Epic and OT Parallels*, 2nd ed. (Chicago, IL: University of Chicago Press, 1949): 143.

[11] *Exp. Luc.* 10.121.

47

Paradise *with him* that very day (Luke 23:42-43)! Weisengoff rightly notes, "Since Christ said 'today' the eschatological paradise can be excluded."[12] On the other hand, where is the locale of this Paradise that Jesus offers the criminal on Good Friday? The meaning and location of Paradise is probably the most debated and controversial issue among the terms for the afterlife in the NT. It is the argument of this section that Paradise and Abraham's bosom are presented as the same locale in Luke-Acts and therefore, is the dwelling place of the righteous dead in the underworld.

The Greek word παράδεισος "Paradise" is a fascinating and peculiar word with rich meaning throughout the ancient world. It is found only three times in the New Testament (Luke 23:43; 2 Cor 12:4; Rev 2:7) and I will argue below that in each instance the locale is different. The earliest religious attestation for παράδεισος in the ancient literature is found in the Septuagint (LXX)[13] beginning in Genesis 2 and 3. Its use throughout the LXX is very religious in tone, as also in the background literature to the New Testament, but παράδεισος originally was used in a secular (non-religious) sense.

It is believed to be a loanword from ancient Persia dating back to the sixth century BC and probably earlier. It comes from the Persian word *pairi-daeza* which can mean "an enclosed space," "park," or "garden." The Zend Avesta, a holy book of Zoroaster, dating somewhere around 600 BC, contains the earliest use of *pairi-daeza*, "but its language is a branch of old Indo-Iranian and the word may easily have been borrowed by Solomon's wide-ranging traders."[14] The secular use of this word has been further defined in the papyri where it is very common as "a garden of fruit trees (protected presumably by a wall)."[15]

Other writers of this time attest to the secular use of παράδεισος, such as Xenophon writing between fifth and sixth century BC. Xenophon uses παράδεισος to describe parks and lush gardens belonging to the Persian king and his nobles. He writes, "And here (at Celaenae) Cyrus held a review and made an enumeration of the Greeks in the park (παράδεισος) . . ."[16] And again, "The Greeks accordingly encamped beside this city, near a large and beautiful park (παράδεισου), thickly covered with all sorts of trees . . ."[17] Paradise is not

---

12 J.P. Weisengoff, "Paradise and St. Luke 23:43," *AER* 103 (1940): 166.

13 Gen 2:8, 9, 10, 15, 16; 3:1, 2, 3, 8 (2x), 10, 23, 24; 13:10, Num 24:6; 2 Chron 33:20; Neh 2:8; Eccl 2:5; Cant 4:13; Isaiah 1:30; 51:3; Jer 29:5; Ezek 28:13; 31:8 (2x), 9; Joel 2:3; cf. *Apocr. Ezek.* 1.4; Sus 1:18, 20, 25, 26, 36 (2x), 38.

14 BDAG, 761. J. Jeremias, "παράδεισος," in *TDNT*, ed. G. Kittel, G. Freidrich, and G. Bromiley, vol. 5 (Grand Rapids: Eerdmans, 1964–76): 5.765.

15 J.H. Moulton and G. Milligan, *The Vocabulary of the Greek Testament: Illustrated from the Papyri and Other Non-Literary Sources* (1930; reprint, Grand Rapids: Eerdmans, 1980): 482a.

16 *Anab* 1. 2, 7 in Xenophon, *Xenophon's Anabasis: Books I–IV*, Greek Series for Colleges and Schools, ed. H.W. Smyth (New York: American Book Company, 1910), 63.

17 *Anab.* 2.4, 14 in Xenophon, *Xenophon's Anabasis.*, 123. cf. *Cyrop.* 1.3.14.

used with any hidden or religious meaning, but only to describe parks and gardens. This secular understanding of παράδεισος continued even on into the first century AD as can be seen by the way Roman writer Aelius Aristides uses it. For he writes, "Indeed, the cities shine with radiance and grace, and the whole earth has been adorned like a pleasure garden (παράδεισος)."[18] Yet, whether the ancient Hebrews borrowed the word from the Persians or the ancient Persians borrowed it from the Hebrews is open for debate. The Hebrew word פַּרְדֵּס "*pardes*" is used in the book of Nehemiah to describe a "forest" (Neh 2:8), in Canticles to depict an "orchard" (Cant 4:13), and in Ecclesiastes to describe the ego-driven campaigns by Solomon to create gardens and "parks" (Eccl 2:5). Solomon's wide ranging traders could have been the source of the Persian word *pairi-daeza* borrowing from the Hebrew word *pardes*. While this is not conclusive, it certainly is as much a possibility as the Hebrews borrowing it from the Persians. In short, from Solomon (1000 BC) to the time before the writing of the Septuagint (250 BC), παράδεισος was a secular word used to describe parks and gardens.

When the ancient world became Hellenized as a result of the conquests of Alexander the Great, the need for a Greek translation of the Hebrew Scriptures became desperate. Jews, who came from Jerusalem, moved to Alexandria to begin translating the Pentateuch into Greek to fill this void.[19] This process continued for over 200 years until all the Hebrew Scriptures had been translated into Greek.[20] These Alexandrian Jews translated the Hebrew words "*pardes*" "*gan/ganna*" and *eden* (once) with the Greek word παράδεισος.[21] It is with the LXX that the religious use of the term παράδεισος begins to take its form. Paradise does not necessarily take on this role in Genesis and Numbers (where it still refers to a garden), but it does have this meaning to the prophets who

---

[18] *Romans* 26, 99 in *Aelius Aristides: The Complete Works*, trans. C.A. Behr, vol. 2: Orations XVII–LIII (Leiden: Brill, 1981).

[19] See the *Letter of Aristeas* in *The Old Testament Pseudepigrapha*. vol. 2, ed. J.H. Charlesworth (Garden City, NY: Doubleday, 1983–85).

[20] The Septuagint was finished at least before the New Testament era because of the numerous citations of the LXX by NT writers. The earliest attestation of the threefold division of the Hebrew Scriptures is from the prologue to Sirach, "Many great teachings have been given to us through the Law and the Prophets and the others that followed them, and for these we should praise Israel for instruction and wisdom." Cf. Luke 24:44, "He said to them, 'This is what I told you while I was still with you: Everything must be fulfilled that is written about me in the Law of Moses, the Prophets and the Psalms.'"

[21] Gen 2:8, 9, 10, 15, 16; 3:1, 2, 3, 8 (2x), 10, 23, 24; 13:10, Num 24:6; 2 Chr 33:20; Neh 2:8; Eccl 2:5; Cant 4:13; Isa 1:30; 51:3; Jer 29:5; Ezek 28:13; 31:8 (2x), 9; Joel 2:3; cf. allusions in Isa 41:18-19; 58:11; 60:13; Jer 32:41; 36:5; Ezek 33:8-9; 36:35; 47:1-12.

hoped for a renewal and restoration of the Garden of Eden from Genesis 2.[22]

The Prophets were actually the first to give this word its eschatological connotations beginning with Isaiah (51:3) writing in the eighth century BC. Isaiah prophesies, "The LORD will surely comfort Zion and will look with compassion on all her ruins; he will make her deserts like Eden (παράδεισον), her wastelands like the garden of the LORD. Joy and gladness will be found in her, thanksgiving and the sound of singing" (Isa 51:3). In the context of the messianic era, Isaiah promises that the eschatological Jerusalem will be like the Garden of Eden, Paradise *redivivus*. Even though the Israelites had been stripped from their land and scattered among the nations, one day the Lord would bring them back to Zion and it would be like the Garden of Eden that Adam and Eve enjoyed. Similarly, Ezekiel foresees Zion becoming like Eden in his picturesque language; he says, "Fruit trees of all kinds will grow on both banks of the river. Their leaves will not wither, nor will their fruit fail. Every month they will bear, because the water from the sanctuary flows to them. Their fruit will serve for food and their leaves for healing" (Ezek 47:12; cf. Rev 22:1-2). In short, as recounted in the Hebrew (and LXX) Scriptures, God planted Paradise for his people (Gen 2), Paradise was taken away as a result of sin (Gen 3), and Paradise will be restored for his people in the messianic age (Isa 51:3; Ezek 47:1-12).

With the LXX as the background for the παράδεισος of God, we can more appreciate how during Second Temple Judaism, Jewish writers formulated their ideas regarding God's eschatological restoration of Eden. The earliest attestation of this idea among the early Jewish writers comes from the Testaments of the Twelve Patriarchs written sometime during the second century BC. The writer of the Testament of Levi says, "And he shall open the gates of paradise, and shall remove the threatening sword against Adam. And he shall give to the saints to eat from the tree of life, and the spirit of holiness shall be on them."[23] Jeremias notes that this is the first instance of a religious use of the term Paradise outside the Hebrew Scriptures.[24] Similarly, the writer of the Testament of Dan says that the New Jerusalem and Eden are synonymous descriptions of the future abode of the saints.[25] Most Second Temple writings are consistent in presenting Paradise as the dwelling place of the righteous, but there is a wide range of opinions on where Paradise is actually located.

1 Enoch is a complex work because of its various stages of composition running from the second century BC to the end of the first century AD. The

---

[22] Gen 13:10 may already be moving in this direction. "Lot looked up and saw that the whole plain of the Jordan was well watered, like the garden of the LORD, like the land of Egypt, toward Zoar."

[23] *T. Levi* 18.10-11.

[24] Jeremias, "παράδεισος," 5.765.

[25] *T. Dan* 5.12.

book of Enoch is only extant in the language of Ethiopic, but was most likely originally written in Aramaic. Moreover, every section of *1 Enoch* was found at Qumran (except the *Similitudes*) and can be safely dated before the New Testament era. Enoch, the seventh from Adam, is transported from this life and taken through journeys of levels of heaven and the underworld, including Paradise. To illustrate, the writer of *1 Enoch* sees Paradise as the restored Eden describing it as a "Garden of righteousness,"[26] dwelling place of the elect and the righteous,[27] "Garden of life,"[28] and it is located in the north (cf. Isa 14:13).[29]

Furthermore, Enoch seems to present this locale for the righteous as one of the compartments of the underworld when he says, "And he answered me and said unto me: 'These three have been made that the spirits of the dead might be separated. And such a division has been made for the spirits of the righteous, in which there is the bright spring of water.'"[30] Enoch does not seem to be consistent here because the dwelling of the righteous can be in the underworld and in the upper heavens.

The author of Psalms of Solomon written within a hundred years of the New Testament era also believes that the Lord's servants will live together forever in the garden of the Lord and are spoken metaphorically as the trees of God's garden.[31] Jubilees, written around a hundred years before Psalms of Solomon, speaks of Eden as the holiest place on earth,[32] hidden on the earth somewhere in the east,[33] and Eden is called the Holy of Holies.[34] All of these writings come before the New Testament era and already bring a lot of color to the word παράδεισος. According to these writings, Paradise seems to be located in the underworld, on the earth, or some other location, probably heaven.

Once we reach the first century AD, παράδεισος is still the abode of the

---

[26] 1 *En.* 24.3; 25.3-5; 32.2-6; 77.3; *L.A.E.* 25.3; cf. Sir 40.17, 27.

[27] 1 *En.* 60.8; 65.2; 70.3; 89.52.

[28] 1 *En.* 61.12.

[29] 1 *En.* 70.3-4; 77.3.

[30] *1 En.* 22.9.

[31] *Ps. Sol.* 14.2-3.

[32] *Jub.* 3.12.

[33] *Jub.* 4.26; 8.16.

[34] *Jub.* 8.19. Interestingly, gold was in the earth for Adam to find in pre-fall Eden (Gen 2:11, 12). It cannot be coincidence that the Holy of Holies in Solomon's temple was a cube made out of pure gold (1Kgs 6:20-35). In the consummation, the New Jerusalem (called the Paradise of God, Rev 2:7; 22:2, 10) has streets made out of pure gold (Rev 21:18, 21). The original Eden was meant to be made into the Holy of Holies, but as a result of the fall its consummation does not take place until Revelation 21-22.

righteous in the afterlife, whether in heaven, on the earth,[35] a metaphor for bliss,[36] or in the underworld. 2 Enoch speaks of παράδεισος as the hidden eschatological place of the righteous,[37] equates the third heaven with Paradise[38] and believes it to be an eternal home.[39] Paradise will also be entered by the righteous in the future, ". . . because it is for you that paradise is opened, the tree of life is planted, the age to come is prepared, plenty is provided, a city is built, rest is appointed, goodness is established and wisdom perfected beforehand" (4 Ezra 8.52; cf. 7.123).

4 Ezra, written in the first century AD, is first during this era (outside the NT) to unambiguously bring out this understanding of παράδεισος as a compartment of the underworld. He speaks of Paradise in the underworld when he says, "The pit of torment shall appear, and opposite it shall be the place of rest; and the furnace of hell shall be disclosed, and opposite it the paradise of delight. Look on this side and on that; here are delight and rest, and there are fire and torments'" (4 Ezra 7.37, 38 cf. Luke 16:19-31). 4 Ezra seems to embrace multiple meanings for Paradise, for he parallels it with heaven when he says, ". . . how many streams are above the firmament, or which are the exits of Hades, or which are the entrances of Paradise?' Perhaps you would have said to me, 'I never went down into the deep, nor as yet into Hades, neither did I ever ascend into heaven'" (4 Ezra 4.7-8). Some of the Rabbis believed that Paradise was in the underworld. They say, "What is the distance between them (Gehinnom and Paradise)? A handbreadth. R. Jonathan said: [They are divided by] a wall. The Rabbis say: They are parallel, so that one should be visible to the other."[40] Others believed that God himself will open the gates of Paradise and it would only be restored during the messianic age.[41] Even if these various writers differed on the actual location of Paradise they all agree that this locale is the abode of the righteous in the present and/or in the future.

Abraham's bosom is also consistently presented as the dwelling place of the

---

[35] Origen *Princ.* 2.11.6, "I think, therefore, that all the saints who depart from this life will remain in some place situated on the earth, which holy Scripture calls paradise, as in some place of instruction, and, so to speak, class-room or school of souls. . . ."

[36] See Luther's interpretation of Paradise on Genesis (2:8) in *Luther's Works* I, 88-89, "Therefore I am of the opinion that in each of the two instances Paradise designates the state in which Adam was in Paradise, abounding in peace, in freedom from fear, and in all gifts which exist where there is no sin. . . . Thus it is an allegorical Paradise, as it were, just as Scripture also gives the name 'Abraham's bosom' (Luke 16:22). . . ." G.W. Macrae, "With Me in Paradise," *Worship* 35 (1961): 238-40.

[37] *2 En.* 8-9.

[38] *2 En.* 8.6; *L.A.E.* 37.5; cf. 2 Cor 12:1-4.

[39] *2 En.* 65.10. Paradise is equated with the very throne room of God in *2 Bar.* 51.11.

[40] Eccl 7.14, 3. *Ecclesiastes*, Midrash Rabbah, ed. A. Cohen and M. Simon (New York: Soncino Press, 1983): 197.

[41] Exod 31.24, 5. *Exodus*, trans. S.M. Lehrman, Midrash Rabbah, ed. H. Freedman and M. Simon (New York: Soncino Press, 1983): 383.

righteous in the afterlife even though some placed it in heaven and others in the underworld. The different legends of Abraham circulating in the first and second centuries AD are fascinating. The phrase τὸν κόλπον Ἀβραάμ "Abraham's bosom" may have its origin from all these legends of the exaltation of Abraham in the afterlife.[42] In the *Testament of Abraham*, he is taken into Paradise (heaven) where Isaac and Jacob dwell.[43] In contrast, in the *Apocalypse of Abraham* he actually sees the Garden of Eden in the underworld along with the abyss and its torments.[44] Philo also exalts Abraham in the afterlife, he speaks of Abraham "leaving mortal things, 'is added to the people of God,' having received immortality, and having become equal to the angels."[45] In addition, the righteous martyrs who have died are received in the afterlife by Abraham. In hope, they say, "After this our passion, Abraham, Isaac, and Jacob shall receive us, and all our forefathers shall praise us."[46] The phrase Abraham's bosom is first found on the lips of Jesus in ancient literature and is only here in the NT.[47] Jesus says in the parable, "Now the poor man died and was carried away by the angels to Abraham's bosom (εἰς τὸν κόλπον Ἀβραάμ); and the rich man also died and was buried. In Hades he lifted up his eyes, being in torment, and saw Abraham far away and Lazarus in his bosom (ἐν τοῖς κόλποις αὐτοῦ)" (Luke 16:22-23; cf. John 1:18; 13:23).

Most scholars agree that Jesus is presenting Abraham's bosom in this parable as an underworld compartment holding the righteous within seeing distance of the abode of the wicked.[48]

---

[42] See LXX Gen 16:5, "And Sarai said to Abram, "May the wrong done me be upon you. I gave my maid into your arms (εἰς τὸν κόλπον σου), but when she saw that she had conceived, I was despised in her sight" (cf. LXX Num 11:12).

[43] *T. Abr.* 20.14-15; cf. *Apoc. Zeph.* 9:1-5; 11:1; *Apoc. Sedr.* 14:5-6; *Hel. Syn. Pr.* 16.4, 12.

[44] *Apoc. Ab.* 21.3-6.

[45] Philo *Sacr.* 5.

[46] *4 Macc* 13:17.

[47] *b. Qidd.* 72a-b uses "Abraham's lap" as a euphemism for death. Ginzberg believes that "Abraham's bosom" represents the same reality as "sleeping with your fathers" from the OT. L. Ginzberg, *The Legends of the Jews*, vol. 5: From the Creation to the Exodus (Philadelphia: Jewish Publication Society of America, 1925, 1953): 5.268.

[48] Luke 16:23; *Apoc. Ab.* 21.3-6; Irenaeus, *Haer.* 5.31.2; Tertullian, *Adv. Marc.* 4.34; *Res.* 17; *Idol* 13; Origen, *Hom. Num.* 26.4; J.B. Green, *The Gospel of Luke*, NICNT, ed. N.B. Stonehouse, F.F. Bruce, and G.D. Fee (Grand Rapids: Eerdmans, 1997): 607. W.R.F. Browning, *The Gospel according to Saint Luke: Introduction and Commentary* (New York: Macmillan, 1960): 135, 164. D.G. Bloesch, "Descent into Hell (Hades)," in *EDT*, ed. W.A. Elwell (Grand Rapids: Baker Academic, 2001): 338. A. Plummer, *A Critical and Exegetical Commentary on the Gospel according to St. Luke*, vol. 2, ICC, ed. A. Plummer, S.R. Driver, and C.A. Briggs (Edinburgh: T. & T. Clark, 1964): 393. J.A. Fitzmyer, *The Gospel according to Luke (X–XXIV)*, AB, ed. W.A. Albright and D.N. Freedman, vol. 28A (Garden City, NY: Doubleday, 1985): 1132. W.F. Arndt, *Luke*, CCCS (St. Louis, MO: Concordia, 1956): 365. W.

This argument is most persuasive in light of the background of *1 En.* 22.[49] In addition, the rich man pleas with Abraham to send Lazarus to his brothers and equates this as Lazarus or someone else coming back "from the dead" ἀπὸ νεκρῶν (Luke 16:30-31). This phrase "from the dead" is equated to the realm of the dead in the underworld everywhere else in the NT (cf. Rom 10:7). Abraham's bosom, therefore, containing Abraham, Lazarus, and presumably many others must be residing in the underworld. Moreover, according to Luke-Acts, the majority of scholars equate Abraham's bosom and Paradise as different titles for the same reality[50] and many argue for Paradise existing in the

---

Manson, *The Gospel of Luke*, MNTC, ed. J. Moffatt (New York: Harper and Brothers Publishers, 1930): 190-91. L. Kreitzer, "Luke 16:19-31 and 1 Enoch 22," *ExpTim* 103 (1991-92): 140. F. Godet, *The Gospel of St. Luke*, trans. M.D. Cusin, vol. 2 (Edinburgh: T. & T. Clark, 1875): 177-79, 335. Weisengoff, "Paradise and St. Luke 23:43," 166-67. A.J. Mattill, *Luke and the Last Things: A Perspecive for the Understanding of Lukan Thought* (Dillsboro, NC: Western North Carolina Press, 1979): 26-34. Goulder, *Luke: A New Paradigm*, 636. Aalen says this was the view of the early church until AD 200. S. Aalen, "St. Luke's Gospel and the Last Chapters of 1 Enoch," *NTS* 13 (1966–67).

[49] The following scholars argue for *1 En.* 22 as the primary background to Luke 16:19-31. L.W. Grensted, "The Use of Enoch in St. Luke xvi. 19-31," *ExpTim* 26 (1914–1915): 334. A.O. Standen, "The Parable of Dives and Lazarus and Enoch 22," *ExpTim* 33 (1921–22): 523. Aalen, "St. Luke's Gospel and the Last Chapters of 1 Enoch," 9, 13. To illustrate, the phrase χάσμα μέγα "great gulf" is only here in the NT, but also in *1 En.* 18:11-12 where Enoch sees a place of torment without water (cf. Luke 16:24). Moreover, in the dwelling place of the righteous there is a spring of water (*1 En.* 22:9). The wicked are in "torment" in both *1 En.* 22:11 and Luke 16:23. Lastly, Hades is presented as an intermediate state in *1 En.* 103:7-8 and so Luke 16:19-31 probably is too.

[50] Jerome, *Hom.* 86 on the Rich Man and Lazarus; Augustine, *Ep.* 187 "Whether that bosom of Abraham where the wicked rich man, when he was in the torment of hell, did behold the poor man resting, were either to be accounted by the name of paradise, or esteemed to appertain unto hell, I cannot readily affirm." MacCulloch, *The Harrowing of Hell*, 271-72, 314. Jeremias, "ᾅδης," 1:147. R.H. Stein, *Luke*, NAC, ed. D.S. Dockery, vol. 24 (Nashville, TN: Broadman, 1992): 593. "'Abraham's bosom' is not a synonym for Paradise, although Abraham may be thought to be in Paradise." I.H. Marshall, *The Gospel of Luke: A Commentary on the Greek Text*, NIGTC, ed. I.H. Marshall and W.W. Gasque (Grand Rapids: Eerdmans, 1978): 636. Godet, *The Gospel of St. Luke*, 335. Weisengoff, "Paradise and St. Luke 23:43," 166-67. Plummer says Abraham's bosom "is not a synonym for paradise; but to repose on Abraham's bosom is to be in paradise, for Abraham is there." Close enough! Plummer, *A Critical and Exegetical Commentary on the Gospel according to St. Luke*, 393. D.L. Bock, *Luke 9:51–24:53*, BECNT, ed. M. Silva, vol. 3B (Grand Rapids: Baker, 1996): 1857. Jeremias, "παράδεισος," 5:769-70. Browning, *The Gospel according to Saint Luke*, 135, 164. C.A. Evans, *Luke*, NIBC, ed. W.W. Gasque (Peabody, MA: Hendrickson Publishers, 1990): 251. Manson, *The Gospel of Luke*, 190-91. Arndt, *Luke*, 365, 471. D.G. Barnhouse, *Revelation: An Expositional Commentary* (Grand Rapids: Zondervan, 1971), 31-32.

underworld.[51] Ellis objects, "However, no Jewish writings view Paradise or Abraham to be a part of the 'underworld.'"[52] In contrast, I believe the evidence presented thus far demonstrates that the *Apocalypse of Abraham, 1 Enoch,* Josephus, the author of 4 Ezra, and Luke 16:19-31 all may have understood Abraham as dwelling in a compartment for the righteous in the underworld. In Paul's writings, Paradise is presented as within or synonymous with the third heaven (2 Cor 12:2, 4)[53] and in Revelation it is synonymous with the New Jerusalem (Rev 2:7; 21:2). This is significant for the transferable nature of the term παράδεισος in the NT.[54] Paradise is clearly distinguished from τοῦ οὐρανοῦ "heaven" in Revelation 21:2, "I saw the Holy City, the new Jerusalem, coming down out of heaven (ἐκ τοῦ οὐρανοῦ) from God, prepared as a bride beautifully dressed for her husband." The New Jerusalem is clearly synonymous with Paradise in Revelation because both contain the tree of life (Rev 2:7; 22:2, 14), but neither are equated with heaven.

Therefore, even though Paradise is equated with the τρίτου οὐρανοῦ "third heaven" in Paul (2 Cor 12:2, 4), Paradise is not heaven in Revelation, but the eternal city that comes down "out of heaven." We must also ask whether Luke meant something different by Paradise since Paul and the author of Revelation did. Luke presents Jesus on Good Friday entering into Paradise (ἐν τῷ

---

[51] Luke 23:43; Acts 2:27, 31; Mattill, *Luke and the Last Things,* 26-34. Browning, *The Gospel according to Saint Luke,* 135, 164. Godet, *The Gospel of St. Luke,* 179, 335. Plummer, *A Critical and Exegetical Commentary on the Gospel according to St. Luke,* 393, 536. Arndt, *Luke,* 365. Goulder, *Luke: A New Paradigm,* 636. Weisengoff, "Paradise and St. Luke 23:43," 166-67. Manson, *The Gospel of Luke,* 190-91. J.A. Seiss, *The Apocalypse: Lectures on the Book of Revelation,* ZCS (Grand Rapids: Zondervan, 1950): 48, 447-50. Barnhouse, *Revelation,* 31-32. Tertullian likens Paradise to the Elysian Fields in *Apol.* 47; *Adv. Marcion* 4.34, but still maintains Paradise is not in the underworld in *Res.* 43.

[52] E.E.Ellis, *The Gospel of Luke,* NCBC, ed. M. Black (Grand Rapids: Eerdmans, 1981): 206. Blomberg says on Luke 23:43, "The doctrine of the descent into hell is a later Christian creation, not conclusively supported by any text of the New Testament. Here Jesus affirms that heaven is available to believers immediately upon death and that he will go there at once in spirit to be with this one 'deathbed' convert." C.L. Blomberg, *Jesus and the Gospels* (Nashville, TN: Broadman and Holman, 1997): 347. Blomberg does not deal with reconciling Jesus' soul being in heaven and in Hades the same day according to the NT (Matt 12:40; Acts 2:27, 31; Rom 10:6-7; cf. John 20:17). Why didn't Jesus say 'Today you will be with me in *heaven*?'

[53] *b.* Chagiga fol. 14; *T. Ab.* 10:15; 11:1-12; *L.A.E.* 25:3; 29:1; 38:5; *Apoc. Mos.* 37:5; 40:1; *2 En.* 8; *T. Levi* 3; Clement of Alexandria, *Strom.* 5.80; *Gos. Nic.* 25-26; W.G.T. Shedd, *Dogmatic Theology,* vol. 2 (New York: Charles Scribner's Sons, 1888): 599-600. William Hendricksen, *Exposition of the Gospel according to Luke,* NTC (Grand Rapids: Baker Book House, 1978): 1032-33. "Paradise is not in Hell." H. Witsius, *Sacred Dissertations on What is Commonly Called the Apostles' Creed,* trans. Donald Fraser, vol. 2 (London: Khull, Blackie, 1823; reprint, 1993): 145.

[54] On the transferable nature of Paradise see Seiss, *The Apocalypse,* 447-50.

παραδείσῳ) (Luke 23:43), but Luke also presents Peter saying that Christ's soul dwelt in Hades (εἰς ᾅδην) between his death and resurrection (Acts 2:27, 31). Luke also says that "David did not ascend to heaven" (Acts 2:34) and Abraham and righteous Lazarus are seen dwelling in the underworld (Luke 16:19-31).

A way to solve the dilemma of Christ being in both Paradise and Hades on Good Friday is if Paradise for Luke was the abode of the righteous in the underworld. Luke and Josephus were contemporary writers and come from the same religious milieu in Jerusalem. Therefore, it should not be forgotten that Josephus believed in good and bad compartments in the underworld[55] and it would be reasonable that Luke did as well. All in all, I agree with Ambrose that, "For life is to be with Christ, because where Christ is, there is the kingdom."[56]

Paradise is a transferable locale because the presence of Christ is what makes the reality Paradise. The criminal was with Christ in Paradise/Abraham's Bosom in the underworld on Good Friday, Paul visited Paradise in the third heaven where Christ currently dwells (2 Cor 12:2, 4; Phil 1:21-26; 3:20), and the saints enter Paradise in the New Jerusalem because the lamb (Christ) will dwell there forever and ever (Rev 2:7; 21:22; 22:1-5, 14). Wherever Christ is, there is Paradise.

Abyss/Tartarus

I will argue in this section that the Abyss and Tartarus are synonymous terms for the same reality in the underworld. Paul speaks of Christ descending into the Abyss (Rom 10:6-7) and Peter arguably says that Christ preached to the spirits imprisoned in Tartarus (1 Pet 3:19; 2 Pet 2:4). The Abyss (ἄβυσσος), which means "bottomless," occurs thirty-four times in the LXX.[57] Thirty of them translate תְּהוֹם, once מְצוֹלָה (Job 41:23), once צוּלָה (Isa 44:27), and two times without translation (Job 36:16; 41:24).[58] It can mean the ocean (Gen 1:2), deep waters (Ps 42:7), but also the realm of the dead (Ps 71:20). The Abyss is also predominantly understood as the dwelling place of fallen angels (demons)

---

[55] *Ant.* 18.14-15.

[56] *Expos. Luc.* 10:121.

[57] Gen 1:2; 7:11; 8:2; Deut 8:7; 33:13; Job 28:14; 36:16; 38:16, 30; 41:23, 24 (2x); Pss 32 (33):7; 34 (35):7; 41 (42):8 (2x); 70:20 (71:20); 76 (77):17; 77 (78):15; 103 (104):6; 105 (106):9; 106 (107):26; 134 (135):6; 147 (148):7; Prov 3:20; 8:24; Isa 44:27; 51:10; 63:13; Ezek 26:19; 31:4, 15; Amos 7:4; Jonah 2:6; Hab 3:10; Wis 10:19; Pr Man 12:3; Sir 1:3; 16:18; 24:5, 29; 42:18; cf. *T. Levi* 3:9; *T. Job* 33:6; *4 Ezra* 4:7-8; *Apoc. Adam* 7:17; *Thom. Cont.*; *Sib. Or.* 1:223; *Dial. Sav.* 36; *As. Mos.* 10:6; *Jub.* 2:2; 5:6; 6:26; 8:12; *Hist. Rech.* 10:7; 1QM 10.13; 4Q246.

[58] H.G. Grether, "Abyss," in *ABD*, ed. D.N. Freedman, vol. 1 (New York: Doubleday, 1992): 49.

in the underworld throughout the interestamental literature.[59] In addition, Abyss occurs nine times in the NT[60] and in every instance (except Rom 10:7) it is the dwelling place of demons. Moreover, Luke and the author of Revelation consistently present the Abyss as the dwelling place of evil powers whether demons, Satan, or the Antichrist. For example, Luke tells the story of Legion and his response to Jesus. Luke records, "And they begged him repeatedly not to order them to go into the Abyss" (Luke 8:31). Bauckham says, "The reference to the abyss is probably not to the place of the dead (which in Revelation is Hades), but rather to the place of the demonic, from which all evil arises (9:1-2, 11; 20:1)."[61]

In Romans 10:7, the Abyss is used in reference to the descent of Christ into the realm of the dead (cf. Ps 71:20). Paul actually changes the Greek word from τῆς θαλάσσης "sea" in the LXX to the more theologically loaded term τὴν ἄβυσσον "the netherworld." In the same way that Paul believed that Christ ascended into heaven he also believed that Christ descended into the Abyss (Rom 10:6-7). The well known passage in 1 Peter concerning Christ's preaching to spirits in prison comes into play here (1 Pet 3:19). The "prison" in which Christ preaches to spirits is the Greek word φυλακῇ which is the same word used as the place Satan is imprisoned for a thousand years in Revelation 20:7.[62] Yet, Satan is first said to be thrown εἰς τὴν ἄβυσσον "into the abyss" (Rev 20:3), but is released ἐκ τῆς φυλακῆς αὐτοῦ "out of his prison" (Rev 20:7). The Abyss and this "prison" are synonymous at least in Revelation and throughout Revelation it is the dwelling place of demons (cf. Rev 18:2). Many Petrine scholars also equate the φυλακῇ "prison" here with Tartarus in 2 Peter 2:4 (see Chapter 5). If correct, this further supports the argument that the reality of the Abyss in the underworld is identical to Tartarus in the NT.

Tartarus is another word used for a compartment of the underworld, but only once in the NT (2 Pet 2:4). Tartarus is only used three times in the LXX (Job

---

[59] *1 En.* 10:4; 18:10-11; 54.5; 88.1-2; 90.25-27; *Jub.* 5:6; *Sib. Or.* 8:196-197, 241; *Apoc. Zeph.* 6:11-17; 7:9; 9:2; *Apoc. Ab.* 21:3-4; *Apoc. El.* (C) 5:35; *Apoc. Dan.* 12:2; *T. Isaac* 5:26-27; *T. Sol.* 6:3, 6; *Acts Thom.* 32; *Apoc. Paul* 11; 32; Pss 152:2, 6; 153:3.

[60] Luke 8:31; Rom 10:7; Rev 9:1, 2, 11; 11:7; 17:8; 20:1, 3.

[61] Bauckham, *The Climax of Prophecy*, 436.

[62] Bertram says, "In 1 Pt. 3:19 φυλακή means "prison" in the sense of the place where departed spirits are kept." G. Bertram, "φυλακή " in *TDNT*, ed. G. Kittel, G. Freidrich, and G. Bromiley, vol. 9 (Grand Rapids: Eerdmans, 1964–76), 9:242. The Syriac version of 1 Pet 3:19 translate 'Scheiul' (Sheol/Hades) for φυλακή in 3:19. MacCulloch, *The Harrowing of Hell*, 51. In the LXX and the rest of the NT, φυλακή usually refers to an earthly prison or dungeon: Gen 40:3-4, 7; 41:10; 42:17, 30; Lev 24:12; Judg 16:25; 1 Kgs 22:27; Isa 42:7; Matt 5:25; 14:3, 10; 18:30; 25:36;, 39, 43, 44; Mark 6:17, 40; Luke 3:20; 12:58; 21:12; 22:33; 23:19, 25; John 3:24; Acts 5:19, 22-23, 25; 8:3; 12:4-6, 17; 16:23, 24, 27, 37, 40; 22:4; 26:10; 2 Cor 6:6; 11:23; Heb 11:36; Rev 2:10.

40:20; 41:24; Prov 30:16). The Greek verb ταρταρόω has its origins in the Greco-Roman world and was known as a murky, dark place located below Hades that imprisoned the Titans of old.[63] The Titans are the children born to Uranos and Gaia, youngest of whom is Kronos.[64] After Kronos takes over from his father Uranos, Zeus then conspires against Kronos and the rest of the Titans. Thus the Titans are imprisoned in the lowest depths of the underworld: Tartarus. Peter finds here a fitting parallel with the fall of the angels in Gen 6:1-4.[65] The Second Temple literature speaks of Tartarus in similar terms as the Greeks, often paralleling it with the Abyss.[66] Green says, "Just as Paul could quote an apt verse of the pagan poet Aratus (Acts 17:28), so could Peter make use of this Homeric imagery."[67] It seems then that Peter, adapting to his Greek audience, uses this word to speak of the dwelling place of disobedient angels of old. I also argued above that Tartarus should be seen as the same locale as φυλακῇ from 1 Peter 3:19. According to that argument, Tartarus is parallel with the Abyss as demonstrated in the interchangeability of the terms in Revelation 20:3, 7. On the other hand, φυλακή is not a technical term for the Abyss or Tartarus since it is used numerous times throughout the NT without this meaning (see Matt 5:25). However, I believe that when it is used in the context of a "prison" in the afterlife (1 Pet 3:19; Rev 20:3, 7) it is referring to this specific realm known as the Abyss/Tartarus.

One might ask whether the authors of the NT really envision more than one compartment in the underworld imprisoning demons? Luke understood the abyss to be this locale (Luke 8:31), Peter called it Tartarus (2 Pet 2:4), Jude said the angels were bound in "darkness" (Jude 1:6), and Revelation sees the abyss as housing all the imprisoned demonic hosts including the Antichrist (Rev 9:1, 2, 11; 11:7; 17:8; 20:1, 3). I believe it makes more sense that these descriptions

---

[63] BDAG, 813, Tartarus is "a subterranean place lower than Hades where divine punishment was meted out, and so regarded in Israelite apocalyptic as well." Cf. Plato, *Gorg.* 523; *Il.* 8.14-15; 14.279; Hesiod *Theog.* 119, 720-25, 735, 868; Apollodorus *Bib.* 1.1.4; 1.2.3; Sextus Empiricus, *Pyr.* 3.210; Virgil *Aen.* 4.511; 6.576; *Hymn. Hom. Merc.* 256, 374; Lycoph. *Alex.* 1197; Plutarch *[Cons. Apoll.]* Vol. 2; Josephus speaks of the beliefs of the Greeks that some are "under the earth" and "bound in hell (Tartarus)" (*Ag. Ap.* 2.240). See Pearson for more references: B.A. Pearson, "A Reminiscence of Classical Myth at II Peter 2.4," *GRBS* 10 (1969). Pearson says that every use he found outside of 2 Pet 2:4 for Tartarus refers "to the theogonic myths of Uranos, Kronos and the Titans, and Zeus." Pearson, "A Reminiscence of Classical Myth at II Peter 2.4," 78.

[64] *Theog.* 132ff.

[65] Josephus even parallels the Titans with the fall of the angels when he says, "The deeds that tradition ascribes to them (the angels) resemble the audacious exploits told by the Greeks of the giants" (*Ant.* 1.73).

[66] LXX Job 41:23-24; *T. Sol.* 6:3, 6; *Sib. Or.* 1:10; *Gk. Apoc. Ezra* 3:15; 5:27; *Apoc. Paul* 18; *Acts Thom.* 32; *Acts of Phil.* 110.

[67] M. Green, *2 Peter and Jude*, TNTC, ed. L. Morris (Grand Rapids: Eerdmans, 1987): 110.

are different terms referring to the same reality rather than referring to three or four different compartments imprisoning demons. Therefore Christ, at his descent, visited the Abyss/Tartarus (Rom 10:7; 2 Pet 2:4) and presumably made a proclamation to the disobedient angels imprisoned there (1 Pet 3:19). This has important implications of the exegesis of the πνεύμασιν "spirits" in 1 Peter 3:19, which is forthcoming.

Gehenna/Lake of Fire

In this last section, we are not dealing with a compartment of the underworld,[68] but instead the future, eternal destiny of the wicked (men and angels) according to Jesus, Revelation and the rest of the NT. These are not compartments in the underworld nor did Christ visit them. However, in order to have a complete theology of the afterlife in the NT we must briefly explore them.[69] It is the consistent testimony of the ancient Jewish and Greco-Roman world that the wicked will suffer eternally in the afterlife, usually by fire.[70] This imagery of the wicked suffering by fire in the afterlife may find its origin in Deuteronomy (32:22) and is demonstrated most clearly in Isaiah (1:31; 33:14; 66:24). This future place of everlasting torment for the wicked later became known as Gehenna.[71] The word Gehenna comes from the Valley of Hinnom which was the boundary between the tribes of Judah and Benjamin (Josh 15:8; 18:16; Isa 31:9; 66:24; Jer 32:35; 2 Chron 33:6) and the northern border of Judah after the captivity (Neh 11:30). The Valley of Hinnom was the location where the Canaanites would sacrifice their children by fire to the pagan gods, Molech and Baal (2 Kgs 16:3; 21:6; Jer 7:31; 19:4-5; 32:35). Josiah had it desecrated (2 Kgs 23:10).

Interestingly, outside of NT and OT Apocrypha (*4 Ezra* 2:29) Gehenna is

---

[68] Contra *2 En.* 40:12.

[69] Friesen says the lake of fire "cannot belong to earth or the underworld because it functions forever, long after the earth and sea have fled from the Almighty judge and are no more." S.J. Friesen, *Imperial Cults and the Apocalypse of John: Reading Revelation in the Ruins* (Oxford: Oxford University Press, 2001): 157.

[70] Deut 32:22; Isa 1:31; 33:14; 66:24; *T. Ab.* 10:15; 11:1-12; Tob 3:6; Jdt 16:17; Wis 11:9; Sir 7:17; Philo *Praem.* 12:70; Lucian *Ver. His.* 2.30; *Men.* 10; *Luct.* 3; *Philops.* 24; *3 Bar.* 4:16; *Ques. Ezra* 3; *4 Macc.* 9:15, 24, 30, 32; 10:11, 15, 21; 11:3, 23; 12:12, 14, 18; 13:15; 17:21; 18:5, 22; 1QM War Scroll 14.15-16; *Ep. Apos. (E)* 39; *3 En.* 44:3; 48D:8; *2 Bar.* 59:10-11; 85:13; *Sib. Or.* 1:100-103, 119; 2:292; 4:178-190; *4 Ezra* 2:29; 7:26-38; *Gk. Apoc. Ezra* 1:10; *Apoc. Ab.*15:6; *Mart. Ascen. Isa.* 1:3; 4:14-18; *5 Ezra* 2.19; *(Apocr.) Ep. Tit.*; *2 Clem.* 5.4; 17.7; Ign. *Eph.* 16.2; *Diogn.* 8.2; 10.7; Eusebius *Dem. Ev.* 13.16; *1 Apol.* 12; 45; 19; 21; Irenaeus *Haer.* 2.28.7; 4.26.2; Clement of Alexandria *Strom.* 5.14.

[71] *m. Ed.* 2:10. Rabbi Aqiba associates Gehenna with the imagery in Isaiah 66. *T. Isa* 30:33.

not found in any sources including LXX, Philo, Josephus, or Greek literature.[72] The Rabbis departed from the NT and the rest of the ancient literature because they started seeing Gehenna as a temporary place of punishment rather than eternal.[73] For example, the most ancient attestation of Gehenna as temporary punishment is found in *b.* Ber. 28b (AD 80). For Rabban Johanan ben Zakkai said, "there are two ways before me, one leading to Paradise and the other to Gehinnom, and I do not know by which I shall be taken, shall I not weep?" And Resh Lakish said, "the wicked are at that time under sentence to suffer in Gehenna, but our father Abraham comes, brings them up, and receives them, except such an Israelite as had immoral intercourse with the daughter of an idolater, since his foreskin is drawn and so he cannot be discovered."[74]

It is more difficult to track down the origin of the imagery behind the Lake of Fire in Revelation.[75] A burning lake where the wicked will remain for eternity is sometimes found in the intertestamental literature.[76] This Lake of Fire that God has prepared for the wicked may be the same "river of fire" (ποταμὸς πυρός) found in Daniel 7:9-10.[77] Daniel writes,

> As I looked, thrones were set in place, and the Ancient of Days took his seat. His clothing was as white as snow; the hair of his head was white like wool. His throne was flaming with fire, and its wheels were all ablaze. A river of fire was flowing, coming out from before him. Thousands upon thousands attended him; ten thousand times ten thousand stood before him. The court was seated, and the books were opened.

Regardless of its origin, scholars are virtually unanimous that γέεννα (Gehenna) and τὴν λίμνην τοῦ πυρὸς (the Lake of Fire) are synonymous titles in the NT referring to the same reality.[78] To illustrate, Jesus consistently uses Gehenna to

---

[72] D.F. Watson, "Gehenna," in *ABD*, ed. D.N. Freedman, vol. 2 (New York: Doubleday, 1992): 926-27.

[73] J. Jeremias, "γέεννα," in *TDNT*, ed. G. Kittel, G. Freidrich, and G. Bromiley, vol. 1 (Grand Rapids: Eerdmans, 1964–76): 1:657.

[74] *b. Erub.* 19a.

[75] Rev 19:20; 20:10, 14 (2x), 15; 21:8.

[76] *1 En.* 17:5; 90:25; *2 En.* 10:2; *Jos. Asen.* 12:10; *Apoc. Peter* 8:23; 11:26; 16:31; *Apoc. Paul* 31, 34, 36; *Sib. Or.* 2:196-199; 1QH 3:28-34.

[77] G.K. Beale, *The Book of Revelation: A Commentary on the Greek Text*, NIGTC, ed. I.H. Marshall and D.A. Hagner (Grand Rapids: Eerdmans, 1999): 969.

[78] Irenaeus *Haer.* 5.35.1. Watson, "Gehenna," 927. Jeremias, "ᾅδης," 1:148. F. Lang, "πυρ," in *TDNT*, ed. G. Kittel, G. Freidrich, and G. Bromiley, vol. 6 (Grand Rapids: Eerdmans, 1964–76): 6:946. S. Shogren, "DLNT," (Hell, Abyss, Eternal Punishment), 460. R.H. Charles, *A Critical and Exegetical Commentary on the Revelation of St. John*, vol. 1, ICC, ed. J.A. Emerton, C.E.B. Cranfield, and G.N. Stanton (Edinburgh: T. & T. Clark, 1966): 239-40. R.L. Thomas, *Revelation 8–22 An Exegetical Commentary* (Chicago, IL: Moody Press, 1995): 398. H.B. Swete, *Commentary on Revelation* (Grand Rapids: Kregel, 1977; reprint, London: Macmillan, 1911): 274. J.M. Ford, *Revelation: Introduction, Translation and*

describe the final destiny of the wicked,[79] and in Revelation their final destiny is the Lake of Fire.[80] Moreover, Jesus says that the Devil and his angels will be cast into the "eternal fire" prepared for them (Matt 25:41), and the Devil and his angels actually get cast into the Lake of Fire (Rev 20:10). Gehenna is consistently distinguished from Hades in the NT as the final Hell of fire for both body and soul, but Hades is temporary punishment for soul only.[81] The Lake of Fire also is the place where body and soul reunite at the resurrection to be cast forever and ever (Rev 20:13-15) and even Hades will be destroyed in the Lake of Fire (Rev 20:13-14).

In sum, I have established in this chapter the consistent theology in the NT of the underworld compartments. I argued that Christ visited these compartments and did not visit Gehenna/Lake of Fire at his descent. Revelation mentions or alludes to all of these compartments, and therefore, exploring these compartments gives us a much better understanding of the author of Revelation's theology of the underworld. This understanding helps significantly in the exegesis of Revelation 1:18. We now move to the primary texts outside of Revelation in the NT that have been used to demonstrate that Christ descended into the underworld between his death and resurrection.

Commentary, AB, ed. W.F. Albright and D.N. Freedman, vol. 38 (Garden City, NY: Doubleday, 1975): 315. R.H. Mounce, *The Book of Revelation*, NICNT, ed. G.D. Fee (Grand Rapids: Eerdmans, 1977): 359. G.R. Osborne, *Revelation*, BECNT, ed. M. Silva (Grand Rapids: Baker Academic, 2002): 690. I. Boxall, *The Revelation of Saint John*, BNTC, ed. M.D. Hooker (London: Hendrickson, 2006): 277. G.E. Ladd, *A Commentary on the Revelation of John* (Grand Rapids: Eerdmans, 1972): 258. Seiss, *The Apocalypse: Lectures on the Book of Revelation*, 450. G.R. Beasley-Murray, *The Book of Revelation*, NCBC, ed. M. Black (Grand Rapids: Eerdmans, 1981): 303. J.F. Walvoord, *The Revelation of Jesus Christ* (Chicago, IL: Moody Press, 1966): 307.

[79] Matt 5:22, 29, 30; 10:28; 18:9; 23:15, 33; Mark 9:43, 45, 47; Luke 12:5; cf. Jas 3:6

[80] Rev 19:20; 20:10, 14 (2x), 15; 21:8.

[81] Matt 10:28; Luke 16:23; Watson, "Gehenna," 927. H. Bietenhard, "Hell, Abyss, Hades, Gehenna, Lower Regions," in *NIDNTT*, ed. Colin Brown (Grand Rapids: Zondervan, 1976, 1986): 208. Jeremias, "γέεννα," 1:657-58. Jeremias, "ᾅδης," 1:148. Osborne, *Revelation*, 690. J.P. Lewis, "'The Gates of Hell Shall Not Prevail against It' (Matt 16:18): A Study of the History of Interpretation," *JETS* 38 (1995): 104-105. Thomas, *Revelation 8–22 An Exegetical Commentary*, 398. Mounce, *The Book of Revelation*, 61. J. Yates, "'He Descended into Hell': Creed, Article and Scripture," *Churchman* 102 (1988): 241. J.W. Cooper, *Body, Soul, and Life Everlasting: Biblical Anthropology and the Monism-Dualism Debate* (Grand Rapids: Eerdmans, 1989): 125. Ellis, *The Gospel of Luke*, 206. Ladd, *A Commentary on the Revelation of John*, 258. Seiss, *The Apocalypse: Lectures on the Book of Revelation*, 450.

CHAPTER 5

DESCENSUS AD INFEROS IN THE NEW TESTAMENT

A Brief Survey of Descending into the Underworld

We now move to the primary texts outside of Revelation in the NT that have been used to argue that Christ descended into the underworld between his death and resurrection. Before I discuss the exegesis of these passages, I will give a brief survey of other stories from the ancient world that involve a descent to the underworld. We will look at some key figures from Mesopotamia, Egypt, Iran, Greco-Roman, the OT, and Second Temple Literature who are reported as descending into the underworld.[1] We will then move to the exegesis of the foundational passages in the NT. It will be demonstrated in this section that while there are parallels between these descents and Christ's descent; most of the features of Christ's descent are unparalleled in the ancient world. Schneider argues that κατάβασις is a technical term for descent to the underworld.[2] This is important because this term is used in three of the key passages used in the NT for Christ's descent into the underworld.[3] In the LXX, καταβαίνω is used to translate יָרַד about eighty percent of the time,[4] mostly speaking about geographical travel, but also in reference to descending into Sheol.[5] According to ancient Mesopotamian beliefs in the afterlife, the "body was laid to rest in the ground, the spirit descended to the underworld to sojourn there throughout

---

[1] For all references and a thorough analysis of descents to the underworld see R. Bauckham, *The Fate of the Dead: Studies on the Jewish and Christian Apocalypses*, Supplements to Novum Testamentum, ed. C.K. Barrett, J.K. Elliott, and M.J.J. Menken, vol. 93 (Leiden: Brill, 1998): 9-48.

[2] J. Schneider, "καταβαίνω," in *TDNT*, ed. G. Kittel, G. Freidrich, and G. Bromiley, vol. 1 (Grand Rapids: Eerdmans, 1964–76): 1:523.

[3] Rom 10:7; Acts 2:27, 31, 34 (implied); Eph 4:9-10; cf. Matt 11:23; Luke 10:15.

[4] W. Mayer, "יָרַד," in *TDOT*, ed. G. Kittel, G. Freidrich, and G. Bromiley, vol. 6 (Grand Rapids: Eerdmans, 1990): 6:316.

[5] LXX Gen 37:35; 42:38; 44:29 (κατάξετέ), 31 (κατάξουσιν); Num 16:30, 33; 1 Sam 2:6; 1 Kgs 2:6, 9; Job 7:9; 17:16; 21:13; Pss 55:15; 88:3-4; Prov 7:27; Isa 14:11, 15; 57:9; Ezek 31:15, 16, 17; 32:21, 27.

eternity."[6] The Mesopotamian myths of *Enlil and Ninlil*, the Descent of Ishtar and the Epic of Gilgamesh clearly illustrate this belief in journeys to the underworld. In addition, Baal's descent and decisive battle with Mot (Death) in the underworld is another example of a popular descent myth.[7]

Herodotus said, in Egypt, that King Rhampsinitus (Ramses III) descended alive into the realm of the dead.[8] However, the myth of Osiris is the most well known story of a descent and resurrection from Egypt. Osiris did not rise from the dead physically like Jesus, but instead his resurrection resulted in ruling over the underworld.[9] The sun god Re, like the sun, appears to descend and ascend every day; this god is said to descend into the underworld every evening and then ascend again every morning.[10] In Iran, there is the journey of Kirdir to heaven and hell who is related to the historical high priest Kirdir (third century BC) during the reign of the Sassanid king Shapur I (240–270 BC).[11] In Greece and Rome, there are numerous accounts of descents to the underworld. Bauckham says, "Many of the descents (*katabaseis*) in Greek mythology are for the purpose of rescuing from death someone who had recently died."[12] The most famous is the story of Orpheus who rescues his wife from Hades.[13] In addition, Aeneas visits Hades[14] and Odysseus seeks the seer Teiresias in Hades.[15]

In the OT, many are said to descend into Sheol. For example, Jacob fears his descent into Sheol when he dies (Gen 37:35; 42:38; 44:29, 31), Korah and his rebels are actually swallowed up alive by Sheol (Num 16:30, 33), and Jonah's descent into the sea is figuratively pictured as a descent into Sheol (Jonah 2:1-9). The mighty kings who are wicked are spoken of as descending into Sheol and reuniting with the spirits of the rest of the wicked (Isa 14:9-11; Ezek 26:19-21; 31:14-18; 32:18-32). In the poetic literature, the Psalmist would frequently speak of going into Sheol metaphorically as being very close to death (Pss 18:5; 30:3; 49:15; 86:13; 116:3; 141:7). King Hezekiah, when he is close to death, speaks of already entering the "gates of Sheol" (Isa 38:10). Cooper argues that Psalm 24:7-10 is a fragment from a lost myth of a god who descends into the

---

[6] A. Heidel, *The Gilgamesh Epic and OT Parallels*, 2nd ed. (Chicago, IL: University of Chicago Press, 1949): 139.

[7] *ANET* 138-42.

[8] Herodotus 2.122.

[9] N.T. Wright, *The Resurrection of the Son of God*, vol. 3 of Christian Origins and the Question of God (Minneapolis, MN: Fortress Press, 2003): 80-81.

[10] E.A.W. Budge, *The Egyptian Heaven and Hell*, vol. 1 (London: Kegan Paul, Trench, Trübner, 1906): 6-7.

[11] Bauckham, *The Fate of the Dead*, 17-19.

[12] Bauckham, *The Fate of the Dead*, 21.

[13] W.K.C. Guthrie, *Orpheus and Greek Religion: A Study of the Orphic Movement* (London: Methuen and Company, 1952): 29-48.

[14] Virgil, *Aen.* 6.

[15] *Od.* 11.626; *Il.* 8.367.

underworld to destroy the powers of death.[16] Most scholars have not agreed with Cooper's theory. On the other hand, the ancient Fathers frequently used Psalm 24:7-10 in reference to Christ's triumphant descent and conquering the powers of the underworld so there could have been an ancient descent tradition associated with this text.

The descent and ascent of Yahweh is spoken of frequently in the OT. Yahweh is said to have descended (κατέβην) to rescue the Israelites from their bondage in Egypt and ascended to bring them out (Ἀναβιβάσω) (LXX Exod 3:8, 17). Moreover, God promises that he will rescue the prisoners out of the pit (ἐκ λάκκου), which is a term frequently used for the underworld (Pss 27:1 [28:1]; 141:7 [142:7]). Finally, the Second Temple Literature speaks of various descents into the underworld. The most ancient is *1 Enoch* where Enoch takes journeys through the underworld and the heavens.[17] In the Testament of Dan, the Lord takes from Beliar the captives which are the souls of the saints.[18] In the Latin text of Sirach 24:32, Wisdom says, "I will pierce all the lowermost parts of the earth, and behold all that are asleep, and enlighten all them that hope in the Lord." This text may be in the background of NT texts where Christ is associated with "wisdom" (1 Cor 1:24, 30; Col 2:3) and his penetration of the underworld (Rom 10:7; Eph 4:9).

It is also important to note that Christ's descent into the underworld, according to the NT, has many unique features that are unparalleled in the ancient world. First, in the Greco-Roman world, the visits are made to Hades while Greek heroes are alive in contrast to Jesus' descent which occurred after his death. Second, Christ's descent is triumphant,[19] which is not true of the others. Lastly and most importantly, Jesus was raised from the dead physically, which has no true parallel in the ancient world.[20] Bauckham determines that the influence of pagan descent myths on the NT teaching of Christ's descent was probably "minimal."[21] Clemen says Christ's descent into Hades "is entirely accounted for without the theory of foreign influences."[22] Jeremias explains the unique details of Christ's descent: "But there are two distinctive points in the NT, first, that Christ preached the Gospel to the souls in Hades (1 Pt. 3:19 ff.; 4:6), and second, that He has the keys of death and Hades (Rev. 1:18), in which there is reference to the preceding overthrow of the powers of death in

---

[16] A. Cooper, "Ps 24:7-10: Mythology and Exegesis," *JBL* 102 (1983): 37-60.

[17] *1 En.* 17-36; 54:1; 90:26.

[18] *T. Dan* 5:10-12.

[19] Bauckham, *The Fate of the Dead*, 15-16.

[20] For an excellent discussion and analysis of the ancient literature on resurrection see Wright, *The Resurrection of the Son of God*, 3-200.

[21] Bauckham, *The Fate of the Dead*, 43.

[22] C. Clemen, *Primitive Christianity and Its Non-Jewish Sources* (Edinburgh: T. & T. Clark, 1912): 200.

conflict."[23] Let us now look at the passages in Matthew, Luke, Paul and Peter recounting Christ's unparalleled, triumphant descent into the underworld.

Matthew (Matt 12:40; 16:18; 27:52-53)

In the Gospel of Matthew, there is a running theme of Christ fulfilling the hope of the righteous OT saints.[24] Jesus says to his disciples, "Blessed are your eyes because they see, and your ears because they hear. For I tell you the truth, many prophets (προφῆται) and righteous (δίκαιοι) men longed to see what you see but did not see it, and to hear what you hear but did not hear it" (Matt 13:17).[25] For Matthew, the δίκαιοι consisted of all true believers from "righteous Abel" to "Zechariah" (Matt 23:35). The προφῆται Matthew had in mind most likely included Moses (Matt 17:3-4), Elijah (17:3-4), Asaph (13:35), Isaiah (1:22; 3:3; 4:14; 8:17; 12:17) Jeremiah (2:17; 16:14; 27:9), Daniel (24:15), Hosea (2:15), Jonah (12:39, 40, 41 (2x); 16:4), Micah (2:5), Zechariah (21:4-5; 23:35), and John the Baptist (11:9; 14:5; 21:26). These "prophets" and "righteous" men of the OT longed and waited for the coming of Christ, but did not experience this hope in their lifetime. In addition, the great patriarchs Abraham, Isaac, and Jacob, even though they have long since been dead, are alive somewhere in some sense (Matt 8:11; 22:32). I have argued in chapter 2 that everyone before Christ (except for Enoch and Elijah), the righteous and the wicked, descended into Hades at death. Matthew seems to agree with this teaching (cf. Matt 11:23; 16:18; 27:52-53). If Abraham and all the rest of the OT worthies are in the underworld according to Matthew (Luke places Abraham there [Luke 16:19-31]), then the descent of Christ to liberate them from the "gates of Hades" solves this tension and fulfills the hope of the OT saints to be rescued from Sheol/Hades. I agree that this is not stated clearly in Matthew, but I believe a further study of these texts in Matthew will make this the most probable solution to this tension.

It is only in Matthew that Jesus himself speaks of his descent into the underworld between his death and resurrection. The Scribes and the Pharisees demand a "sign" (σημεῖον) from Jesus and he tells them that the only sign that will be given to them is "the sign of the Prophet Jonah" (τὸ σημεῖον Ἰωνᾶ τοῦ

---

[23] J. Jeremias, "ᾅδης," in *TDNT*, ed. G. Kittel, G. Freidrich, and G. Bromiley, vol. 1 (Grand Rapids: Eerdmans, 1964–76): 1:149. Origen (*Cels.* 2:56) also comments on the uniqueness of Christ's descent. He says, "But since the Jew says that these histories of the alleged descent of heroes to Hades, and of their return thence, are juggling impositions, maintaining that these heroes disappeared for a certain time, and secretly withdrew themselves from the sight of all men, and gave themselves out afterwards as having returned form Hades…let us endeavor to show that the account of Jesus being raised from the dead cannot possibly be compared to these."

[24] Matt 4:16; 8:11; 12:40; 13:17; 16:18; 22:32; 27:52-53.

[25] *Haer.* 4.22.1 Irenaeus cites Matthew 13:17 in support of the descent of Christ to release the OT saints.

προφήτου). Jesus further explains the sign, "For as Jonah was three days and three nights in the belly of a huge fish, so the Son of Man will be three days and three nights in the heart of the earth (ἐν τῇ καρδίᾳ τῆς γῆς)" (Matt 12:40). Therefore, the origin of the doctrine of the *Descensus* may be able to be traced to the very *ipsissima verba* of Christ. To illustrate, the phrase "heart of the earth" (τῇ καρδίᾳ τῆς γῆς) only occurs here in the entire NT. If this was put on the lips of Jesus by Matthew or the early church we would expect to see it used elsewhere. Jesus also refers to himself in this passage as the "Son of Man." This seems to be Jesus' favorite self-designating title and the later NT writers and the early church did not use it. Lastly, I would argue that this passage passes the criteria of embarrassment because Jesus did not spend "three days and three nights" in the tomb, but instead a day and a half to two days at most. As early as Irenaeus, Tertullian, and Cyprian,[26] Matthew 12:40 is already being used in reference to the *Descensus*. Many scholars since have argued that the *Descensus* is being taught in this passage,[27] while others directly oppose it.[28]

The allusion to Jonah[29] is significant because Jonah, in figurative language, descends to Sheol/Hades in Jonah 2:1-9 (death and descent) and then is vomited onto dry land (resurrection) (Jonah 2:10-3:3).[30] Thus, the "sign of the

---

[26] Irenaeus *Haer*. 5.31.1-2; Tertullian *An*. 55; Cyprian *Test*. 2.24-27.

[27] Bauckham, *The Fate of the Dead*, 39. T.R. McLay, *The Use of the Septuagint in New Testament Research* (Grand Rapids: Eerdmans, 2003): 159-70. R.H. Gundry, *Matthew: A Commentary on His Handbook for a Mixed Church under Persecution*, 2nd ed. (Grand Rapids: Eerdmans, 1994): 576-77. D.G. Murray, "The Sign of Jonah," *Downside Review* 107 (1989): 224-25. J. Yates, "'He Descended into Hell': Creed, Article and Scripture," *Churchman* 102 (1988): 303. D.A. Hagner, *Matthew 1–13*, WBC, ed. D.A. Hubbard, R.P. Martin, and J.D.W. Watts, vol. 33A (Dallas, TX: Word, 1993): 354. J. Woodhouse, "Jesus and Jonah," *RTR* 43 (1984): 36. W. Grundman, *Das Evangelium nach Matthaus* (Berlin: Evangelische, 1971): 334.

[28] W. Bieder, *Die Vorstellung von der Höllenfahrt Jesu Christi: Beitrag zur Entstehungsgeschichte der Vorstellung vom sog. Descensus ad Inferos*, ATANT 19, ed. W. Eichrodt and O. Cullmann (Zürich: Zwingli-Verlag, 1949): 36-43. W.A. Grudem, "He Did Not Descend into Hell: A Plea for Following Scripture Instead of the Apostles' Creed," *JETS* 34 (March 1991): 107. U. Luz, *Matthew 8–20*, trans. James E. Crouch, Hermeneia, ed. H. Koester et al. (Minneapolis, MN: Fortress Press, 2001): 217-18. Most commentators do not mention the *Descensus* at all, but just see this as speaking of Christ's burial in death.

[29] Matthew has six references to Jonah (Matt 12:39, 40, 41 (2x); 16:4, 17) as opposed to Luke who mentions Jonah four times (Luke 11:29, 30, 32 (2x). Mark and John do not mention Jonah at all. It should also be noted that the texts that are used from Matthew to argue that the *Descensus* motif is behind the Gospel are all special material unique to Matthew (Matt 12:40; 16:4, 17-19 (Σίμων Βαριωνᾶ, πύλαι ᾅδου); 27:52-53).

[30] The evidence suggests that the phrase "heart of the earth" (ἐν τῇ καρδίᾳ τῆς γῆς) is a synonym for Hades in the Septuagint and other background literature (cf. Sir 51:5). "Then Jonah prayed to the LORD his God from the stomach of the fish (ἐν τῇ κοιλίᾳ τοῦ κήτους), and he said, "I called out of my distress to the LORD, And He answered me. I cried for help from the depth of Sheol (ἐκ κοιλίας ᾅδου); You heard my voice.

Prophet Jonah" that Jesus applied to himself would include his real death, descent, and resurrection all of which was foreshadowed in Jonah's figurative descent into the heart of the great fish (death and descent) and ascent onto the dry land (resurrection).[31] In Jewish tradition on the story of Jonah, the most emphasis is on Jonah's time in the fish and his liberation was seen as deliverance from death.[32] The Scribes and the Pharisees are witnesses to both the death of Jesus and at least second hand witnesses to the resurrection (Matt 27:41, 62-66; 28:11-15). The very sign that brought the Ninevites (Gentiles) to faith (Jonah 3) is the very sign that condemns the Jewish leadership (Matt 8:11-12; 12:22-37; 23:1-39). This fits well with Matthew's emphasis on rejection of Jewish leadership and the Gospel going to all the nations (Gentiles) (Matt 24:14; 28:18-20). Even though Christ's descent into the underworld is not the primary teaching here, it is nevertheless assumed by his allusion to Jonah's descent.

Another significant phrase used only by Matthew in the NT is Jesus' promise that the "gates of Hades (πύλαι ᾅδου) will not overpower" the new community of God (Matt 16:18). We already explored this passage in detail in Chapter 3, but will reference it again to follow Matthew's theme of Christ's descent throughout his Gospel. Similar to Matthew 12:40, I do not believe that the *Descensus* is the primary point of Jesus' promise here, but neither can it simply mean that Christ's church will overcome death.[33] For this promise to be true throughout the ages it is a logical necessity for the new community to not be enclosed in the gates of Hades.[34] How could Christ's promise be true if his

---

"For You had cast me into the deep, Into the heart of the seas (καρδίας θαλάσσης), And the current engulfed me. All Your breakers and billows passed over me. I descended to the roots of the mountains (κατέβην εἰς γῆν). The earth with its bars *was* around me forever, But You have brought up my life from the pit, O LORD my God" (Jonah 2:1-4, 6). "'Arise (Ἀνάστηθι), go to Nineveh the great city and proclaim to it the proclamation which I am going to tell you.' So Jonah arose (καὶ ἀνέστη Ιωνας) and went to Nineveh according to the word of the LORD" (Jonah 3:2-3). Since this is the only background we have for this phrase, the weight of evidence leans toward Matthew understanding it as a synonym for Hades.

[31] Justin Martyr sees Christ's resurrection as the sign (*Dial.* 107.1-2).

[32] Josephus *Ant.* 9.10.2, 208-14; *b.* Sanhedrin 89ab; *b.* Erubin 19a; *m.* Ta'an 2:4; *T. Neofiti* Deut 30:13.

[33] Contra C.S. Keener, *Revelation*, NIVAC, ed. T. Muck (Grand Rapids: Zondervan, 2000): 428. D.A. Hagner, *Matthew 14–28*, WBC, ed. D.A. Hubbard, R.P. Martin, and J.D.W. Watts, vol. 33B (Dallas, TX: Word, 1995): 472. R.T. France, *The Gospel of Matthew*, NICNT, ed. N.B. Stonehouse, F.F. Bruce, and G.D. Fee (Grand Rapids: Eerdmans, 2007): 624. J.P. Lewis, "'The Gates of Hell Shall Not Prevail against It' (Matt 16:18): A Study of the History of Interpretation," *JETS* 38 (1995): 366-67.

[34] Bousset argues for the *Descensus* as the primary point of the passage. W. Bousset, *Kyrios Christos: A History of the Belief in Christ from the Beginnings of Christianity to Irenaeus*, trans. J.E. Steely (Nashville, TN: Abingdon Press, 1970): 65. Cf. McLay, *The Use of the Septuagint in New Testament Research*, 159-70.

disciples went to Hades at death? This would also include the righteous saints and prophets, mentioned above, from ages past who had longed and hoped for the new age (Matt 13:17). It cannot be by coincidence that only here in the NT is Peter referred to as "Simon, son of Jonah" (Σίμων Βαριωνᾶ) by Jesus in light of his earlier allusion to descending like Jonah into the heart of the earth (Matt 16:17). In short, Jesus is promising that the impenetrable gates of Hades will not enclose him (Matt 12:40) or his new community (Matt 16:18; 27:52-53).

The climax of Matthew's Gospel[35] demonstrates that the gates of Hades cannot contain his new community in that "many" of the "saints" (ἁγίων) of old are released from Hades' grip at his death and appear to many in Jerusalem (Matt 27:52-53). This is clearly the most ancient interpretation of Matthew 27:52-53.[36] Moreover, many scholars today see the *Descensus* in the background of this passage,[37] but still others deny it.[38] In the same way Jonah's

---

[35] This passage may form an *inclusio* within Matthew's Gospel. At the beginning of Christ's ministry, the heavens are "opened" (ἠνεῴχθησαν) (Matt 3:16) and at his death the tombs of the dead are "opened" (ἀνεῴχθησαν) (Matt 27:52). Christ truly has the keys of the kingdom of heaven (Matt 16:19; Rev 3:7) and the keys of death and Hades (Rev 1:18).

[36] *Fr.* of Papias 5; Ign. *Magn.* 9:2; *T. Benj.* 9.3-5; Irenaeus *Frag.* 28; *Haer.* 4.34.3; Clement of Alexandria *Strom.* 6.6; Cyril of Jerusalem *Catech.* 14.18-19; *Gos. Nic.* 17.1; Eusebius *H. E.*. 1.13.20; *Apoc. Ezra* 7:1-2; Hilary of Poiters *on Matt. 23.7.* It should also be noted that Matt 27:52-53 seems to be the passage that Ignatius (*Magn.* 9:2) is alluding to in the earliest reference to the *Descensus* from the Fathers.

[37] Bousset, *Kyrios Christos*, 65. McLay, *The Use of the Septuagint in New Testament Research*, 159-70. F. Loofs, "Descent to Hades (Christ's)," in *ERE*, ed. J. Hastings, vol. 4 (Edinburgh: T. & T. Clark, 1908–1921): 662. Hans Urs von Balthasar, "The Descent into Hell," *CS* 23 (1984): 230. K. Gschwind, *Die Niederfahrt Christi in der Unterwelt: Ein Beitrag zum Exegese des Neuen Testaments und zum Geschichte der Taufsymbols* (Münster: Aschendorff, 1911): 185-99. J. Kroll, *Gott und Hölle: Der Mythos vom Descensuskampfe*, Studien der Bibliothek Warburg 20 (Leipzig-Berlin: B.G. Teubner, 1932): 8. Ragnar Leivestad, *Christ the Conqueror: Ideas of Conflict and Victory in the New Testament* (London: SPCK, 1954): 69, 271-72. J. Schniewind, *Das Evangelium nach Matthäus*, 8th ed., NTD 2 (Göttingen: Vandenhoeck and Ruprecht, 1956): 273. J. Gnilka, *Das Matthäusevangelium*, vol. 2, HThKNT1/1-2 (Freiburg: Herder, 1986–88): 2:478. A.H. McNeile, *The Gospel According to St. Matthew* (1915; reprint, London: Macmillan, 1965). R.C. Fuller, "The Bodies of the Saints (Matt. xxvii, 52-3)," *Scripture* 3 (1948): 86-87. J.W.C. Wand, *The General Epistles of St. Peter and St. Jude* (London: Methuen and Company, 1934), 109-10.

[38] W.D. Davies and D.C. Allison Jr., *A Critical and Exegetical Commentary on the Gospel According to Saint Matthew*, vol. 3, ICC, ed. J.A. Emerton, C.E.B. Cranfield, and G.N. Stanton (Edinburgh: T. & T. Clark, 1991): 3:633. D. Hutton, "The Resurrection of the Holy Ones (Mt 27:51b-53): A Study of the Theology of the Matthean Passion Narrative" (Th.D. diss., Harvard Divinity School, 1970): 5-6. E. Lohmeyer, *Das Evangelium des Matthäus*, Kritisch-exegetischer Kommentar über das Neue Testament (Göttingen: Vandenhoeck and Ruprecht, 1967): 397. Grundman, *Das Evangelium nach Matthaus*, 563. R.E. Brown, *The Death of the Messiah, from*

figurative descent and resurrection saved 120,000 Ninevites; Christ's literal death, descent, and resurrection saved his saints from ages past.[39] Matthew says that "many" were raised implying that this was only a foretaste to the resurrection of all on the last day (Matt 27:51).[40] Which saints from the past were raised? Christian tradition have listed Zechariah, Simeon, Simeon's two sons, Anna and Joseph, among others.[41] More than likely, Matthew has in mind those saints from old that he has mentioned throughout his Gospel (see above), but the text does not provide a conclusive answer.[42]

Another difficult question that the text does not clearly address is whether or not these saints were merely resuscitated like Lazarus[43] or resurrected to immortality like Jesus. If they were resuscitated then that solves the seemingly doctrinal difficulty that Jesus should be the first to rise from the dead (1 Cor 15:12-57; Col 1:18; 1 Thess 4:14; Rev 1:5).[44] However, this would be a weak

---

Gethsemane to the Grave: A Commentary on the Passion Narratives in the Four Gospels, vol. 2, AB, ed. D.N. Freedman (New York: Doubleday, 1994): 2:1127-29. Hagner, *Matthew 14–28*, 849. Bieder, *Die Vorstellung von der Höllenfahrt Jesu Christi: Beitrag zur Entstehungsgeschichte der Vorstellung vom sog. Descensus ad Inferos*, 49-56. G.R. Osborne, *Matthew*, ZECNT, ed. C.E. Arnold (Grand Rapids: Zondervan, 2010): 486. E. Schweizer, *The Good News According to Matthew*, trans. David E. Green (Atlanta, GA: John Knox Press, 1966): 516. D. Senior, "Matthew's Special Material in the Passion Story: Implications for the Evangelist's Redactional Technique and Theological Perspective," *ETL* 63 (1987): 278.

[39] "He saved others," they said, "but he can't save himself!" (Matt 27:42).

[40] Bruner says, "The 'Friday resurrections,' if we may call them that, are simply the hors d'oeuvres before the Big Celebration of the Sunday Resurrection." F.D. Bruner, *Matthew: A Commentary*, vol. 2: The Churchbook *Matthew* 13–28 (Grand Rapids: Eerdmans, 1990): 761.

[41] See *Gos. Nic.* 17.1.

[42] There may be a parallel between the tombs of the prophets and the righteous in Jerusalem and the tombs of the saints opened in Jerusalem as a result of the earthquake. Jesus says, "Woe to you, teachers of the law and Pharisees, you hypocrites! You build tombs for the prophets and decorate the graves of the righteous" (Matt 23:29). One thing is for sure, King David was not among this group because if his tomb was empty, Peter's argument on the day of Pentecost would have been moot (see Acts 2:29-34)! Already in Augustine on his comments concerning Acts 2:29, "a statement which would have had no force as an argument unless the body of David was still undisturbed in the sepulchre; for of course the sepulchre might still have been there even had the saint's body been raised up immediately after his death, and had thus not seen corruption" (*Ep.* 164).

[43] One ancient tradition interprets these as resuscitations. *Fr.* of Papias 5, "As for those who were raised from the dead by Christ, he states that they survived until the time of Hadrian." Philip of Side quoting Papias on Matt 27:52-53.

[44] "After his resurrection" can be taken with either ἐξελθόντες (as in the NRSV) or εἰσῆλθον (as in the NIV). The tombs are ripped open at the death of Jesus but not until "after his resurrection" are they raised. Wenham rightly places a period between 52a and 52b-53 placing the earthquake and opening of the tombs with the death of Jesus, but their resurrection awaits Easter morning. J.W. Wenham, "When Were the

foreshadowing of the general resurrection and what Christ's death accomplished if all of these saints rose only to die again. Also, many OT passages concerning resurrection are alluded to here and so would argue strongly against resuscitation.[45] Therefore, we should see these as resurrections to eternal life like Jesus. The text should be punctuated as Wenham recommends so Jesus is truly the "firstfruits" of the resurrection.[46] Lastly, what happened to them? The text does not answer, but the best solution is that they were translated to heaven with Christ similar to Enoch and Elijah around the time of his ascension.[47]

In sum, Matthew's special material has a theme of the OT saints, prophets, and righteous waiting and looking for the Christ. Their great hope was not fulfilled in their lifetime and since that time they have dwelt in the righteous compartment of Hades. Christ's descent into the underworld to release them from the "gates of Hades" may be the best explanation for some of Christ's activity during the three day interval (Matt 12:40), Christ's promise to Peter concerning the "gates of Hades not overpowering" his new community, and the imagery behind many saints' souls returning to their bodies (resurrection) after Christ's death (Matt 27:52-53).

Luke (Luke 23:43; Acts 2:25-31)

Luke is arguably one of the strongest voices in this discussion because he actually records that Christ's soul was in Hades between his death and resurrection (Acts 2:27, 31). *Descendit ad Inferna* "He descended into hell" from the Apostles' Creed finds its clearest justification in the NT when Peter says twice of Christ "You will not abandon my soul to Hades" (οὐκ ἐγκαταλείψεις τὴν ψυχήν μου εἰς ᾅδην) (Acts 2:27, 31).[48] As Moule rightly notes, "Acts 2:27, 31 clearly means nothing else than in Hades, whatever the

---

Saints Raised? A Note on the Punctuation of Matthew xxvii. 51-53," *JTS* 32 (1981): 150-52.

[45] Zech 14:4-5; Isa 26:19; Ezek 37:14; Dan 12:1-2. Interestingly, on Ezek 37, a painting at the synagogue of Dura Europos presents in pictorial form scenes strikingly similar to Matt 27:51-53. There is a split mountain from an earthquake, ten men dressed in white represent OT saints raised, and a figure in pink is the Davidic Messiah raising the dead from their tombs! J. Grassi, "Ezekiel XXXVII.1-14 and the New Testament," *NTS* 11 (1964-65): 162-64.

[46] Jerome *Hom.* Matt. 27:52-53.

[47] Epiphanius *Pan.* 75.7.6-7; J. Nolland, *The Gospel of Matthew*, NTGTC, ed. I.H. Marshall and D.A. Hagner (Grand Rapids: Eerdmans, 2005), 1217.

[48] Pearson says on Acts 2:27, 31, "Now from this place the Article is clearly and infallibly deduced thus: If the soul of Christ were not left in Hell at his resurrection, then his soul was in hell before his resurrection: but it was not there before his death; therefore upon or after his death, and before his resurrection, the soul of Christ descended into hell. . . . and no Christian can deny it." J. Pearson, *An Exposition of the Creed* (Oxford: Oxford University Press, 1857): 410.

original (Ps. 16) may mean."[49] In addition, Luke records Peter saying, "But God raised him from the dead, freeing him from the agony of death (τὰς ὠδῖνας τοῦ θανάτου),[50] because it was impossible for death to keep its hold on him" (Acts 2:24; cf. Rom 6:9). Mattill comments on this passage, "Here Luke conceives of Hades as travailing with countless souls in her womb. When God brought forth Jesus out of the womb of Hades, these travail pangs were loosed or ended and the way was opened for others to follow in the general resurrection at the end of the age."[51] Even though Mattill sees the promise of the general resurrection from this passage (not a liberation from Hades at his descent), he does see Christ's descent and victory over the realm of Hades as the foundation for this later general resurrection. The interpretation of Acts 2:25, 27, 31 as teaching Christ's descent into Hades is found as early as Polycarp (possibly), Irenaeus, Clement of Alexandria, Origen, and Cyprian.[52] Most modern scholars admit some kind of descent of Christ to Hades from this passage,[53] but still others deny it.[54]

---

[49] C.F.D. Moule, *An Idiom Book of New Testament Greek* (Cambridge, MA: Cambridge University Press, 1953): 68. F. Blass and A. Debrunner, *A Greek Grammar of the New Testament and Other Early Christian Literature*, trans. Robert W. Funk (Chicago, IL: University of Chicago Press, 1961): 110-11. A.T. Robertson, *Word Pictures in the New Testament*, vol. 3 (New York: Harper and Row, 1930–33).

[50] Pol. *Phil.* 1.2 "Pangs of Hades."

[51] A.J. Mattill, *Luke and the Last Things: A Perspecive for the Understanding of Lukan Thought* (Dillsboro, NC: Western North Carolina Press, 1979): 32. Bertram similarly says, "The Abyss can no more hold the Redeemer than a pregnant woman can hold the child in her body." G. Bertram, "ὠδίν," in *TDNT*, ed. G. Kittel, G. Freidrich, and G. Bromiley, vol. 9 (Grand Rapids: Eerdmans, 1964–76): 9:673.

[52] Pol. *Phil.* 1.2; Irenaeus *Haer.* 5.31.1-2; Clement of Alexandria *Strom.* 6.6; Origen *Comm. John* 6.18; Cyprian *Test.* 2.24-27.

[53] E. Haenchen, *The Acts of the Apostles: A Commentary* (Philadelphia: Westminster Press, 1971): 181; J.-M Vosté, *Commentarius in Epistolam ad Ephesios* (Paris: Gabalda, 1921): 182-84. A.T. Hanson, *The New Testament Interpretation of Scripture* (London: SPCK, 1980): 151-55. W. Sanday and A.C. Headlam, *A Critical and Exegetical Commentary on the Epistle to the Romans*, ICC, ed. S.R. Driver, A. Plummer, and C.A. Briggs (Edinburgh: T. & T. Clark, 1902): 288. R.B. Rackham, *The Acts of the Apostles* (Grand Rapids: Baker, 1978): 29. D.M. Williams, *Psalms 1– 72*, The Communicator's Commentary, ed. L.J. Ogilvie (Waco, TX: Word, 1986): 128. Bertram, "ὠδίν," 9:667-74. Bauckham, *The Fate of the Dead*, 38-39. E.G. Selwyn, *The First Epistle of St. Peter: The Greek Text with Introduction, Notes, and Essays*, 2nd ed. (Grand Rapids: Baker, 1981): 320. J.A. MacCulloch, *The Harrowing of Hell: A Comparative Study of an Early Christian Doctrine* (Edinburgh: T. & T. Clark, 1930): 63. E. H. Merrill, "מָוֶת," in *NIDOTTE*, ed. W.A. VanGemeren, vol. 2 (Grand Rapids: Zondervan, 1997): 888. Pearson, *An Exposition of the Creed*, 410. J. Jeremias, "κλείς," in *TDNT*, ed. G. Kittel, G. Freidrich, and G. Bromiley, vol. 3 (Grand Rapids: Eerdmans, 1964–1976): 3:746-47. D.L. Bock, *Luke 9:51–24:53*, BECNT, ed. M. Silva, vol. 3B (Grand Rapids: Baker, 1996): 1370. E.H. Plumptre, *The Spirits in Prison and Other Studies on the Life After Death* (New York: Thomas Wittaker, 1889): 102. J.W. Cooper, *Body, Soul, and Life Everlasting: Biblical*

Bock expresses the best objection to this passage teaching that Christ descended into Hades. He writes, "Luke 23:43 has Jesus express the confidence that this death will take him to paradise 'today' and so apparently not to hades" (cf. Wesley).[55] On the other hand, Luke 23:43 can also be produced as one of the best arguments that Christ descended into the underworld if "Paradise" for Luke is located within Hades. In chapter 4, I have already discussed Luke 23:43 in detail and the background of the word Paradise. The conclusion drawn was that Paradise and Abraham's bosom are synonymous in Luke as the righteous compartment in the underworld. This solves the ancient dilemma of how Christ could be in both Paradise and Hades on Good Friday (Matt 12:40; Luke 23:43, 46; John 20:17; Acts 2:27, 31; Rom 10:7). My proposed solution is that according to Luke, Paradise/Abraham's bosom is the righteous compartment contained within Hades (Luke 16:19-31).

The only other objection to this passage teaching the descent is to argue that descending to Hades means nothing more than being dead and buried i.e. "the grave."[56] We must look at Luke's theology of the afterlife in detail to see if Luke equates being buried with descending into Hades. Luke clearly separates being physically buried and one's soul descending into Hades as two separate realities. Luke records Jesus saying, ". . . and the rich man also died and was buried (καὶ ἐτάφη). 'In Hades (καὶ ἐν τῷ ᾅδῃ) he lifted up his eyes, being in torment'" (Luke 16:23).[57] Moreover, Luke envisions the rich man's body

---

Anthropology and the Monism-Dualism Debate (Grand Rapids: Eerdmans, 1989): 129-32. K. Rahner, *On the Theology of Death* (New York: Herder and Herder, 1961): 65. Mattill, *Luke and the Last Things*, 32, 34. P. King, *The History of the Apostles' Creed, with Critical Observations on its Several Articles* (London, 1737): 264-65.

[54] H. Conzelmann, *Acts of the Apostles*, trans. James Limburg, A. Thomas Kraabel, and Donald H. Juel, Hermeneia, ed. H. Koester et al. (Philadelphia: Fortress Press, 1987): 20-21. However, Conzelmann agrees that grammatically εἰς ᾅδην means "leave in Hades." R.P.C. Hanson, "The Journey of Paul and the Journey of Nikias: An Experiment in Comparative Historiography," in *Studies in Christian Antiquity*, ed. R.P.C. Hanson (Edinburgh: T. & T. Clark, 1985). Grudem, "He Did Not Descend into Hell," 107. R.E. Otto, "*Descendit in Inferna*: A Reformed Review of a Doctrinal Conundrum," *WTJ* 52 (1990): 148. J.B. Polhill, *Acts* NAC, ed. D.S. Dockery, vol. 26 (Nashville, TN: Broadman Press, 1992): 113. D.L. Bock, *Acts*, BECNT, ed. R.W. Yarbrough and R.H. Stein (Grand Rapids: Baker Academic, 2007): 124-25. S.J. Kistemaker, *Exposition of the Acts of the Apostles*, NTC (Grand Rapids: Baker, 1990): 96. R.C.H. Lenski, *The Interpretation of the Acts of the Apostles* (Minneapolis, MN: Augsburg, 1961): 90-91.

[55] Bock, *Acts*, 124-25.

[56] So NIV; Otto, "*Descendit in Inferna*: A Reformed Review of a Doctrinal Conundrum," 148. It must be remembered from the survey in the introduction that no one believed that Hades was merely synonymous with "the grave" until Martin Bucer in the 16th century. For the first 1,500 years of the church, Hades was viewed as the unseen dwelling place of departed spirits, good or bad.

[57] In the earliest creed of the NT, Paul says, "For I delivered to you as of first importance what I also received, that Christ died for our sins according to the

buried in the earth, but his soul experiences conscious torment in Hades. Furthermore, Luke many times emphasizes the departure of a person's soul at death. Luke records the story of Jesus raising Jarius' daughter, "And they began laughing at Him, knowing that she had died. He, however, took her by the hand and called, saying, "Child, arise!" And her spirit returned (καὶ ἐπέστρεψεν τὸ πνεῦμα αὐτῆς), and she got up immediately; and He gave orders for something to be given her to eat" (Luke 8:53-55).[58] Where did her "spirit" (τὸ πνεῦμα) go according to Luke? If the parable of the rich man and Lazarus is any indication, her spirit was probably residing in Abraham's bosom, but I admit this is mere conjecture. In addition, Luke says, "They went on stoning Stephen as he called on the Lord and said, "Lord Jesus, receive my spirit (δέξαι τὸ πνεῦμά μου)!" Stephen's body is then said to be buried, "Some devout men buried Stephen, and made loud lamentation over him" (Acts 8:2). Luke believed that Stephen's body could be buried in the earth and his "spirit" enjoys conscious existence with Christ in heaven. In short, Luke does not see physical death and burial to be synonymous with one's soul descending into Hades.[59] These are different realities for Luke as they are with the other writers of the NT.

Luke, like Matthew, believes that Abraham, Isaac and Jacob are still alive in some sense (Luke 13:28; 20:37), David did not ascend into heaven[60] and was buried (Acts 2:29, 34), and Luke directly places Abraham and Lazarus in the

---

Scriptures, and that He was buried (ὅτι ἐτάφη), and that He was raised on the third day according to the Scriptures" (1 Cor 15:3-4). In light of Luke's use of this same word καὶ ἐτάφη (Luke 16:23) and Paul's allusion to the descent elsewhere (Rom 10:7; Eph 4:9?), could the phrase "he was buried" have implied that Christ's soul was in Hades?

58 This is special Lukan material (Matthew and Mark record this story but say nothing about the girl's spirit returning).

59 "But Paul went down and fell upon him, and after embracing him, he said, "Do not be troubled, for his soul is in him (ἡ γὰρ ψυχὴ αὐτοῦ ἐν αὐτῷ ἐστιν)" (Acts 20:10; cf. Ant. 8.326; 9.119; J. W. 6.309; 7.354-355). "And Jesus, crying out with a loud voice, said, 'Father, into your hands I commit my spirit (εἰς χεῖράς σου παρατίθεμαι τὸ πνεῦμά μου)' (Luke 23:46). Some would use this text as an argument that Christ's spirit did not descend into Hades, but ascended into the hands of the Father on Good Friday. We should remember that the same author, Luke, clearly places Christ's soul in Hades (Acts 2:27, 31). This would also contradict the risen Jesus' words to Mary, "Jesus said, 'Do not hold on to me, for I have not yet returned to the Father. Go instead to my brothers and tell them" (John 20:17). Furthermore, MacCulloch says, "To whom did Christ commend his spirit (23:43)? 'The Father's care is still exercised in Hades, and will not leave Christ's Soul (the word is taken from Ps. xvi. 10) in Hades.'" MacCulloch, The Harrowing of Hell, 63. Cf. Psalm 139:8.

60 If David did not go to heaven when he died, where did he go? After David's child dies he says, "But now that he is dead, why should I fast? Can I bring him back again? I will go to him, but he will not return to me" (2 Sam 12:23). David believed that he would be with his son in Sheol after death, not heaven. Luke most likely believed that David was in the same place Abraham and Lazarus was (Luke 16:19-31).

righteous compartment of the underworld (Luke 16:19-31).[61] MacCulloch's comment bears repeating, "The current popular Jewish doctrine of the life after death was probably represented by the parable of Dives and Lazarus. All souls passed to an intermediate state, or place of waiting, called Hades (Sheol), in which there were two divisions—one for the righteous (Abraham's bosom), and one for the wicked."[62] I have demonstrated that this was Luke's view of the after life from the many examples cited from Luke-Acts.

In Luke-Acts, I have argued that the OT saints dwell in Abraham's bosom in the underworld before the coming of Christ (Luke 16:19-31; 20:38; Acts 2:29, 34), Christ descended (with the criminal) to Paradise/Abraham's bosom in Hades on Good Friday (Luke 23:43; Acts 2:27, 31), and ever since Christ's resurrection and ascension believers ascend immediately to heaven at death to be with Christ (Acts 7:55-60).

Paul (Rom 10:6-7; Eph 4:8-10; Phil 2:10)

The first occurrence of a possible reference to the descent of Christ in the NT is found in Paul's letter to the Romans (10:6-7). Even though Paul never uses the word Hades throughout his thirteen epistles, it is clear from his writings that he believed in an underworld with conscious living beings (angels and men). For he writes, "that at the name of Jesus every knee should bow, in heaven and on earth and under the earth (καταχθονίων)" (Phil 2:10). It will be argued in this section that Paul believed that Christ descended into this underworld between his death and resurrection, but beyond that Paul does not say anything definitive of Christ's activity there. The primary passages from Paul's letters produced to argue for the *Descensus* are Romans 10:6-7, Ephesians 4:8-10 and Philippians 2:10.

Paul believed that Christ was the "firstborn of the dead" (Col 1:15, 18),[63] that he had died and returned to life so that he would the Lord of both the dead and the living (Rom 14:9;[64] cf. 2 Tim 4:1), and that death at one time had mastery over Christ (Rom 6:9). This last verse parallels Acts 2:25 because if death no longer has mastery over him then it did have mastery over him for a

---

[61] Irenaeus *Haer.* 2.34.1. Irenaeus says this parable proves the existence of souls in afterlife.

[62] MacCulloch, *The Harrowing of Hell*, 312.

[63] *Haer.* 5.31.2. Irenaeus calls Christ the "firstborn of the dead" in reference to his descent cf. *Haer.* 3.22.4; *Sib. Or.* 8:310-314; Victorinus of Pettau *Apoc.* on Rev 1:5 (see quote in Chapter 6). MacCulloch believes that the title "firstborn of the dead" means that Christ was the first to be delivered from Hades. MacCulloch, *The Harrowing of Hell*, 63.

[64] Romans 14:9 and Revelation 1:18; 2:8 have some striking parallels. Εἰς τοῦτο γὰρ Χριστὸς ἀπέθανεν καὶ ἔζησεν, ἵνα καὶ νεκρῶν καὶ ζώντων κυριεύσῃ (Rom 14:9). Καὶ ὁ ζῶν, καὶ ἐγενόμην νεκρὸς καὶ ἰδοὺ ζῶν εἰμι εἰς τοὺς αἰῶνας τῶν αἰώνων καὶ ἔχω τὰς κλεῖς τοῦ θανάτου καὶ τοῦ ᾅδου (Rev 1:18). Τάδε λέγει ὁ πρῶτος καὶ ὁ ἔσχατος, ὃς ἐγένετο νεκρὸς καὶ ἔζησεν (Rev 2:8).

time, but he loosed the pangs of death or Hades. Caesarius of Arles rightly noted, "When death first had dominion over Christ, it was only with his consent."[65] However, the primary passages used for the *Descensus* are Romans 10:6-7, Ephesians 4:8-10 and Philippians 2:10 and to these I now turn.

In Romans 10:6-7, Paul's primary purpose is not to discuss the descent of Christ, but he does so incidentally and reveals what seems to be assumed knowledge by Paul and his Christian Roman readers. He says, "But the righteousness that is by faith says: 'Do not say in your heart, 'Who will ascend into heaven?' (that is, to bring Christ down) or 'Who will descend into the abyss (τίς καταβήσεται εἰς τὴν ἄβυσσον)?' (that is, to bring Christ up from the dead [τοῦτ' ἔστιν Χριστὸν ἐκ νεκρῶν ἀναγαγεῖν])" (Rom 10:6-7).[66] Paul is speaking about what is impossible such as snatching Christ from heaven (which cannot be done because he is already there) or bringing Christ up from the underworld (which cannot be done because he has already been resurrected). In contrast to what is impossible to reach, Paul is saying that the "word of faith" (τὸ ῥῆμα τῆς πίστεως) is near us and within everyone's grasp (Rom 10:8). Many scholars agree that Paul assumes the truth of the doctrine of the *Descensus* in this passage,[67] but still others deny it.[68] Even Grudem, who

---

[65] Caesarius of Arles *Serm.* 69.2.

[66] In the Peshitta version of Rom 10:6-7 an explicit mention of Sheol is found. J.M. Magiera, *Aramaic Peshitta New Testament Translation* (Truth or Consequences, NM: LWM Publications, 2005): 380.

[67] E. Käsemann, *Commentary on Romans*, trans. Geoffrey W. Bromiley (Grand Rapids: Eerdmans, 1980): 288-89; H.B. Swete, *The Apostles' Creed: Its Relation to Primitive Christianity* (London: University Press, 1908): 60. O. Michel, *Der Brief an die Römer*, Kritisch-exegetischer Kommentar über das Neue Testament, ed. H.A.W. Meyer (Göttingen: Vandenhoeck and Ruprecht, 1966): 328. Sanday and Headlam, *A Critical and Exegetical Commentary on the Epistle to the Romans*, 288. J. Murray, *The Epistle to the Romans: The English Text with Introduction, Exposition, and Notes*, vol. 2, NICNT, ed. N.B. Stonehouse and F.F. Bruce (Grand Rapids: Eerdmans, 1965). J.A. Zeisler, *Paul's Letter to the Romans*, TPI New Testament Commentaries (Philadelphia: Trinity Press International, 1989): 261. Clemen, *Primitive Christianity and Its Non-Jewish Sources*, 198. Vosté, *Commentarius in Epistolam ad Ephesios*, 182-84. Hanson, *The New Testament Interpretation of Scripture*, 135-36. MacCulloch, *The Harrowing of Hell*, 45-47. M. McNamara, *The New Testament and the Palestinian Targum to the Pentateuch* (Rome: Pontifical Biblical Institute, 1966): 75-77. Selwyn, *The First Epistle of St. Peter: The Greek Text with Introduction, Notes, and Essays*, 320-21. Jeremias, "κλείς," 3:746-47. Balthasar, "The Descent into Hell," 231. J.G. Davies, *He Ascended into Heaven: A Study in the History of Doctrine* (London: Lutterworth, 1958): 27-28. E.E. Ellis, *The Gospel of Luke*, NCBC, ed. M. Black (Grand Rapids: Eerdmans, 1981): 129. F.F. Bruce, *The Epistle to the Ephesians* (London: Pickering and Inglis, 1961): 83-84. H. P. Liddon, *Explanatory Analysis of St. Paul's Epistle to the Romans* (Minneapolis, MN: James and Klock, 1977): 182-83. J.D.G. Dunn, *Romans 9–16*, WBC, ed. D.A. Hubbard and G.W. Barker, vol. 38B (Dallas, TX: Word, 1988): 606. M. Black, *Romans*, 2nd ed., NCB, ed. M. Black and R.E. Clements (Grand Rapids: Eerdmans,

denies the descent, admits that Paul is expressing a belief that Christ descended into the abyss. He writes,

> Some may object, however, that Paul could not have anticipated these questions as possible thoughts of his readers unless it was widely known that Christ did in fact descend "into the deep." This may in fact be true, but even in that case Scripture would not be saying or implying that Christ went into 'hell' in the sense of a place of punishment for the dead (which would ordinarily be expressed by *geenna*) but rather implies here that he went into "the deep" (*abyssos*).[69]

Grudem is misunderstanding the Fathers' teaching on Christ's descent. It was not until the 15th century (see Introduction) that anyone taught that Christ descended to Gehenna or the place of punishment (properly called "hell"). Therefore, Grudem admits that Paul assumes a descent of Christ into the abyss and rejects an aspect of the descent of Christ that is inaccurate. If Christ descended into the abyss, the next question that should be asked is: what did Paul mean by a descent into the abyss? Is this just a figurative way of saying Christ was dead and buried or something more in Paul's thinking?

Paul actually changes the Greek word from "sea" (τῆς θαλάσσης) to the more theologically loaded term "the netherworld" (τὴν ἄβυσσον).[70] Himmelfarb says, "Paul (Rom 10:7) uses "abyss" to mean hell, and the abyss of Revelation is more or less equivalent to hell."[71]

Paul's use of abyss in Rom 10:7 may be from *T. Deut* 30:13 as a reference to Jonah 2:6 where Jonah says that the *tehom* surrounded him and LXX translates *abyssos*. This is significant because Jonah also is said to have descended into Sheol/Hades (Jonah 2:1-9) as I discussed above. Whether Paul is working with

---

1989): 143. P. Stuhlmacher, *Paul's Letter to the Romans: A Commentary*, trans. Scott J. Hafemann (Louisville, KY: Westminster/John Knox Press, 1994): 156. Moo says it is possible. D.J. Moo, *The Epistle to the Romans*, NICNT, ed. N.B. Stonehouse, F.F. Bruce, and G.D. Fee (Grand Rapids: Eerdmans, 1996): 656. Aquinas says in his commentary on Rom 10:7, "This explanation prevents any doubt about two articles of Christian faith, namely Christ's ascension and his death and descent into hell, the first of which pertains to his supreme exaltation and the second to his lowest humiliations."

[68] D.E.H. Whiteley, *The Theology of St. Paul*, 2nd ed. (Eugene, OR: WIPF and Stock, 1974): 153. G.R. Osborne, *Romans*, IVP New Testament Commentary Series, ed. G.R. Osborne (Downers Grove, IL: InterVarsity Press, 2004): 268-69. Bieder, *Die Vorstellung von der Höllenfahrt Jesu Christi*, 71-75. Grudem, "He Did Not Descend into Hell," 108. Most commentators don't mention the doctrine of the *Descensus*, but just say Paul is speaking about what is impossible.

[69] Grudem, "He Did Not Descend into Hell," 108.

[70] In every other reference to the abyss in the NT, it refers to the dwelling place of demons in the underworld (Luke 8:31; Rev 9:1, 2, 11; 11:7; 17:8; 20:1, 3). The abyss represents the realm of the dead in LXX Psalm 70:20 (71:20).

[71] M. Himmelfarb, *Tours of Hell: An Apocalyptic Form in Jewish and Christian Literature* (Philadelphia: University of Pennsylvania, 1983): 108.

the Targum or the Septuagint here, he clearly is adapting it for his own use. Walvoord comments on this passage, "Romans 10:7 implies hypothetically that Christ descended into the spirit world between His death and resurrection."[72] Since most would agree that Paul believed in a literal ascension to heaven (Eph 4:8-10; cf. Acts 1:9-11), it should follow that Paul also believed in a literal (not hypothetical) descent of Christ into the abyss.

I believe Acts 2:27, 31 and Romans 10:7 are the two strongest passages to be reckoned with if one believes that the doctrine of Christ's descent is not taught in the NT. It is very difficult to read these passages in any other way. It is true that neither of these passages says anything about Christ's activity in the underworld or the purpose for this journey. However, if it is granted that they do teach his descent, then it gives more weight to the *Descensus* option in other controversial passages that may be teaching the purpose and the activity of Christ in the underworld. Ephesians 4:8-10 is one of these passages.[73]

As early as Irenaeus, Tertullian, and Origen, this passage was understood as teaching the descent of Christ to the underworld and his liberation of the righteous OT saints there.[74] This has been the predominant interpretation throughout church history and still has a large following to this day.[75] The two

---

[72] J.F. Walvoord, *The Revelation of Jesus Christ* (Chicago, IL: Moody Press, 1966): 159.

[73] The other passages are Matthew 27:52-53; 1 Peter 3:18-19; 4:6; Revelation 1:18.

[74] Irenaeus *Frag.* 42; *Haer.* 4.22.1; 5.31.1-2; Tertullian *An.* 55; *Adv. Prax.* 30; Origen *Hom. Exod.* 6.6. Cf. *T. Dan* 5:10-12; *Odes of Sol.* 22:1.

[75] Jerome: R.E. Heine, ed. *The Commentaries of Origen and Jerome on St Paul's Epistle to the Ephesians* (Oxford: Oxford University Press, 2002): 173. Pelagius: A. Souter, *Pelagius' Expositions of Thirteen Epistles of St Paul: Text and Apparatus Criticus* vol. 2 (Cambridge, MA: Cambridge University Press, 1926): 2.364. Thomas Aquinas, *Commentary on Saint Paul's Epistle to the Ephesians*, trans. M.L. Lamb (Albany, NY: Magi Books, 1966): 159-61. H.A.W. Meyer, *Critical and Exegetical Handbook to the Epistle to the Ephesians*, trans. M.J.Evans, ed. W.P. Dickson (New York: Funk and Wagnalls, 1884): 450-51. Swete, *The Apostles' Creed: Its Relation to Primitive Christianity*, 60. B.F. Westcott, *Saint Paul's Epistle to the Ephesians* (Grand Rapids: Eerdmans, 1952): 61. J.A. Robinson, *Commentary on Ephesians* (Grand Rapids: Kregel, 1979): 180. E. Bröse, "Der Descensus ad Inferos Eph. 4, 8-10," *NKZ* 9 (1898): 447-55. Clemen, *Primitive Christianity and Its Non-Jewish Sources*, 198. Vosté, *Commentarius in Epistolam ad Ephesios*, 182-84. H. Odeberg, *The View of the Universer in the Epistle to the Ephesians* (Lund: Gleerup, 1934): 17-18. E.F. Stroter, *Die Herrlichkeit des Leibes Christi: Der Epheserbrief*, 2nd ed. (Gumligen-Bern: Siloah, 1952): 99-100. F.W. Beare, "The Epistle to the Ephesians," *IB* 10 (1953): 689; F. Büchsel, "κατώτερος," in *TDNT*, ed. G. Kittel, G. Friedrich, and G. Bromiley, vol. 3 (Grand Rapids: Eerdmans, 1964-1976): 3:641-42. J. Schneider, "μέρη," in *TDNT*, ed. G. Kittel, G. Freidrich, and G. Bromiley, vol. 4 (Grand Rapids: Eerdmans, 1964–76): 4:597-98. Hanson, *The New Testament Interpretation of Scripture*, 136-41. Selwyn, *The First Epistle of St. Peter: The Greek Text with Introduction, Notes, and Essays*, 321. MacCulloch, *The Harrowing of Hell*, 45-47. J.D.G. Dunn, *Christology in the Making: A New Testament Inquiry into the*

other interpretations that have gained a strong following in the last few centuries are: Christ descended to the earth in his incarnation[76] and the other is that Christ descended in the Holy Spirit at Pentecost.[77]

Origins of the Doctrine of the Incarnation (London: SCM, 1980): 186-87. Bauckham, *The Fate of the Dead*, 38. Balthasar, "The Descent into Hell," 229-30. Plumptre, *The Spirits in Prison and Other Studies on the Life After Death*, 108-109. Blass and Debrunner, *A Greek Grammar of the New Testament and Other Early Christian Literature*, 92. Larry J. Kreitzer, "The Plutonium of Hierapolis and the Descent of Christ into the 'Lowermost parts of the Earth' (Ephesians 4,9)," *Biblica* 79 (1998): 381-93. C.E. Arnold, *Ephesians*, ZECNT, ed. C.E. Arnold (Grand Rapids: Zondervan, 2010): 252-54. C.J. Ellicott, *St. Paul's Epistle to the Ephesians: with a Critical and Grammatical Commentary and a Revised Translation* (Cambridge, MA: Cambridge University Press, 1859): 84. Bruce, *The Epistle to the Ephesians*, 82-84. W. Bales, "The Descent of Christ in Ephesians 4:9," *CBQ* 72 (2010): 84-100. J. Muddiman, *A Commentary on the Epistle to the Ephesians*, BNTC, ed. H. Chadwick (New York: Continuum, 2001): 192-93. F. Thielman, *Ephesians*, BECNT, ed. R.W. Yarbrough and R.H. Stein (Grand Rapids: Baker Academic, 2010): 270-72.

[76] Schneider, "καταβαίνω," 1:523. Theodore of Mopsuestia, "Ad Ephesios," in *Epistolas B. Pauli Commentarii*, ed. H.B. Swete (Cambridge, MA: Cambridge University Press, 1880): 1.112-96. J. Calvin, *Sermons on the Epistle to the Ephesians*, trans. Arthur Golding (1562; reprint, Edinburgh: Banner of Truth Trust, 1973): 350-51. M. Dibelius, *An die Kolosser, Epheser, An Philemon* (Tübingen: Mohr, 1953): 80. M. Barth, *Ephesians: Translation and Commentary on Chapters 4– 6*, AB, ed. W.F. Albright, D.N. Freedman, and R.E. Brown, vol. 34A (Garden City, NY: Doubleday, 1974): 432-34. R. Schnackenburg, *Ephesians: A Commentary* (Edinburgh: T. & T. Clark, 1991): 177-82. C.H. Talbert, *Ephesians and Colossians*, Commentaries on the New Testament, ed. M.C. Parsons and C.H. Talbert (Grand Rapids: Baker Academic, 2007): 112. F. Foulkes, *The Letter of Paul to the Ephesians: An Introduction and Commentary*, TNTC, ed. L. Morris (Grand Rapids: Eerdmans, 1989): 124. C.L. Mitton, *Ephesians*, NCBC, ed. M. Black (Grand Rapids: Eerdmans, 1973): 147. E. Best, *A Critical and Exegetical Commentary on Ephesians*, ICC, ed. J.A. Emerton, C.E.B. Cranfield, and G.N. Stanton (Edinburgh: T. & T. Clark, 1998): 386. Bieder, *Die Vorstellung von der Höllenfahrt Jesu Christi: Beitrag zur Entstehungsgeschichte der Vorstellung vom sog. Descensus ad Inferos*, 81-90. K. Snodgrass, *Ephesians*, NIVAC, ed. T. Muck (Grand Rapids: Zondervan, 1996): 202. A. Lindemann, *Der Epheserbrief*, Züricher Bibelkommentare, ed. H.H. Schmid and S. Schulz (Zürich: Theologischer Verlag, 1985): 77. J. Ernst, *Die Briefe an die Philipper, an Philemon, an die Kolosser, an die Epheser*, Regensburger Neues Testament, ed. O. Kuss (Regensburg: Friedrich Pustet, 1974): 351-52. G.B. Winer, *A Treatise on the Grammar of New Testament Greek*, trans. W.F. Moulton, 3rd ed. (Edinburgh: T. & T. Clark, 1882): 410. R.K. Hughes, *Ephesians: The Mystery of the Body of Christ*, Preaching the Word, ed. R.K. Hughes (Wheaton, IL: Crossway, 1990): 132. A. Barnes, *Epistles of Paul to the Ephesians, Philippians, and Colossians* (New York: Harper and Brothers, 1854): 88. J.R.W. Stott, *The Message of Ephesians: God's New Society*, BST, ed. J.R.W. Stott (Downers Grove, IL: Inter-Varsity Press, 1979): 157-58. C. Hodge, *A Commentary on the Epistle to the Ephesians* (New York: Robert Carter and Brothers, 1856): 220-22.

[77] W. Hall Harris III, *The Descent of Christ: Ephesians 4:7-11 and Traditional Hebrew Imagery*, Arbeiten zur Geschichte des antiken Judentums und des Urchristentums

The third interpretation was first introduced a century ago by von Soden and later followed by Abbott; and more recently Caird and Harris. Proponents of this view believe that Christ's descent was *after* his ascent in the Holy Spirit on the day of Pentecost. This view makes use of *Tg.* Psalm 68 and other ancient traditions about Moses ascending to heaven to receive the Torah.[78] If it is true that Paul was aware of these traditions about Moses and was working with this Targum on Psalm 68 (instead of the OT version of Psalm 68), then I would agree that this is the best interpretation of the passage. However, I will argue below that the LXX version of Psalm 67 (68) is sufficient to supply the background to Paul's argument of Christ's descent and ascent. In addition, the "and" (καὶ) of Ephesians 4:9 argues that the descent was before the ascent and not after (cf. Rom 10:6-7). Paul also adds the word "himself" (αὐτός) in Ephesians 4:10 making it emphatic that the same one who ascended (Christ) is the same one who descended. Lastly, the giving of gifts also seems to be associated with his ascent and not his descent (Eph 4:8-13).[79]

The debate between the other two interpretations largely centers on how to understand the meaning of "descended into the lower parts of the earth" (κατέβη εἰς τὰ κατώτερα [μέρη] τῆς γῆς) (Eph 4:9). Should we understand this genitive as appositional ("he descended to the lower parts, namely the earth") or should it be translated as a partitive genitive ("he descended to the lower(est)

(Leiden: E.J. Brill, 1996; reprint, Grand Rapids: Baker, 1998). G.B. Caird, "The Descent of Christ in Ephesians 4,7-11," in *Studia evangelica*, ed. F.L. Cross, vol. 2 (Berlin: Akademie-Verlag, 1964): 535-45. H. von Soden, *Die Briefe an die Kolosser, Epheser, Philemon; die Pastoralbriefe*, 2nd ed., HTKNT 3 (Freiburg/Leipzig: Mohr, 1893): 135-36. T.K. Abbott, *A Critical and Exegetical Commentary on the Epistles to the Ephesians and to the Colossians*, ICC, ed. S.R. Driver, A. Plummer, and C.A. Briggs (Edinburgh: T. & T. Clark, 1897): 115. C.H. Porter, "The Descent of Christ: An Exegetical Study of Ephesians 4:7-11," in *One Faith: Its Biblical, Historical, and Ecumenical Dimensions. A Series of Essays in Honor of Stephen J. England on the Occasion of His Seventieth Birthday*, ed. R.L. Simpson (Enid, OK: Phillips University Press, 1966): 45-55. A.T. Lincoln, *Ephesians*, WBC, ed. B.M. Metzger et al. (Nashville, TN: Thomas Nelson, 1990): 155-63. R.P. Martin, *Ephesians, Colossians, and Philemon*, Interpretation: A Bible Commentary for Teaching and Preaching, ed. J. Luther and P.J. Achtemeier (Atlanta, GA: John Knox Press, 1991): 50-51. D.E. Garland, "A Life Worthy of the Calling: Unity and Holiness. Ephesians 4:1-24," *RevExp* 76 (1979): 517-27. J.C. Kirby, *Ephesians, Baptism and Penetecost: An Inquiry into the Structure and Purpose of the Epistle to the Ephesians* (Montreal: McGill University Press, 1968): 145-46.

[78] For an excellent and detailed analysis of *Tg.* Ps. 68 and these traditions concerning Moses in the background of Ephesians 4:8-10 see W. Hall Harris III, *The Descent of Christ: Ephesians 4:7-11 and Traditional Hebrew Imagery* (Grand Rapids: Baker, 1998): 64-142.

[79] This section is too brief to give the appropriate pros and cons of this persuasive interpretation of Ephesians 4:8-10. See Harris for the most thorough analysis to date and a fair treatment of the pros and cons of all three interpretations. Harris III, *The Descent of Christ: Ephesians 4:7-11 and Traditional Hebrew Imagery*.

parts under the earth")? Τὰ κατώτερα is the comparative of κατώ. Furthermore, is it used in the sense of the superlative ("lowest regions under the earth") or the positive ("the regions of the earth, on the earth")? Proponents of Christ's descent at the incarnation argue that if Paul wanted to mean the underworld then he would have used the superlative instead of the comparative. It is true that this word appears in the superlative when it is used of the underworld in the Septuagint.[80]

On the other hand, it may not be in the superlative form in Ephesians 4:9 because the comparative form of the adjective had largely replaced the superlative in Koine Greek.[81] Moreover, if Paul meant only "the earth" then why even use this adjective and not just say κατέβη εἰς τῆς γῆς as Paul makes clear in other passages contrasting heaven and earth.[82] Bales says, "So prevalent was the idea of an 'underworld' in the Greco-Roman culture of the day that it can be reasonably assumed that the average person would have understood the phrase 'he descended to the lower regions of the earth' as indicating, first and foremost, a descent (of some sort) to the underworld, the realm of the dead."[83] By adding this adjective, Paul seems to want to follow those passages in the Septuagint that speak of the underworld.

Philippians 2:10 is very important to this discussion because it reveals that Paul envisioned a three-tiered universe with creatures in heaven, on earth, and under the earth (καταχθονίων).[84] As early as Ignatius, this passage is very likely

---

[80] Pss 62:10 (63:9) εἰς τὰ κατώτατα τῆς γῆς; 138:15 (139:15) ἐν τοῖς κατωτάτοις τῆς γῆς; Lam 3:55 ἐκ λάκκου κατωτάτου; Neh 4:7 (4:13) εἰς τὰ κατώτατα τοῦ τόπου; Tob 4:19 ἕως ᾅδου κατωτάτω; 13:2 κατάγει ἕως ᾇ δου κατωτάτω τῆς γῆς. Cf. Isa 44:23 (Aquila) τὰ κατώτατα τῆς γῆς.

[81] J.H. Moulton, *A Grammar of New Testament Greek*, 3rd ed., vol. 1: *Prolegomena* (Edinburgh: T. & T. Clark, 1908): 78. Robinson, *Commentary on Ephesians*, 668. Bales, "The Descent of Christ in Ephesians 4:9," 92.

[82] Eph 1:10; 3:15; Col 1:16, 20; 3:2; cf. Acts 2:19; Rev 9:1; 12:4, 9, 13.

[83] Bales, "The Descent of Christ in Ephesians 4:9," 90.

[84] There is some debate on whether Paul envisions fallen angels (demons): Irenaeus *Haer.* 1.10.1; Chrysostom *Hom.* on Phil 2:10; E. Lohmeyer, *Kyrios Jesus: Eine Untersuchung zu Phil. 2,5-11*, Sitzungsberichte der Heidelberger Akademie der Wissenschaften (Heidelberg: Winter, 1928): 59. The souls of the dead: J. Reumann, *Philippians: A New Translation with Introduction and Commentary*, AB, ed. J.J. Collins, vol. 33B (London: Yale University Press, 2008): 357. or just a figurative way of saying the entire universe: J. Eadie, *A Commentary on the Greek Text of the Epistle of Paul to the Philippians* (Edinburgh: T. & T. Clark, 1894; reprint, Minneapolis, MN: James and Klock, 1977): 122-23. J.B. Lightfoot, *St. Paul's Epistle to the Philippians* (London: Macmillan, 1913; reprint, Grand Rapids: Zondervan, 1975): 115. H.C.G. Moule, *Studies in Philippians* (Cambridge, MA: Cambridge University Press, 1893; reprint, Grand Rapids: Kregel, 1977): 69. R.P. Martin, *Carmen Christi: Philippians ii.5-11 in Recent Interpretation and in the Setting of Early Christian Worship* (Grand Rapids: Eerdmans, 1967): 257-65. W. Carr, *Angels and Principalities: the Background, Meaning, and Development of the Pauline Phrase ταῖς ἀρχαῖς καὶ ταῖς ἐξουσίαις*, Society for New Testament Studies (Sheffield:

being used in reference to the *Descensus*.[85] To those who just want to see "those under the earth" as the dead who are buried, Sasse responds, "It is a mistake, and betrays misunderstanding of the liturgical and poetic nature of the language in Phil. 2:6 ff., to classify the beings mentioned in 2:10f. and to see in the καταχθόνιοι only the dead who rest in the earth. This is refuted by Greek usage, in which the καταχθόνιοι are always θεοί or δαίμονες."[86]

This is an especially compelling argument for those who attest to Pauline authorship of both Philippians and Ephesians. Did Paul's cosmology change from when he wrote Ephesians to within a year or so of writing Philippians? This is very doubtful. Furthermore, Bröse argues that if Paul presents Christ as ascending "above the heavens" (ὑπεράνω πάντων τῶν οὐρανῶν) in order to fill all things, then it is difficult to see why Paul would not include "those under the earth" at his descent (Eph 4:8-10). How does Christ fill all things and how are all things subject to him if he did not descend to "those under the earth"?[87]

Proponents of the incarnation view respond that the author of Ephesians believes in a two-tiered universe: things in heaven and things on earth (Eph 1:10; 3:15) and therefore, Christ does not need to descend into the underworld to fill all things.[88] They also parallel Christ descent and ascent in the Gospel of John which is clearly from heaven to the earth in his incarnation (John 3:13). Bröse counters that καταβαίνω never means incarnation for Paul as it does clearly in John (cf. Rom 10:7).[89] In the same way we should not interpret σάρξ the same in both John and Paul, but instead should interpret it based on the context of each author; we should interpret καταβαίνω the same.

University of Sheffield Press, 1981): 86-89. A both/and approach is probably more accurate here.

[85] Ign. *Trall.* 9.1, "Jesus Christ . . . who really was crucified and died while those in heaven and on earth and under the earth (ὑπόχqόniwn) looked on." cf. Ign. *Magn.* 9.1-2; Poly. *Phil.* 2.1; Hippolytus *Antichr.* 26; Origen *Hom. 1 Reg.* 28.8; *T. Sol.* 16:3; Homer *Il.*, 9, 457; Soph. *Ant.* 75; *Ajax* 865; Aeschyl. *Cho.* 855.

[86] H. Sasse, "καταχθόνιος," in *TDNT*, ed. G. Kittel, G. Freidrich, and G. Bromiley, vol. 3 (Grand Rapids: Eerdmans, 1964–1976): 3:634.

[87] Bröse, "Der Descensus ad Inferos Eph. 4, 8-10," 447-55. Heaven and Sheol/Hades are contrasted throughout the Scriptures as the highest and lowest places in the universe (Job 11:8, 19; Ps 138:8 (139:8); Prov 9:18; Isa 7:11; 14:11, 13, 15; 44:23; Am 9:2; Matt 11:23; Luke 10:15).

[88] However, the case can be made that the author of Ephesians (Paul or someone else) did believe in a three-tiered universe because of his mentioning of "from the dead" (ἐκ νεκρῶν) two times (Eph 1:20; 5:14). Did the author of Ephesians believe the "realm of the dead" (ἐκ νεκρῶν) was somewhere in heaven or on the earth?

[89] Bröse, "Der Descensus ad Inferos Eph. 4, 8-10," 447-55. Hoehner says Paul does not mean the underworld here because "he could have used specific terms referring to Hades (ᾅδης) or the abyss (ἄβυσσος)." H.W. Hoehner, *Ephesians: An Exegetical Commentary* (Grand Rapids: Baker Academic, 2002): 535. However, Paul does make clear he believes in the descent of Christ into the abyss elsewhere (Rom 10:7 τίς καταβήσεται εἰς τὴν ἄβυσσον).

Barth gives six arguments for why the *Descensus* interpretation should be removed from this passage. First, τὰ κατώτερα is not "exactly" the same as τὰ κατώτατα used so often in the Septuagint. Second, Ephesians 2:2, 3:15 and 6:12 place the demonic hosts in the heavenly realms and not in the underworld. Third, Christ's victory was at his resurrection and ascension and not his descent. Fourth, Paul pictures a two step descent from heaven to earth and not a three step from earth to hell. Fifth, Ephesians 4:8-10 parallels John 3:13 where Christ's descent refers to his incarnation. Sixth, Christ's conquest of the realm of the dead is alien to Ephesians 4:9.[90] The first and fifth arguments were answered above. As for the second, the demonic hosts are pictured in the heavenly realms in Ephesians and Colossians, but that does not negate the fact that other angelic beings are in the underworld according to the NT and Paul (Phil 2:10; 2 Pet 2:4; Jude 6; Rev 5:3, 13; 9:1-3). Barth does not see a victory at Christ's descent because he rejects the doctrine of the descent from every passage in the NT. Lastly, whether Christ's conquest of the realm of the dead is referenced in Ephesians 4:9 largely depends on how Paul is using Psalm 68:17-18.

Psalm 68 is a victory psalm recounting the triumphal victories of Yahweh against Israel's enemies.[91] The Psalmist recounts how Yahweh from Egypt to Canaan, from Canaan to Jerusalem has taken Israel's enemies captive ("he led captivity captive"). Yahweh receives gifts from his enemies and distributes the plunder to his people as he ascends Mt. Zion (Ps 68:15-18). There is great debate on why Paul changed "received" to "gave" here or whether he was using a Targum where "gave" is used.[92]

It is important to note that after Yahweh receives gifts from his enemies, Yahweh then gives blessing after blessing to his people (Ps 68:19ff, 35). Augustine said both "gave" and "receive" bring out the fullest meaning of the text.[93] Chrysostom says, "The one [word] is the same was the other'; to 'receive' is to take for the purpose of going to another." Acts 2:33 illustrates this well. Peter says, "Exalted to the right hand of God, he has *received* from the Father the promised Holy Spirit and has *poured out* what you now see and hear." Moreover, ancient battles involved both receiving gifts from the conquered enemies and distributing the spoils to the victors.[94]

Most of the parallels fit nicely for Paul between Yahweh and Christ. Yahweh conquers his enemies, takes them captive, and gave blessings to his people as he ascends Mt. Zion. Similarly, Christ conquered his enemies at the cross, stripped them bare of their plunder (Col 2:14-15), and gave spiritual gifts

---

[90] Barth, *Ephesians: Translation and Commentary on Chapters 4–6*, 433-34.

[91] Hans-Joachim Kraus, *Psalms 60–150: A Commentary*, trans. H.C. Oswald (Minneapolis, MN: Fortress Press, 1993): 49-51.

[92] See *Tg.* Ps. 68.

[93] Augustine *Trin.* 15.5.34.

[94] Gen 14; Judg 5; 1 Sam 30.

to his people as he ascended to the heavenly Jerusalem (Eph 4:8-10).[95] How does Christ's descent into the underworld fit in? First we must answer how Paul understood "he led captivity captive" (ἠχμαλώτευσεν αἰχμαλωσίαν). As early as Irenaeus[96] this phrase was understood as Christ's conquest of the demonic hosts at his ascension and I believe this is the correct interpretation of the passage. The other predominant interpretation in the Fathers is that it referred to taking captive the souls of the OT saints and bringing them to heaven.[97] Chrysostom was the first to argue that it referred to Satan, death, the curse, and sin.[98] While it is true that both the souls of the righteous were liberated at Christ's descent and Satan, death, the curse, and sin were defeated by Christ in his passion; I believe Paul primarily had in mind the demonic hosts that he references all throughout Ephesians (1:20-23; 2:1-3; 3:10; 6:10-16).

The phrase ἠχμαλώτευσεν αἰχμαλωσίαν consistently refers to the hostile capture of enemies through battle and therefore, could hardly mean Christ's saints. Christ's leading captivity captive also occurs at his ascension (Eph 4:8; Col 2:15) and not in his descent because Paul sees the demonic hosts in the

---

[95] "The Psalmist pictures to himself a triumphal procession, winding up the newly conquered hill of Zion, the figure being that of a victor, taking possession of the enemy's citadel, and with his train of captives and spoil following him in triumph." Robinson, *Commentary on Ephesians*, 179.

[96] *Epid.* 83; *Haer.* 2.20.3; cf. Selwyn, *The First Epistle of St. Peter: The Greek Text with Introduction, Notes, and Essays*, 321. T.R. Schreiner, *1, 2 Peter, Jude*, NAC, ed. E.R. Clendenen, vol. 37 (Nashville, TN: Broadman and Holman, 2003): 167. Büchsel, "κατώτερος," 3:642. A.G. Patzia, *Ephesians, Colossians, Philemon*, NIBC, ed. W.W. Gasque (Peabody, MA: Hendrickson, 1984, 1990): 237. Barth, *Ephesians: Translation and Commentary on Chapters 4–6*, 432. Bruce, *The Epistle to the Ephesians*, 82-83. Lincoln, *Ephesians*, 242. Stott, *The Message of Ephesians: God's New Society*, 157-58.

[97] *Acts of Thom.* 10; *Od. Sol.* 17:12; 22:1-5; *Gos. Nic.* 20-27; Jerome *Comm. Matt.* 12.29; Robert Murray, *Symbols of Church and Kingdom* (New Jersey: Gorgias Press, 2004): 65. J.F. Brug, "Psalm 68:19—He received Gifts Among Men," *WLQ* 96 (Spring 1999): 126. 126; MacCulloch, *The Harrowing of Hell*, 45-47. W. Hendricksen, *More Than Conquerors: An Interpretation of the Book of Revelation* (Grand Rapids: Baker Academic, 1967): 191. R. Dormandy, "The Ascended Christ and His Gifts Among Men," *ExpTim* 109 (April 1998): 207.

[98] Chrysostom *Hom.* 11 on Eph 4:9-10 "Why does he descend upon this region here? And of what captivity does he speak? Of that of the devil; for He took the tyrant captive, the devil, I mean, and death, and the curse, and sin. Behold His spoils and His trophies." Cf. J. Calvin, *Sermons on the Epistle to the Ephesians*, trans. Arthur Golding (Edinburgh: Banner of Truth Trust, 1577), 175. Ellicott, *St. Paul's Epistle to the Ephesians: with a Critical and Grammatical Commentary and a Revised Translation*, 84. Meyer, *Critical and Exegetical Handbook to the Epistle to the Ephesians*, 210. Abbott, *A Critical and Exegetical Commentary on the Epistles to the Ephesians and to the Colossians*, 113. Hoehner, *Ephesians: An Exegetical Commentary*, 529-30.

heavenly realms which Christ passed through at his ascension.[99] We should include Satan in this captivity (Eph 2:2), but death, the curse, and sin are not in view here. This does not mean that Christ did not also release the captives of the righteous dead in the underworld (see below), but I do not think that is what is being taught in the phrase "he led captivity captive." This is dealing with his overpowering the demonic hosts at his ascent, not his descent.

On the other hand, in keeping with the imagery Paul is using from Psalm 68, if Paul sees Christ taking demonic hosts captive and stripping them of their plunder, who receives the gifts Christ distributes (Eph 4:8) and who is released from the demonic hosts? Clearly all who are a part of the "church" receive these gifts (Eph 4:11-13) and are released from their bondage (Eph 2:1-3; cf. Heb 2:14), but should this not also include all the saints who were in Christ from the foundation of the world (Eph 1:4-5)? If the demonic hosts are led captive then Paul mentioning the descent into the underworld may be because all the saints from ages past are recipients of these gifts, are truly released from the bondage of the demonic hosts, and thus transferred to heaven. Once again this is not the primary purpose of the passage, but it does explain why Paul would bring up the descent along with his desire to say that Christ penetrated every place in the entire universe to bring it under his subjection (Eph 1:22-23). Paul also could be alluding to Christ's appearance to the dead in Christ and releasing them when he says, "Wake up, O sleeper, rise from the dead, and Christ will shine on you" (Eph 5:14).[100] However, the meaning of this passage in reference to the *Descensus* is uncertain.

All in all, it has been argued from these passages, especially Romans 10:7 and Ephesians 4:9 that Paul believed that Christ descended into the underworld between his death and resurrection. These passages were interpreted this way by the majority of commentators throughout church history and Ephesians 4:9 and Philippians 2:10, as early as the second century. Paul may implicitly be saying that Christ released the souls of the saints of old in his battle imagery from Psalm 68 and descent into the lower parts under the earth, but this is not conclusive. What is for certain is that Paul believed in intelligent beings who lived under the earth (Phil 2:10), Christ descended to the abyss (Rom 10:7), and for Christ to truly be Lord of all things, he must have penetrated all the regions of the underworld (Eph 4:9-10).

Peter (1 Pet 3:18-22; 4:5-6)

Peter wrote two of the most obscure and debated passages in the entire NT (1 Pet 3:18-22; 4:5-6). On 1 Pet 3:18-22, Martin Luther wrote, "This is a strange

---

[99] LXX Gen 34:29; Judges 5:12; Isa 14:2; Ps 67:19; cf. Jer 15:2; Amos 1:15; Num 31:12; Jdth 2:9; 1 Esdr 6:5, 8; 1 Macc 9:70, 72; 2 Macc 8:10; Rev 13:10; *Ant.* 10.68; 11.1; Ep Aristeas 23; *T. Zeb* 9:6; *Asc. Isa.* 3:2.

[100] Already seen in reference to the *Descensus* in Irenaeus *Haer.* 4.20.11.

text and certainly a more obscure passage than any other passage in the NT. I still do not know for sure what the apostle means."[101] St. Augustine said similarly, "Who can be otherwise than perplexed by words so profound as these?"[102] As a result of this obscurity, I do not believe that the doctrine of the *Descensus* in any way stands or falls on these two passages from Peter. In fact, it has been demonstrated in the Introduction that Clement of Alexandria was the first to directly cite 1 Peter 3:18-22 in support of the descent in AD 200. The doctrine of the *Descensus* arose independently of 1 Peter 3:18-22; 4:6 as early as Ignatius as a result of such texts as Matthew 12:40; 27:52-53; Acts 2:27, 31; and Ephesians 4:8-10. It must be admitted that if this passage is discussing Christ's descent, it has the most detail of Christ's activity during this time period of all the passages in the NT. However, even if it did not we would still have hints of the purpose of Christ's journey to the underworld from Matthew, Luke, Paul and especially Revelation.

It does seem that this passage is being alluded to in reference to the *Descensus* as early as the *Gospel of Peter* in the mid-second century and possibly by Irenaeus.[103] On the other hand, Clement of Alexandria, Hippolytus, Origen and Athanasius are surely speaking of these Petrine passages in reference to the *Descensus* by the third and fourth centuries of the church.[104] Grudem rejects the *Descensus* in this passage and says, "Some have taken 'he went and preached to the spirits in prison' to mean that Christ went into hell and preached to the spirits who were there, either proclaiming the gospel and offering a second chance to repent or just proclaiming that he had triumphed over them and that they were eternally condemned."[105] This is misleading. The Fathers (except for Clement of Alexandria and Origen) overwhelmingly condemned the teaching that Christ proclaimed a second chance to repent in the underworld as heretical (see Introduction). Instead, they consistently taught that Christ preached the Gospel to the righteous dead who had looked forward to him when they were alive on earth. This clearly reveals that Grudem has not understood the Fathers on this doctrine because these are not the two options they have left us.

---

[101] *Luther's Works* 30, 113.

[102] *Ep.* 164.

[103] *Gos. Pet.* 10.39-42; MacCulloch, *The Harrowing of Hell*, 64. Irenaeus *Haer.* 4.27.1-2.

[104] Clement of Alexandria *Strom.* 6.6; Origen *Comm. John* 6.18; Athanasius *Ep. Epict.* 109.5. Syriac fragment from Hippolytus cited in B. Reicke, *The Disobedient Spirits and Christian Baptism* (Copenhagen: Ejnar Munksgaard, 1946): 24-25.

[105] Grudem, "He Did Not Descend into Hell," 109. See also Erickson and Otto who make this same error. Erickson says, "The Roman Catholic idea of a second chance to accept the gospel message after death seems inconsistent with other teachings of Scripture." M.J. Erickson, *Christian Theology*, 2nd ed. (Grand Rapids: Baker, 1998): 793. Otto, "*Descendit in Inferna*: A Reformed Review of a Doctrinal Conundrum," 146.

There are three main interpretations of 1 Peter 3:18-22 that have carried through the centuries. First, the traditional understanding is that Christ descended into the underworld to preach the Gospel to the souls of those who had lived before his coming.[106] As noted above, the vast majority of the Fathers believed it was only to those who had believed while they were alive that Christ preached to and therefore, unbelievers who died did not receive a second chance (contra Clement of Alexandria and Origen). Second, originally argued by Augustine, Christ in the Spirit preached through Noah to his contemporaries during the time he built the ark.[107] If this interpretation is correct, then Peter would be speaking of the pre-existent Christ and this passage would have nothing to do with his descent. Proponents of this view point to Christ's spirit speaking through the prophets of old (1 Pet 1:11; cf. Eph 2:17) and Noah being presented as a "preacher of righteousness" (δικαιοσύνης κήρυκα) (2 Pet 2:5). The spirits are not in a literal prison then, but were in the figurative prison of sin during Noah's day. Moreover, Feinberg takes ἐν ᾧ as referring to the

---

[106] *Gos. Pet.* 10.39-42; Irenaeus *Haer.* 4.27.1-2; Clement of Alexandria *Strom.* 6.6; Origen *Comm. John* 6.18; Athanasius *Ep. Epict.* 109.5; Vosté, *Commentarius in Epistolam ad Ephesios*, 182-84. Swete, *The Apostles' Creed: Its Relation to Primitive Christianity*, 58-59. MacCulloch, *The Harrowing of Hell*, 50-66. Clemen, *Primitive Christianity and Its Non-Jewish Sources*, 198. W. Schmithals, "θάνατος," in *NIDNTT*, ed. C. Brown, vol. 1 (Grand Rapids: Zondervan, 1986): 438. H. Bietenhard, "Hell, Abyss, Hades, Gehenna, Lower Regions," in *NIDNTT*, ed. Colin Brown (Grand Rapids: Zondervan, 1976, 1986): 208. Jeremias, "κλείς," 3:746-47. Lewis, "'The Gates of Hell Shall Not Prevail against It' (Matt 16:18)," 105. A. Grillmeier, *Christ in Christian Tradition: From the Apostolic Age to Chalcedon (451)*, trans. John Bowden, vol. 1 (Atlanta: John Knox Press, 1975): 73. Wolfhart Pannenberg, *The Apostles' Creed: In the Light of Today's Questions* (Philadelphia: Westminster Press, 1972): 92-93. Leivestad, *Christ the Conqueror: Ideas of Conflict and Victory in the New Testament*, 172-77. Sanday and Headlam, *A Critical and Exegetical Commentary on the Epistle to the Romans*, 288. Dunn, *Romans 9–16*, 606. C. Bigg, *A Critical and Exegetical Commentary on the Epistles of St. Peter and St. Jude*, ICC, ed. J.A. Emerton, C.E.B. Cranfield, and G.N. Stanton (Edinburgh: T. & T. Clark, 1956): 162-63. Leonhard Goppelt, *A Commentary on 1 Peter*, trans. John E. Alsup, ed. F. Hahn (Grand Rapids: Eerdmans, 1993): 255-60. E.H. Plumptre, *The General Epistles of St. Peter and St. Jude*, Cambridge Bible for Schools and Colleges, ed. J.J. S. Perowne (Cambridge, MA: Cambridge University Press, 1899): 131-34. F.W. Beare, *The First Epistle of Peter: The Greek Text with Introduction and Notes* (Oxford: Blackwell and Mott, 1958): 144-45. R. Bultmann, *Theology of the New Testament*, trans. Kendrick Grobel, vol. 1 (New York: Charles Scribner's Sons, 1951): 176. N. Turner, *Grammatical Insights into the New Testament* (Edinburgh: T. & T. Clark, 1965): 171.

[107] Augustine *Ep.* 164; Aquinas *Summa* 3.52.2; Grudem, "He Did Not Descend into Hell," 109-12. W.A. Grudem, *The First Epistle of Peter: An Introduction and Commentary*, TNTC, ed. L. Morris (Grand Rapids: Eerdmans, 1988): 203-39. Bede, *The Commentary on the Seven Catholic Epistles of Bede the Venerable* (Kalamazoo, MI: Cistercian Publications, 1985): 102-104. J. Feinberg, "1 Peter 3:18-20: Ancient Mythology and the Intermediate State," *WTJ* 48 (October 1986): 303-36.

antecedent "spirit" (πνεύματι) and sees Christ as a spirit without his body, preaching through Noah.[108]

One significant weakness of this view is that the participle πορευθείς must be taken figuratively in 1 Peter 3:19, but literally in 1 Peter 3:22. The same participle is used in both passages and in 3:22 it is agreed upon by all that it is speaking of Christ's journey to heaven at his ascension. However, if the Augustinian view is correct, then Christ did not "go" anywhere when he preached to Noah (3:19), but did "go" to heaven at his ascension (3:22). Second, "spirits" (πνεύμασιν) are much more likely to be referring to angels and not humans throughout the NT (see arguments below). Freidrich says of the Augustinian view, "This is highly artificial. In any case, πορευθείς seems to be in temporal antithesis to ἀπειθήσασίν ποτε."[109] Furthermore, speaking about Christ's pre-existence here is out of place and does not fit with Peter's chronological creedal language of Christ's passion: Christ suffered (3:18a), died (3:18b), "went" to preach (descended) (3:19), resurrected (3:18b, 21b), "went" to heaven (ascended) (3:22a) and is exalted to God's right hand (3:22b).[110]

Lastly, the majority of scholars of recent times argue that 1 Enoch is the primary background of Peter's language.[111] Therefore, Christ preached not to the souls of dead men, but to the disobedient angels from Genesis 6:1-4. There is still a further division in this interpretation because some argue for Christ's descent to this prison (Tartarus) in the underworld to preach to demons between

---

[108] Feinberg, "1 Peter 3:18-20: Ancient Mythology and the Intermediate State," 318.

[109] G. Freidrich, "κηρύσσω," in *TDNT*, ed. G. Kittel, G. Freidrich, and G. Bromiley, vol. 3 (Grand Rapids: Eerdmans, 1964–1976): 3:707.

[110] The creedal order here finds interesting parallels with Peter's speech recorded in Acts 2:23-35. To illustrate, Christ was put to death in the flesh (Acts 2:23-24; 1 Pet 3:18), his spirit/soul descended into the underworld (Acts 2:27, 31; 1 Pet 3:18-19), he resurrected from the dead (Acts 2:31-32; 1 Pet 3:18b, 21), he ascended/exalted to the right hand of God (Acts 2:33-34; 1 Pet 3:22) and all enemies have been brought into subjection to him (Acts 2:35; 1 Pet 3:22). Selwyn says, "St. Peter does not, in fact, in this Epistle speak of Christ going to 'Hades,' though his speech in Acts ii. suggests that he would have done so had he been asked the *locale* of 'the spirits in prison.'" Selwyn, *The First Epistle of St. Peter*, 319.

[111] In fact, some scholars beginning with William Bowyer in 1772 have argued that "Enoch" was originally in the text of 1 Peter 3:19 so it read "Enoch went and preached to the spirits in prison." B.M. Metzger, *Chapters in the History of New Testament Textual Criticism* (Grand Rapids: Eerdmans, 1963): 158-59. This interpretation has not gained much of a following. For it would be very strange for Peter to introduce Enoch in the text when Christ is the subject of 1 Peter 3:18 and 22 and then never bring him up again. Scholars who argue for this emendation: R. Harris, "An Unobserved Quotation from the Book of Enoch," *The Expositor* 6 (1901): 348-49. J. Moffatt, *The General Epistles: James, Peter, and Judas* (London: Hodder and Stoughton, 1928): 141. E.J. Goodspeed, "Enoch in 1 Pet 3:19," *JBL* 73 (1954): 91-92.

his death and resurrection[112] and others believe that Christ preached to them *after* his resurrection and during his ascension in a prison located within the heavens.[113] I believe a combination the first and third interpretation mentioned above is the correct understanding of these passages.

To argue conclusively for any of these interpretations, five exegetical questions need to be answered from 1 Peter 3:18-22; 4:6. France says, "Here, in these nine words, all the controversy centres."[114] First, what does ἐν ᾧ mean in 1 Peter 3.19? It could be in reference to its antecedent πνεύματι used instrumentally[115] or it means "in a state of spiritual existence" in contrast to

---

[112] R.P. Lightner, "Excursus: The Spirits in Prison in 1 Peter 3," in *Understanding Christian Theology*, ed. C.R. Swindoll and R.B. Zuck (Nashville, TN: Thomas Nelson, 2003): 592-93. Reicke, *The Disobedient Spirits and Christian Baptism*, 163. B. Reicke, *The Epistles of James, Peter, and Jude*, AB, ed. W.F. Albright and D.N. Freedman, vol. 37 (Garden City, NY: Doubleday, 1964): 109-10. D.J. Moo, *2 Peter and Jude*, NIVAC, ed. T. Muck (Grand Rapids: Zondervan, 1996): 102. J.N.D. Kelly, *A Commentary on the Epistles of Peter and of Jude*, HNTC, ed. H. Chadwick (New York: Harper and Row,, 1969): 152-57. J. Macarthur, *Ephesians* (Chicago: Moody Press, 1986): 139-40. F. Hauck, "πορεύομαι " in *TDNT*, ed. G. Kittel, G. Freidrich, and G. Bromiley, vol. 6 (Grand Rapids: Eerdmans, 1964–76): 6:577; Selwyn, *The First Epistle of St. Peter*, 315, 26. E. Best, *1 Peter*, NCBC, ed. R.E. Clements and M. Black (Grand Rapids: Eerdmans, 1971): 140-46. A.M. Stibbs, *The First Epistle General of Peter*, TNTC, ed. R.V.G. Tasker (Grand Rapids: Eerdmans, 1959): 142-43. D.E. Hiebert, *1 Peter* (Chicago: Moody Press, 1992): 243. Wand, *The General Epistles of St. Peter and St. Jude*, 100. Schreiner, *1, 2 Peter, Jude*, 188.

[113] W.J. Dalton, *Christ's Proclamation to the Spirits: A Study of 1 Peter 3:18–4:6* (Rome: Pontifical Biblical Institute, 1965): 159, 165, 186. Yates, "'He Descended into Hell'," 309. Kelly, *A Commentary on the Epistles of Peter and of Jude*, 155-56. P.J. Achtemeier, *1 Peter: A Commentary on First Peter*, Hermeneia, ed. H.W. Attridge et al. (Minneapolis: Fortress Press, 1996): 257-58. J.R. Michaels, *1 Peter*, WBC, ed. D.A. Hubbard, G.W. Barker, and R.P. Martin (Waco, TX: Word, 1988): 209. S. Mcknight, *1 Peter*, NIVAC, ed. T. Muck, S. Mcknight, and K. Snodgrass (Grand Rapids: Zondervan, 1996): 216-17. D. Harink, *1 & 2 Peter*, BTCB, ed. R.R. Reno et al. (Grand Rapids: Brazos Press, 2009): 99. Gschwind, *Die Niederfahrt Christi in der Unterwelt*, 119.

[114] R.T. France, "Exegesis in Practice: Two Examples," in *New Testament Interpretation: Essays on Principles and Methods*, ed. I.H. Marshall (Grand Rapids: Eerdmans, 1977): 268. France is referring to the nine Greek words in 1 Peter 3:19.

[115] Bigg, *A Critical and Exegetical Commentary on the Epistles of St. Peter and St. Jude*, 162. MacCulloch, *The Harrowing of Hell*, 51. Beare, *The First Epistle of Peter*, 171. H. Windisch, *Die katholischen Briefe*, Handbuch zum Neuen Testament 15 (Tübingen: Mohr-Siebeck, 1930): 70. Kelly, *A Commentary on the Epistles of Peter and of Jude*, 152. C.E.B. Cranfield, "The Interpretation of I Peter iii.19 and iv.6," *ExpTim* 69 (1957–58): 369-72. Dalton sees πνεύματι as the Holy Spirit not Christ's spirit. Dalton, *Christ's Proclamation to the Spirits: A Study of 1 Peter 3:18–4:6*, 138. cf. Bieder, *Die Vorstellung von der Höllenfahrt Jesu Christi*, 105.

σαρκὶ "a state of mortal existence,"[116] or it is a conjunction and should be translated "when," "in these circumstances," or "in which process."[117] Bigg rightly says, "There can be no doubt that the event referred to is placed between the Crucifixion and the Ascension."[118] Most commentators would agree with Bigg, except for those who argue that Christ preached through Noah. However, did this preaching tour occur between Christ's death and resurrection or after Christ's resurrection and during his ascension? Both interpretations have strong arguments in their favor. If πνεύματι were the antecedent and it was contrasting Christ's risen, spiritual existence in contrast to his fleshly, mortal existence (σαρκὶ) then there would be no doubt that Christ's preaching occurred *after* his resurrection (ζωοποιηθεὶς δὲ πνεύματι).[119] I believe, however, that ἐν ᾧ should be translated as a conjunction ("during which time") because this is how Peter uses this grammatical construction four other times in his letter (1 Pet 1:6; 2:12; 3:16 (temporal); 4:4).[120] Therefore, did this preaching tour of Christ happen between his death and resurrection or between his resurrection and ascension? I believe how we understand the "spirits" (πνεύμασιν) and the location of this "prison" (φυλακῇ) in Peter's mind will determine the answer to this vexing question.

Second, who are the πνεύμασιν? There are only two options that have been

---

[116] Kelly, *A Commentary on the Epistles of Peter and of Jude*, 152. France, "Exegesis in Practice: Two Examples," 267. Selwyn, *The First Epistle of St. Peter*, 197. E.P. Clowney, *The Message of 1 Peter: The Way of the Cross*, BST, ed. J.A. Motyer and J.R.W. Stott (Downers Grove, IL: InterVarsity Press, 1988): 158.

[117] Reicke, *The Disobedient Spirits and Christian Baptism*, 111-13. Selwyn, *The First Epistle of St. Peter*, 315. Goppelt, *A Commentary on 1 Peter*, 255-56. Bieder, *Die Vorstellung von der Höllenfahrt Jesu Christi*, 106. E. Schweizer, "πνεῦμα," in *TDNT*, ed. G. Kittel, G. Freidrich, and G. Bromiley, vol. 6 (Grand Rapids: Eerdmans, 1964–76): 6:447-48. P.H. Davids, *The First Epistle of Peter*, NICNT, ed. F.F. Bruce (Grand Rapids: Eerdmans, 1990), 138. Moule, *An Idiom Book of New Testament Greek*, 131-32. Best, *1 Peter*, 140.

[118] Bigg, *A Critical and Exegetical Commentary on the Epistles of St. Peter and St. Jude*, 162.

[119] Hanson says, "ζωοποιηθεὶς πνεύματι is a strange way to describe the resurrection of Christ's body." Hanson, *The New Testament Interpretation of Scripture*, 129. On the other hand, even though the phrase may be unique in the NT to describe the resurrection of Christ's body, this word is used consistently to refer to physical resurrection all throughout the NT (John 5:21; 6:63; Rom 4:17; 8:11; 1 Cor 15:22, 45). In short, Peter means Christ's physical resurrection by this phrase.

[120] France, who argues that πνεύματι is the antecedent, counters, "It is to be noted, however, that in none of these cases is there any masculine or neuter noun in the preceding clause which could be taken as the antecedent." France, "Exegesis in Practice: Two Examples," 269. On the other hand, Selwyn says that σαρκὶ and πνεύματι are adverbial datives and "there is no example in the NT of a dative being the antecedent to a relative sentence." Selwyn, *The First Epistle of St. Peter*, 315. See also discussion in D.B. Wallace, *Greek Grammar Beyond the Basics: An Exegetical Syntax of the New Testament* (Grand Rapids: Zondervan, 1996): 343.

proposed. Either they are the rebellious angels spoken of in Genesis 6:1-4 or they are the spirits of human beings who are physically dead.[121] Those who argue for the spirits of dead humans here point to Hebrews 12:23 (πνεύμασι cf. Heb 12:9; LXX Num 16:22; 27:16) as an example of the dead referred to as "spirits." However, πνεύμασι is qualified here by δικαίων where there is no qualification in 1 Peter 3:19. In fact, there is a qualification in every example produced where πνεύμα refers to dead humans.[122] In contrast, disobedient angels are referred to as "spirits" numerous times and without qualification.[123] The author of 2 Peter also seems to be interpreting these "spirits" as the disobedient angels of Genesis 6:1-4 (2 Pet 2:4-9; cf. Jude 1:6-7).[124] Peter even speaks of humans as ψυχαί in the very next verse (1 Pet 3:20),[125] but both Greek words could be used synonymously during this period so this is not conclusive. Spitta[126] was the first modern commentator to interpret the πνεύμασιν as disobedient angels and the majority of scholars follow this interpretation today.[127] I believe that the disobedient angels in Genesis 6:1-4

---

[121] Freidrich specifically believes the "spirits" only refer to the sinners who perished in the flood (1 Pet 3:20): Freidrich, "κηρύσσω," 3:707. Others limit it to the spirits of the righteous of the OT, and the rest argue it refers to the spirits of all mankind before Christ's incarnation paralleling 1 Peter 4:5-6. See discussions in Hanson, *The New Testament Interpretation of Scripture*, 130. Cranfield, "The Interpretation of I Peter iii.19 and iv.6," 369-72. J. Dublin, "The Descent into Hades and Christian Baptism (A Study of 1 Peter III.19 ff.)," *The Expositor* 8, 88 (April 1916): 241-74. Bigg, *A Critical and Exegetical Commentary on the Epistles of St. Peter and St. Jude*, 162, 170-71. Best, *1 Peter*, 140.

[122] Luke 24:37, 39 (a ghost); LXX Num 16:22; 27:16 θεὸς τῶν πνευμάτων καὶ πάσης σαρκός; Dan 3:86 πνεύματα καὶ ψυχαι δικαίων; *1 En.* 20.3 "spirits of men"; 22:3 "spirits of the souls of the dead"; cf. *Apoc. Zeph.* 6:11-17.

[123] LXX 1 Kgs 22:21; Luke 10:20; Acts 23:8-9; Heb 1:14; Tob 6:6; 2 Macc 3:24; *Jub.* 15:31; *1 En.* 60.11; *T. Dan* 1.7; 5.5; 1QS 3.17; 1QM 12.8; 13:10.

[124] Whether Peter wrote 2 Peter or not, it is clear that the author of 2 Peter had read 1 Peter and this was his interpretation of the "spirits" (2 Pet 3:1-2).

[125] Ψυχαί is the normative designation for humans in the NT (Acts 2:41; 1 Pet 1:9, 22; 2:25; 4:19; 2 Pet 2:14; Jude 15), even dead ones (Rev 6:9).

[126] Dublin, "The Descent into Hades and Christian Baptism," 69.

[127] Kelly, *A Commentary on the Epistles of Peter and of Jude*, 154. Davids, *The First Epistle of Peter*, 140. Hiebert, *1 Peter*, 243. J.H. Elliott, *1 Peter: A New Translation with Introduction and Commentary*, AB, ed. W.F. Albright and D.N. Freedman, vol. 37B (New York: Doubleday, 2000): 656. S.J. Kistemaker, *Peter and Jude*, NTC (Grand Rapids: Baker, 1987): 143. Schweizer, "πνεῦμα," 6:447-48. Michaels, *1 Peter*, 207-209. Achtemeier, *1 Peter: A Commentary on First Peter*, 255-56. I.H. Marshall, *1 Peter*, IVP New Testament Commentary Series, ed. G.R. Osborne (Downers Grove, IL: InterVarsity Press, 1991): 126-28. Mcknight, *1 Peter*, 217. France, "Exegesis in Practice: Two Examples," 269-70. Bauckham, *The Fate of the Dead*, 39. Gschwind, *Die Niederfahrt Christi in der Unterwelt*, 119. C.F. Dickason, *Angels: Elect and Evil* (Chicago, IL: Moody Press, 1995): 227. K.S. Wuest, *First*

are the "spirits" that Peter had in mind and this designation would have been familiar to his audience.

Moreover, *1 Enoch* seems to have played a very important role for the authors of 1 Peter, 2 Peter, Jude and the early Christian community.[128] France says, "To try to understand 1 Peter 3:19-20 without a copy of the Book of Enoch at your elbow is to condemn yourself to failure."[129] The parallels between 1 Peter 3:19-20 and *1 Enoch* are striking. For example, Enoch is sent[130] to pronounce a message of condemnation to disobedient angels called *pneumata*![131] The angels that Enoch preached to had "transgressed the commandment of the Lord"[132] and were thus disobedient (1 Pet 3:20). Lastly, Enoch condemned them eternally through the proclamation: "you will have no peace."[133] The greatest weakness of this interpretation is that if this would have been obvious to Peter's audience because they knew *1 Enoch* so well, then why did none of the Fathers argue for this interpretation? A possible answer is that since we do not have clear comments on these passages until Clement of Alexandria, *1 Enoch* could have lost its influence among Christians from the third century on. The Apostolic Fathers, Justin Martyr, Irenaeus and others may have understood the "spirits" this way, but if they wrote on this passage their writings did not survive. In short, the πνεύμασιν are the disobedient angels of Genesis 6:1-4 that have been kept in "prison" since the days before Noah, and these are most likely the very "angels, authorities, and powers" (ἀγγέλων καὶ ἐξουσιῶν καὶ δυνάμεων) that are now in subjection to Christ (1 Pet 3:22).

Third, what is meant by ἐν φυλακῇ? At this point, the crux of the debate falls with the correct interpretation of φυλακῇ. If according to Peter, this "prison" is located in the underworld then the preaching would likely have occurred between his death and resurrection,[134] but if it is in the heavenlies, then the preaching almost certainly occurred at Christ's ascension. φυλακή is used predominantly in the LXX and the rest of the NT to refer to an earthly prison or dungeon.[135] In all of these uses it is never a positive place, but consistently a

---

Peter in the Greek New Testament for the English Reader, 2nd ed. (Grand Rapids: Eerdmans, 1944), 100.

[128] *1 En.* 1:9 is cited in Jude 1:14-15, the story of Gen 6:1-4 is discussed heavily in *1 Enoch* and is alluded to in Jude 6-7; 2 Pet 2:4, and *1 En.* 80:65-67 is cited as "Scripture" in *Barn.* 16:5.

[129] France, "Exegesis in Practice: Two Examples," 265.

[130] *1 En.* 12:4; 13:3; 15:2 (πορεύομαι used in all three instances).

[131] *1 En.* 10:15; 13:6; 15:4.

[132] *1 En.* 21:6; 106:13.

[133] *1 En.* 16:3-4; cf. 12:4-6; 13:1; 14:3-6.

[134] This is not for certain, because Christ could have visited this prison in the underworld after his resurrection as well.

[135] Gen 40:3-4, 7; 41:10; 42:17, 30; Lev 24:12; Judg 16:25; 1 Kgs 22:27; Isa 42:7; Matt 5:25; 14:3, 10; 18:30; 25:36;, 39, 43, 44; Mark 6:17, 40; Luke 3:20; 12:58; 21:12;

place of punishment or confinement.[136] In its more figurative uses in the NT, it is used to refer to the dwelling place of demons and Satan.[137] In Revelation 20:7, it is the prison of Satan located under the earth because it is synonymous with the abyss (Rev 20:3). It is also found in the only other place in the NT where φυλακή and πνεύματος appear together (other than 1 Pet 3:19), and here it is a prison for unclean spirits (demons) (Rev 18:2). Those who argue that the preaching took place at Christ's ascension must find the "prison" spoken of here located somewhere in the heavenlies. While there are some texts in the Jewish background literature that place disobedient angels in a prison in the heavenlies,[138] there is no evidence that these texts formed the background of Peter's thinking. In fact, *1 Enoch*, which seems to be in the background of Peter's thinking, places the disobedient angels in the underworld.[139]

Moreover, no one would deny that the author of 2 Peter places these very angels in confinement in Tartarus (2 Pet 2:4; cf. Jude 1:6), which for the entire Greco-Roman world was located in the lowest depths of the underworld (see Chapter 4 above). Therefore, despite a few texts from *2 Enoch* and other literature, the evidence seems to be conclusive that the "prison" that Peter was thinking of was located in the lowest depths of the underworld.

Fourth, what does it mean that Christ went there to ἐκήρυξεν "preach"? The LXX use of this word is not very helpful here because it in most cases just means some sort of proclamation: good or bad.[140] In the NT, κηρύσσω is used sixty-one times and in the vast majority of cases to speak of the proclamation of the "kingdom of God" or the "Gospel." However, the interpretation of a word should be based on context and not a word count. It is used in a neutral sense in the NT as well (Luke 4:19; 8:39; 12:3; Rom 2:21; Rev 5:2). If our interpretation is correct that the "spirits" are disobedient angels then the proclamation of

---

22:33; 23:19, 25; John 3:24; Acts 5:19, 22-23, 25; 8:3; 12:4-6, 17; 16:23, 24, 27, 37, 40; 22:4; 26:10; 2 Cor 6:6; 11:23; Heb 11:36; Rev 2:10.

[136] This argues against the "spirits" in 1 Peter 3:19 being at least righteous OT saints because they would be in a locale of punishment and not of bliss (compare Luke 16:19-31).

[137] Bertram says, "In 1 Pt. 3:19 φυλακή means "prison" in the sense of the place where departed spirits are kept." G. Bertram, "φυλακή " in *TDNT*, ed. G. Kittel, G. Freidrich, and G. Bromiley, vol. 9 (Grand Rapids: Eerdmans, 1964–76): 9:242. The Peshitta version of 1 Pet 3:19 translated 'Sheol' for φυλακή in 1 Peter 3:19. Magiera, *Aramaic Peshitta New Testament Translation*, 547. Some see φυλακή as synonymous with Hades in 1 Peter 3:19. Bietenhard, "Hell, Abyss, Hades, Gehenna, Lower Regions," 207. Jeremias, "ᾅδης," 1:148. Selwyn, *The First Epistle of St. Peter*, 319.

[138] *2 En.* 7:1-5; 18:3-6; *T. Lev.* 3:2; *Odes Sol.* 22:1. Cf. *T. Naph.* 3.5; *T. Reub.* 5.6; *2 Bar.* 56:13.

[139] *1 En.* 18:14; 21:10; cf. *Jub.* 5:6.

[140] LXX Gen 41:43; Exod 32:5; 36:6; 2 Kgs 10:20; Esth 6:9; Jonah 1:2. Jonah's use of this word is very interesting because both πορεύθητι and κήρυξον appear together as in 1 Peter 3:19. Whether this was in the author's mind or just mere coincidence is hard to say.

Christ could not be an offer of redemption or salvation to them (see Heb 2:16), but must be one of condemnation and triumph. In addition, if *1 Enoch* is the appropriate background to seek the content of this preaching then a proclamation of condemnation and victory by Christ over the disobedient angels, authorities and powers would make the most sense (1 Pet 3:22). Christ does speak harshly and in condemnation to Satan and demons throughout the Gospels and so should not be surprising here.[141] In fact, the demons called Legion expected Jesus himself to torture them at the appointed time (Matt 8:29; Mark 5:7). The promise of victory over Satan and the demonic hosts was a consistent source of encouragement for the believers throughout the NT.[142]

Moreover, when Peter wanted to speak of the proclamation of the good news of salvation he uses εὐαγγελίζω (1 Pet 1:12, 25; 4:6), but κηρύσσω only in 1 Peter 3:19. In sum, if our exegesis of this passage is correct then Peter is saying that between Christ being put to death in the flesh and resurrected to a spiritual existence, he "went" to the underworld to declare victory over the disobedient angels confined in Tartarus. Peter then references Noah because he builds the ark after this event (Gen 6), and like Noah and his family, Peter's audience was baptized and both were a very small number compared to the pagan world around them. The participle ἀπειθήσασίν Peter uses can mean "after they were disobedient long ago" (adverbial) or describing the "spirits" "who had once been disobedient" (adjectival). This same participle has a substantival use in 1 Peter 2:7. Achtemeier argues that it is an "adverbial participle of cause ('because they were disobedient') indicating the reason either why Christ announced his victory over them, or why they had been imprisoned."[143] I believe the latter makes the most sense in the context. The disobedient generation of Noah followed the disobedience of the angels in Genesis 6 (cf. 2 Pet 2:4-5). After the resurrection, Christ then "went" to heaven in his ascension and exaltation with all angels, authorities, and powers now under his control.

Finally, what does 1 Peter 4:6 mean? The first question that must be answered is whether or not this passage refers back to 1 Peter 3:19? Most scholars today believe that these two passages are not related,[144] but still others see Peter expanding on 3:19.[145] I believe that Peter is discussing a different

---

[141] Matt 4:10; 25:41, 46; Mark 1:25; 5:8-9, 12-13; Luke 4:35; John 8:44; cf. Rev 14:9-11.

[142] Matt 10:1; Mark 1:27; 6:7; 9:25; Luke 4:36; 10:17-20.

[143] Achtemeier, *1 Peter: A Commentary on First Peter*, 262.

[144] Achtemeier, *1 Peter*, 291. Dalton, *Christ's Proclamation to the Spirits*, 42-51. Davids, *The First Epistle of Peter*, 154. Elliott, *1 Peter*, 730-31. N. Hillyer, *1 and 2 Peter, Jude*, NIBC, ed. W.W. Gasque (Peabody, MA: Hendrickson, 1992): 122. Kistemaker, *Peter and Jude*, 163-64. Michaels, *1 Peter*, 237-38. K.H. Jobes, *1 Peter*, BECNT, ed. R.W. Yarbrough and R.H. Stein, vol. 6 (Grand Rapids: Baker Academic, 2005): 272-73.

[145] *Herm. Sim.* 9:16:2-7 (possibly); Cyprian *Test.* 2.27 (this is the earliest direct citation of 1 Peter 4:6); Bigg, *A Critical and Exegetical Commentary on the Epistles of St.*

proclamation[146] and a different audience in 1 Peter 4:6 than in 3:19,[147] but this proclamation of the Gospel by Christ most likely occurred during the same time period and so this should be seen as further expansion on what Peter says in 1 Peter 3:18-20.

The hardest question in this passage is the identity of the νεκροῖς in 1 Peter 4:6? We can easily identify the νεκροῖς of 1 Peter 4:5 because Peter says, "But they will have to give account to him who is ready to judge the living and the dead (κρῖναι ζῶντας καὶ νεκρούς)."[148] Since all mankind will be judged (living or dead), Peter has in mind everyone who has ever lived and will live. In addition, since Peter has just spoken of the literal dead in 4:5 it is extremely doubtful he would use the same word to refer to the spiritually dead in 4:6 (contra Augustine, Aquinas, Grudem).[149] In fact, if the νεκροῖς in 4:5 means all the dead will be judged, but in 4:6 νεκροῖς only means the spiritually dead whom Christ preached to while he was on earth, then we have only a very small segment of the νεκροῖς being preached to. MacCulloch quips, "All the dead are judged, therefore to all the dead the Gospel has been preached."[150] This, however, must be further qualified. Peter could not have in mind all the dead (both believers and unbelievers) who had ever lived hearing the Gospel in the underworld because this would imply a second chance. Peter's audience undergoing significant persecution (1 Pet 4:12-13) and being encouraged to persevere would hardly be encouraged by hearing that there is a second chance in the afterlife even for their persecutors (cf. 1 Pet 2:7-8; Heb 9:27; Luke 16:26). We must then revisit the context.

Peter throughout his epistle lifts up Christ as the example par excellence to imitate as believers. In the midst of theological and ethical teaching, Peter presents Christ's voluntary suffering and death as an example to follow (1 Pet

---

Peter and St. Jude, 162. Wand, *The General Epistles of St. Peter and St. Jude*, 105. Reicke, *The Disobedient Spirits and Christian Baptism*, 205. Schweizer, "πνεῦμα," 6:447-48. MacCulloch, *The Harrowing of Hell*, 58. Hanson, *The New Testament Interpretation of Scripture*, 132-33. Moo, *2 Peter and Jude*, 102. Kelly, *A Commentary on the Epistles of Peter and of Jude*, 152-57. Michaels, *1 Peter*, 205-11. Beare, *The First Epistle of Peter*, 156.

[146] Εὐηγγελίσθη "the good news was proclaimed" (1 Pet 1:12, 25; 4:6) is used here instead of the more generic proclamation ἐκήρυξεν "he proclaimed" (1 Pet 3:19).

[147] Christ preaches the good news to the "dead (humans)" (νεκροῖς) rather than to the angelic "spirits" (πνεύμασιν).

[148] Cf. Acts 10:42; 2 Tim 4:1; Rom 14:9; *Barn.* 7:2; Pol. *Phil.* 2:1; 2 Clem. 1:1; *Sib. Or.* 8:82-83, 223; *Apoc. Pet.* 1.

[149] The νεκροῖς can be those who are physically dead in the NT (Matt 10:8; 11:5; 28:4; Luke 7:22; 24:5; 1 Thess 4:16; Heb 6:1; 9:14, 17; 11:35; 1 Pet 1:3, 21; 4:5; Rev 11:18; 14:13; 20:5, 12 (2x), 13 (2x)) or spiritually dead (Matt 8:22 (2x); Luke 9:60 (2x); 15:24, 32; Rom 6:11; Eph 2:1, 5; Col 2:13; Rev 3:1). Every other place this word is used in Peter's epistle it is referring to the physically dead (1 Pet 1:3, 21; 4:5).

[150] MacCulloch, *The Harrowing of Hell*, 58.

2:21-25). Similarly, 1 Peter 3:18-22 is another clear example of Peter calling his readers to walk in Christ's cosmic victory over the spiritual forces at work and to persevere like Noah and his family did despite the pagan world around them and were saved. Peter then brings more ethical application (4:1-4) for the reason to bring up the eschatological teaching (4:5-6). The "they" in "they will have to given an account" (4:5) are the wicked, pagan persecutors around them who are enticing them to sin. Christ is the judge of the living and the dead, so one day they will have to meet Christ in judgment. Peter then says, "For this is the reason the gospel was preached even to the dead (νεκροῖς), so that they might be judged according to men in regard to the body, but live according to God in regard to the spirit" (1 Pet 4:6). Since Peter says that they "might be judged according to men in regard to the body" he must be thinking of believers who had been martyred in the flesh. They had heard the good news, accepted it, and so could "live according to God in regard to the spirit."

However, Peter does not limit believers to Christians who had died since Christ,[151] but Peter includes all who are true believers from Noah (1 Pet 3:20-21) to the Prophets (1 Pet 1:10-12) to the suffering Christians of his time (1 Pet 4:12-19).[152] As the writer to the Hebrews says, "These were all commended for their faith, yet none of them received what had been promised. God had planned something better for us so that only together with us would they be made perfect" (Heb 11:39-40; cf. 4:2, 6; Gal 3:8-9). This would require a preaching tour in the underworld even to those who had died before Christ's incarnation (all true believers since the beginning of the world). This is not teaching a second chance for those who had died, but instead giving believers great hope that all who had died in faith would hear the Gospel, and "who through faith are shielded by God's power until the coming of the salvation that is ready to be revealed in the last time" (1 Pet 1:5). In short, Christ's descent to the saints of old and his preaching the Gospel to them is the only way for Peter's readers to be confident that no matter where the believer is (dead or alive), Christ will be with them.

In my survey of Matthew, Luke, Paul and Peter on their references to the descent of Christ, I have argued that not only is Christ's descent to the underworld assumed by them, but each of them could imply the liberation of the OT saints and Peter discusses his preaching tour. It is important to remember that the origin of the doctrine of Christ's descent is from the lips of Christ himself (Matt 12:40). Matthew and Peter would have heard this as eyewitnesses because they were two of Christ's twelve disciples. Jesus may have discussed these things in more detail during his forty days of teaching the apostles between his resurrection and ascension (Acts 1:3). Paul spent fifteen

---

[151] So Selwyn, *The First Epistle of St. Peter*, 316. Harink, *1 & 2 Peter*, 110. Kelly, *A Commentary on the Epistles of Peter and of Jude*, 174. Clowney, *The Message of 1 Peter*, 175.

[152] Rightly, Achtemeier, *1 Peter*, 288-90.

days with Peter (Gal 1:18) and during this time Peter may have discussed Christ's descent when he gave Paul the earliest creed chronicling Christ's passion (1 Cor 15:3-5). We can also envision Paul teaching these things to Luke during their many travels on his missionary journeys. John, the author of Revelation, also was present for Jesus' teaching on his descent (Matt 12:40) and about things concerning the "kingdom of God" during this forty day period (Acts 1:3). It is to his contribution to the *Descensus* we now turn.

CHAPTER 6

DESCENSUS AD INFEROS IN REVELATION 1:18

History of Interpretation of Revelation 1:18

The fundamental contribution of this book is to give a full exegetical and theological study on Revelation 1:18. Many commentators from the Fathers until now have commented on this passage, but there is yet to be a detailed study on the background, imagery and theology behind this powerful declaration by the risen Christ. It will be shown through this survey of commentators on Revelation 1:18 that the majority of them understood it in light of the *Descensus*, and even those who do not, allow for the possibility.

The history of interpretation of Revelation 1:18 began with Irenaeus of Lyons in AD 180. Although Irenaeus only cites Rev 1:18 once in his writings,[1] it has been demonstrated above that Irenaeus argued for Christ's descent into Hades and it is very likely that he understood the background of this passage in the same way. Origen only cites Revelation 1:18 two times.[2] However, one of these citations[3] occurs in a context when Origen is expounding on what it means that Christ is the first and the last and he references the descent of Christ. Origen says, "His birth from the Virgin and His life so admirably lived showed Him to be more than man, and it was the same among the dead. He was the only free person there, and His soul was not left in hell. Thus, then, He is the first and the last."[4] In addition, Epiphanius[5] and the Acts of Thomas[6] also cite parts of Revelation 1:18.

Cyprian is the first to use Revelation 1:17-18 in reference to Christ's conquest after his death, descent into hell, and resurrection. Cyprian says:

---

[1] Irenaeus *Haer.* 4.20.11.

[2] Origen *Comm. John* 1.23, 35. In the first citation of Rev 1:18, Origen does not have the last phrase καὶ ἔχω τὰς κλεῖς τοῦ θανάτου καὶ τοῦ ᾅδου and in the second he only calls Christ the "living and the dead."

[3] Origen *Comm. John* 1.35.

[4] Origen *Comm. John* 1.34.

[5] Epiphanius *Gem.* 130.27.

[6] *Acts of Thom.* 1.129.

That He was not to be overcome of death, nor should remain in Hades. In the twenty-ninth Psalm: "O Lord, Thou hast brought back my soul from hell." Also in the fifteenth Psalm: "Thou wilt not leave my soul in hell, neither wilt Thou suffer Thine Holy One to see corruption".... That after He had risen again He should receive from His Father all power, and His power should be everlasting. ... Also in the Apocalypse: And He laid His right hand upon me, and said, "Fear not; I am the first and the last, and He that liveth and was dead; and, lo, I am living for evermore and I have the keys of death and of hell." Likewise in the Gospel, the Lord after His resurrection says to His disciples: "All power is given unto me in heaven and in earth. Go therefore and teach all nations, baptizing them in the name of the Father, and of the Son, and of the Holy Ghost, teaching them to observe all things whatsoever I have commanded you."[7]

Cyril of Jerusalem clearly alludes to Revelation 1:18 and the descent when he says of Christ, "He is called Dead; not as abiding among the dead, as all in the nether world, but alone 'free among the dead.'"[8] The Fathers frequently cited Psalm 87:5 (88:5) in reference to Christ being free in Hades and only in Revelation 1:18 is Christ ever given the title "Dead" (νεκρός) in the NT. Victorinus (third century AD) wrote the earliest commentary on Revelation that has survived. Victorinus does not comment on Revelation 1:17-18, but he says the following on Revelation 1:5, "He freed us by His blood from sin; and having vanquished hell, He was the first who rose from the dead, and 'death shall have no more dominion over Him.'"[9] Oecumenius (seventh century AD), another ancient commentator on Revelation, alludes to this battle with Death and Hades at Christ's descent. Oecumenius puts these words in the mouth of Christ when he comments on 1:17-18,

> For if I who am living and am the wellspring of life became dead for you, and trampled death underfoot and lived again, how is it possible that you who are living become dead on account of me and my appearance? And if I have the keys of death and of hades,; so that I make dead and make alive those whom I wish, and that I will bring down to hades and bring up again, as it is written concerning me, and that, as the prophet says, escape from death belongs to me.[10]

During the Middle Ages, Nicholas of Lyra (AD 1329) wrote a commentary on Revelation. He believed Revelation 1:18 not only alluded to the descent, but taught that Jesus released the OT saints from the underworld. He comments on 1:18, "'And I have the keys of Death. ...' That is, the power of leading the just from thence, which he also did in his own resurrection, and the power to shut up the impious there, which he will specifically do at the last judgment, saying

---

[7] Cyprian *Test.* 2.24-26.

[8] Cyril of Jerusalem *Catech.* 10.4.

[9] Victorinus of Pettau *Apoc.* on Rev 1:5.

[10] Oecumenius *Apoc.* 1.29.

that terrible word, 'Depart you evil ones into the eternal fire' (Mt 25:41)."[11]

The Reformers largely ignored the book of Revelation and few wrote commentaries on it.[12] However, Matthew Henry, who wrote a commentary on the entire Bible, said this on Revelation 1:17-18, "*I have the keys of hell and of death,* a sovereign dominion in and over the invisible world, opening and none can shut, shutting so that none can open, opening the gates of death when he pleases and the gates of the eternal world, of happiness or misery, as the Judge of all, from whose sentence there lies no appeal."[13] In the notes of John Wesley on the NT, he writes concerning Revelation 1:18, "And I have the keys of death and of hades—That is, the invisible world. In the intermediate state, the body abides in death, the soul in hades. Christ hath the keys of, that is, the power over, both; killing or quickening of the body, and disposing of the soul, as it pleaseth him. He gave St. Peter the keys of the kingdom of heaven; but not the keys of death or of hades."[14] In addition, the famous preacher Jonathan Edwards spoke on Revelation 1:18 in one of his sermons. Edwards proclaimed,

> He says, for the comfort of his saints, Rev i. 18. "I am he that liveth and was dead: and behold, I am alive for evermore, Amen; and have the keys of hell and death." Death not only cannot destroy a Christian, but it cannot hurt him; Christ carries him on eagle wings aloft on high, out of the reach of death. Death, with respect to him, is disarmed of his power: and every Christian may say, "O death, where is thy sting?" Death was once indeed a terrible enemy, but now he has become weak. He spent all his strength on Christ; in killing him, he killed himself; he was conquered then, and has now no power to hurt his followers.[15]

Modern commentators on Revelation over the last few centuries have predominantly seen the imagery behind Revelation 1:18 as Christ's descent into the underworld between his death and resurrection. Plumptre, writing at the

---

[11] *Nicholas of Lyra's Apocalypse Commentary*, trans. P.D.W. Krey (Kalamazoo, MI: Medieval Institute Publications, 1997): 40.

[12] John Calvin wrote a commentary on every book of the NT except for Revelation. Martin Luther said of the book of Revelation, "About this Book of Revelation of John, I leave everyone free to hold his own opinion. I miss more than one thing in this book and it makes me consider it to be neither apostolic nor prophetic. . . . I can in no way detect that the Holy Spirit produced it. . . . They are supposed to be blessed who keep what is written in this book and yet no one knows what it is, to say nothing of keeping it. . . . My spirit cannot accommodate itself to this book. . . . Christ is neither taught nor known in it. . . . Many have tried their hands at it. But until this very day they have also let it alone until now, especially because some of the ancient fathers held it was not the work of St. John the Apostle. . . . For our part, we share this doubt." *Luther's Works* 35:398-400.

[13] M. Henry, *Commentary on the Whole Bible, Genesis to Revelation*, ed. L.F. Church (Grand Rapids: Zondervan, 1961).

[14] . Wesley, *Wesley's Notes on the Bible* (Grand Rapids: Francis Asbury Press, 1987).

[15] Cf. Charles Spurgeon's sermon "Christ with the Keys of Death and Hell" (Sermon #894).

turn of the nineteenth century, says on Revelation 1:18, "It is all but impossible not to believe that He speaks here as one who had passed into that world of the shadow of death, and had come forth as a conqueror, who had burst open those 'gates of Hades, of which He had said that they should not prevail against His Church."[16] Renowned Bible scholars Franz Delitzsch and von Hofmann had a fascinating correspondence debating the Scriptural basis for the *Descensus*. Delitzsch, who argued for the truth of the *Descensus*, brought Revelation 1:18 into the discussion. He wrote to Hofmann, "Therefore Christ's descent into Hades must have also been His victory over Hades; and for this reason the risen Lord carries the keys of Hades and of death, having triumphed over both."[17] Hofmann countered, "Because He was dead, and is alive, He calls himself (Rev. 1.18) the holder of the keys of death and of Hades, and not because, after He had become alive, He entered into Hades."[18]

At the turn of the twentieth century, Loofs wrote one of the best exegetical and theological arguments for the *Descensus* from Scripture. In his discussion, he says that the belief of the *Descensus* may be presupposed in Revelation 1:18.[19] Soon after, MacCulloch wrote what is still probably the definitive work on the *Descensus*, and uses the imagery of Revelation 1:18 frequently to support it. He says, "As His resurrection proves, Christ, though He died and was one of the dead in Hades, could not be held by Death or Hades: thus He is superior to them, and thus, possessing their keys, can open the doors of the Underworld to the faithful souls there."[20] He later wrote, "Hence, as in Rev. i. 18, He has the keys of death and Hades, because He has entered their realm as a Conqueror; He who was dead is alive and makes the dead live."[21] Seiss argues from Revelation 1:18:

> Though once dead, and an inmate of hades, he is alive now for all the ages of ages. In this eternal life, which he had from all eternity, he walks among his people, locking and unlocking death and hades, disposing of souls and bodies as to him seems best, and keeping them in his power for that Apocalypse and

---

[16] E.H. Plumptre, *The Spirits in Prison and Other Studies on the Life After Death* (New York: Thomas Wittaker, 1889): 110-111.

[17] F. Delitzsch and von Hofmann, "The Descent of Christ into Hades: A Correspondence between Professor Franz Delitzsch and Professor von Hofmann," *Expositor* 4th Series 3 (1891): 243.

[18] Delitzsch and von Hofmann, "The Descent of Christ into Hades," 246.

[19] F. Loofs, "Descent to Hades (Christ's)," in *ERE*, ed. J. Hastings, vol. 4 (Edinburgh: T. & T. Clark, 1908–1921): 662. Selwyn also cites Revelation 1:18 in support of his argument for the *Descensus*. E.G. Selwyn, *The First Epistle of St. Peter: The Greek Text with Introduction, Notes, and Essays*, 2nd ed. (Grand Rapids: Baker, 1981): 322.

[20] J.A. MacCulloch, *The Harrowing of Hell: A Comparative Study of an Early Christian Doctrine* (Edinburgh: T. & T. Clark, 1930): 49.

[21] MacCulloch, *The Harrowing of Hell*, 239. Cf. J. Kroll, *Gott und Hölle: Der Mythos vom Descensuskampfe*, Studien der Bibliothek Warburg 20 (Leipzig-Berlin: B.G. Teubner, 1932): 10-11.

administration which it is the office of this book to describe.[22]

Stroter had the interesting theory that Christ was given the keys after his resurrection on the third day and so could visit the dead in the underworld as he pleased.[23] This, however, is unique to him and there is no clear evidence that Christ visited the underworld after his resurrection.

Some of the strongest advocates of the *Descensus* in the background of Revelation 1:18 in recent times are W. Bousset, R.H. Charles, Joachim Jeremias, and Richard Bauckham. To illustrate, Bousset uses this battle imagery when he says, "One who holds in his hand the keys of the rulers of the underworld has won them in victorious battle with the dread powers there below; the journey to Hades was a journey of struggle and of victory."[24] On the other hand, Bousset sees the Gnostic Redeemer as the background of the descent imagery of Christ in the NT and very few have followed him in that aspect. Jeremias, Charles, and Bauckham were much more in line with the ancient Fathers' threefold view of Christ as preaching to and releasing the OT captives and conquering Death and Hades through a triumphant victory. Jeremias writes, "Rev. 1:18 refers to the keys which Death and Hades carry as lords of the underworld. But if Death and Hades are personified, it is quite plain that the possession of their keys implies a preceding battle between them and Christ."[25]

Charles, in his commentary, argues concerning Revelation 1:18, "Again we have here one of the earliest traces in Christian literature of the Descent of Christ into Hades, and the conquest of its powers."[26] He continues,

> Neither death nor Hades can resist the power of the risen Christ. It is not only that they cannot withhold from Him the faithful that have already died, but that Christ has entered their realm as a conqueror and preached there the Gospel of Redemption to those that had not yet heard it. This interpretation of the text is in keeping with the universal proclamation of the Gospel to the heathen world, which according to xiv.6-7, xv.4, was to precede the end. All—wherever they

---

[22] J.A. Seiss, *The Apocalypse: Lectures on the Book of Revelation*, ZCS (Grand Rapids: Zondervan, 1950): 48.

[23] E.F. Stroter, *Die Herrlichkeit des Leibes Christi: Der Epheserbrief*, 2nd ed. (Gumligen-Bern: Siloah, 1952): 99-100.

[24] W. Bousset, *Kyrios Christos: A History of the Belief in Christ from the Beginnings of Christianity to Irenaeus*, trans. J.E. Steely (Nashville, TN: Abingdon Press, 1970): 65.

[25] J. Jeremias, "κλείς," in *TDNT*, ed. G. Kittel, G. Freidrich, and G. Bromiley, vol. 3 (Grand Rapids: Eerdmans, 1964–1976): 3:746.

[26] R.H. Charles, *A Critical and Exegetical Commentary on the Revelation of St. John*, vol. 1, ICC, ed. J.A. Emerton, C.E.B. Cranfield, and G.N. Stanton (Edinburgh: T. & T. Clark, 1966): 32.

were—were to hear the Gospel before the Final Judgment.[27]

Bauckham argues, "Revelation 1:18 ('I have the keys of Death and Hades') presupposes that the gates of Hades, which release none who has entered them, have been for the first time opened for a man to leave."[28]

Many other recent commentators of Revelation have discussed Revelation 1:18 in support of the *Descensus*. Hendrickson comments on this passage, "Had He not Himself been in Hades? (See Acts 2:27, 31)?". . . . "Does not the Son of man reveal that He has the keys of death whenever He welcomes the soul of a believer into heaven? And does He not prove that He has the keys of Hades when at His second coming He reunites the soul and body of the believer, a body now gloriously transformed?"[29] Furthermore, Barnhouse sees Revelation 1:18 as a sequel to Hebrews 2:14-15 discussing Christ's battle with the devil. He says,

> He secured the keys of death and Hades. This is a most interesting sequel to the story of the struggle recounted in the book of Hebrews. There we read that our Lord Himself took part of flesh and blood so that through death He might destroy him that had the power of death, that is, the devil (Heb. 2:14). He took a body that He might die in order to destroy the malignant enemy who had the power of death, but though he had it, Christ brought back the keys with Him so that Satan has it no more.[30]

Other scholars arguing for the *Descensus* from this passage include Doehler,[31] Pannenberg,[32] Hughes,[33] Roloff,[34] and Orthodox commentator Taushev.[35] One

---

[27] Charles, *A Critical and Exegetical Commentary on the Revelation of St. John*, 32.

[28] R. Bauckham, *The Fate of the Dead: Studies on the Jewish and Christian Apocalypses*, Supplements to Novum Testamentum, ed. C.K. Barrett, J.K. Elliott, and M.J.J. Menken, vol. 93 (Leiden: Brill, 1998): 39. R. Bauckham, "God Who Raises the Dead: The Resurrection of Jesus in Relation to Early Christian Faith in God," in *The Resurrection of Jesus Christ*, ed. Paul Avis (London: Darton, Longman and Todd, 1993): 150.

[29] W. Hendricksen, *More Than Conquerors: An Interpretation of the Book of Revelation* (Grand Rapids: Baker Academic, 1967): 57.

[30] D.G. Barnhouse, *Revelation: An Expositional Commentary* (Grand Rapids: Zondervan, 1971): 32.

[31] "Christ descends as Victor, as the Triumphant One into Hell with the keys of hell and death in His hand." G. Doehler, "The Descent into Hell," *The Springfielder* 39 (June 1975): 8.

[32] "Rev. 1:18 adds to this assertion that Christ freed the dead in Hades by overcoming death for himself and for them." Wolfhart Pannenberg, *Jesus–God and Man*, trans. Lewis L. Wilkins and Duane A. Priebe, 2nd ed. (Philadelphia: Westminster Press, 1977): 272.

[33] P.E. Hughes, *The Book of Revelation: A Commentary* (Grand Rapids: Eerdmans, 1990): 29.

of the most influential commentators of Revelation today, Greg Beale, also seems to agree that Christ's descent is in the background of Revelation 1:18. He writes, "It is utilized to indicate that through the victory of the resurrection Christ became king even over the realm of the dead in which he was formerly imprisoned. Now, not only is he no longer held in death's bonds but he also holds sway over who is released and retained in that realm."[36]

Some scholars, such as Caird, use the battle imagery between Christ and the powers of the underworld, but do not believe in a real *Descensus*, because for them Death and Hades are only a metaphor for the grave. For example, Caird writes on Revelation 1:18, "Not only had he burst out of the prison, he had carried away the keys. His followers may pass confidently into the dungeons of death and the grave, knowing that he holds the authority to unlock the gates and set them free."[37] Many commentators acknowledge the possibility that the *Descensus* may be in the background of Revelation 1:18, but generally make the argument that it is not. For instance, Aune argues that "the possessive genitive is often understood as implying the tradition of the *descensus ad inferos*, '(Christ's) descent to Hell,' for if the keys formerly belonged to the personified Death and Hades, they must have been forcibly taken from them."[38] Similarly, Beasley-Murray says the language "would undoubtedly suit the doctrine of the *descensus ad inferos*, but whether this language demands it, as many commentators have suggested, is doubtful."[39]

---

[34] J. Roloff, *The Revelation of John: A Continental Commentary*, trans. John E. Alsup (Minneapolis, MN: Fortress Press, 1993): 38.

[35] "One might add here that Christ has authority over hell and death in that He Himself tasted of death in the body and descended to hell in His soul after death (1 Peter 3:19), but in His resurrection gained victory over both." A. Taushev, *The Apocalypse in the Teachings of Ancient Christianity* (Platina, CA: St. Herman of Alaska Brotherhood, 1995): 71.

[36] G.K. Beale, *The Book of Revelation: A Commentary on the Greek Text*, NIGTC, ed. I.H. Marshall and D.A. Hagner (Grand Rapids: Eerdmans, 1999): 215.

[37] G.B. Caird, *The Revelation of Saint John*, BNTC, ed. Henry Chadwick (Peabody, MA: Hendrickson Publishers, 1966): 26. "In His death and resurrection, Christ wrested from Satan any authority the devil may have had over death (cf. Heb 2:14-15)." J.F. Walvoord, *The Revelation of Jesus Christ* (Chicago, IL: Moody Press, 1966): 47. M. Barker, *The Revelation of Jesus Christ Which God Gave to Him to Show to His Servants What Must Soon Take Place (Revelation 1.1)* (Edinburgh: T. & T. Clark, 2000): 366. C.S. Keener, *Revelation*, NIVAC, ed. T. Muck (Grand Rapids: Zondervan, 2000): 98. "Revelation 1:18 says that Christ has the keys of hell and of death. It is presupposed here that the exalted Lord who lives from eternity to eternity has victoriously withstood the conflict." H. Thielicke, "The Evangelical Faith," in *The Doctrine of God and of Christ*, trans. Geoffrey W. Bromiley, vol. 2 (Grand Rapids: Eerdmans, 1977): 418.

[38] D.E. Aune, *Revelation 1–5*, WBC, ed. D.A. Hubbard, G.W. Barker, and R.P. Martin, vol. 52A (Dallas, TX: Word, 1997): 104.

[39] G.R. Beasley-Murray, *The Book of Revelation*, NCBC, ed. M. Black (Grand Rapids: Eerdmans, 1981), 68. Cf. H.B. Swete, *Commentary on Revelation* (Grand Rapids:

In sum, from commentators on Revelation such as Cyprian to Beale, the foundation for the battle imagery of between Christ and Death and Hades has been argued for from Revelation 1:18. Moreover, as most of these commentators suggest this battle between Christ and Death and Hades most likely took place at his descent between his death and resurrection. No scholars would argue that Christ received the keys before his death and resurrection. Only Stroter argued that Christ received them after his resurrection. Revelation 1:18 illuminates further the purpose for which Christ descended into the underworld, namely to conquer Death and Hades. I will discuss this in much more detail as we focus on the exegesis and theology of Revelation 1:18 in the next section.

Revelation (Rev 1:5, 17-18; 5:3, 13; 6:8-9; 20:13-14)

At the end of the first century, the risen Christ said to John, "Do not be afraid. I am the First and the Last. I am the Living One; I was dead, and behold I am alive for ever and ever! And I hold the keys of death and Hades" (Rev 1:17-18). Jesus Christ's majestic claim to have the keys of Death and Hades is one of four divine declarations made in John's first vision (Rev 1:12-20).[40] These four claims to deity on the lips of Christ are found nowhere else in the NT, but only here in the book of Revelation. It is the last description καὶ ἔχω τὰς κλεῖς τοῦ θανάτου καὶ τοῦ ᾅδου "and I have the keys of Death and Hades" that we are most interested in. Of all the declarations made by Christ in the book of Revelation, this claim to be the possessor of the keys is the most mysterious. When did Christ receive these keys? Is Christ claiming to possess the keys to the realm of death and the underworld or is Christ saying he took the keys by force in a previous battle with personified Death and Hades? Moreover, if we presume the personification of Death and Hades, is this transferring of the keys all metaphor or should we take any of it literally? I hope to answer these challenging questions in this section on the exegesis and theology of Revelation 1:18.

The book of Revelation is outlined by some commentators according to Revelation 1:19-20, "Now write what you have seen, what is, and what is to take place after this." "What is" (ἃ εἰσὶν) would include chapters two and three

---

Kregel, 1977; reprint, London: Macmillan, 1911): 20. W. Barclay, *The Revelation of John* (Philadelphia: Westminster Press, 1959): 65.

[40] In this first vision, Christ makes four unique declarations of deity. First, ἐγώ εἰμι ὁ πρῶτος καὶ ὁ ἔσχατος "I am the First and the Last" (1:17a). Second, καὶ ὁ ζῶν "and I am the Living One" (1:17b). Third, καὶ ἐγενόμην νεκρὸς καὶ ἰδοὺ ζῶν εἰμι εἰς τοὺς αἰῶνας τῶν αἰώνων "I became dead but behold I am alive forevermore" (1:18a). And finally, καὶ ἔχω τὰς κλεῖς τοῦ θανάτου καὶ τοῦ ᾅδου "And I have the keys belonging to Death and Hades" (1:18b). I will focus primarily on the last declaration by Jesus that he possesses the keys, but all of these statements get developed throughout Revelation.

concerning the seven churches, and "What is to take place after these things" (ἃ μέλλει γενέσθαι μετὰ ταῦτα) covers Revelation 4:1 through 22:5 (with Rev 1:1-9 as introduction and Rev 22:6-21 as epilogue). Moreover, "Write what you have seen" (γράψον οὖν ἃ εἶδες) must be what was revealed to John in Revelation 1:10-20, but very specifically John's vision of Christ in Revelation 1:12 and 17-18. The primary support for this is in Revelation 1:12 and 17a because only in those verses does it say that John "saw" something (Καὶ ὅτε εἶδον αὐτόν). Interestingly, the risen Christ speaks from Revelation 1:17a through 3:22, but only in 1:17-18 do we have Christ speaking freely and not in reference to the seven churches. Moreover, what Christ decides to say in these two short verses must be very important.

The risen Christ begins by saying "Do not fear!" (μὴ φοβοῦ), which appears only here in Revelation. A very appropriate command given the horrific and terrifying images that John would see as the Revelation unfolds. Then Christ claims to be the God of Isaiah when he says, "I am the first and the last."[41] "I am" (ἐγώ εἰμι) declarations are consistently used throughout Revelation by both God the Father and Christ.[42] Only Christ claims the title of "the First and the Last" in the NT.[43] In addition, Christ's title "the living One" (ὁ ζῶν) does not occur in the OT or in the NT except for here.[44] However, God is frequently referred to as the "living God" in both the OT and NT.[45] "The living One" (ὁ ζῶν) then would be an exclusive title for Christ used only here in Revelation (1:17b). The transitional marker "and behold" (καὶ ἰδού) occurs twelve times in Revelation[46] always highlighting what takes place immediately after the preceding text. This is the first use of that term in Revelation. Aune says, "Here it functions as a marker emphasizing the truth of the statement that immediately follows."[47] Christ also declares that he is alive "forevermore" (εἰς τοὺς αἰῶνας

---

[41] Isa 41:4; 44:6; 48:12; cf. Surah 57:2 where Allah is called "the first and the last."

[42] I am the Alpha and Omega by God the Father (Rev 1:8; 21:6) and by Christ (22:13). I am the beginning and the end by God the Father (Rev 21:6) and by Christ (22:13). I am the First and the Last only by Christ (Rev 1:17; 2:8; 22:13). I am alive forevermore only by Christ (Rev 1:18). I am coming only by Christ (Rev 2:5, 16; 3:11; 16:15; 22:7, 13, 20). I am he who searches minds and hearts only by Christ (Rev 2:23). I am making all things new only by God the Father (Rev 21:5). I am the root and descendant of David, the bright morning star only by Christ (Rev 22:16).

[43] Rev 1:17; 2:8; 22:13; cf. Isa 41:4; 44:6; 48:12.

[44] cf. LXX Num 14:21; 1 Kgs 3:22-26; Luke 24:5; Sir 18:1; Tob 13:2; 2 Apoc. Bar. 21:9, 10; Sib. Or. 3.763.

[45] Deut 5:26; Josh 3:10; 1 Sam 17:26, 36; Pss 42:2; 84:2; Jer 10:10; 23:36; Dan 6:27; Hos 1:10; Pss 42:3; 84:3; Josh 3:10; Matt 16:16; 26:63; Acts 14:15; Rom 9:26; 2 Cor 3:3; 6:16; 1 Thess 1:9; 1 Tim 3:15; 4:10; Heb 3:12; 9:14; 10:31; 1 Pet 1:23; Rev 7:2; 2 Clem. 20:2; Hermas Vis. 2.3.2; 3.7.2; Sim. 6.2.2; Bel 1:5, 25; 3 Macc. 6:28; Jub. 1:25; 21:4. "Living Lord" only occurs in LXX Esth 16:16; 2 Macc 7:33; 15:4.

[46] Rev 1:18; 4:1, 2; 6:2, 5, 8; 7:9; 12:3; 14:1, 14; 19:11; 22:7.

[47] Aune, Revelation 1–5, 103.

τῶν αἰώνων) (1:18a). This phrase "forevermore" is used a total of eight times in Revelation of both God the Father and Christ.[48] It is clear that these declarations are essential to seeing the deep Christology of the book of Revelation in its presentation of both Christ and God the Father as the one true God.[49]

The fourth and last phrase is the most fascinating and difficult of the declarations of Christ. "And I became dead and behold I am alive forevermore and I have the keys belonging to Death and Hades" (καὶ ἐγενόμην νεκρὸς καὶ ἰδοὺ ζῶν εἰμι εἰς τοὺς αἰῶνας τῶν αἰώνων καὶ ἔχω τὰς κλεῖς τοῦ θανάτου καὶ τοῦ ᾅδου) (1:18b). "Death and Hades" (τοῦ θανάτου καὶ τοῦ ᾅδου) appear here for the first time in Revelation, but they will appear three more times always together and always in this order (Rev 6:8; 20:13, 14). Aune rightly notes, "They are always in this order, suggesting that 'Death' is considered the ruler over the realm 'Hades.'"[50] Hades never appears in Revelation without Death, but Death does appear alone a few times. For example, in Revelation 9:6 Death is personified as fleeing from those being tortured. Also, in Revelation 21:4, Death seems to be personified in contrast to mourning, pain, and crying because it is articular (ὁ θάνατος).

The grammar of the last clause is constructed in a complex and interesting way. Osborne comments, "First is the switch from adjective (νεκρός) to participle (ζῶν); second is the switch from ἐγενόμην (*egenomen*, I was) to εἰμι (*eimi*, I am)."[51] "I became" (ἐγενόμην) is functioning as an aorist ingressive, "I became dead and behold I am alive forevermore." Furthermore, "And behold I am alive" is a "periphrastic present, a rare construction in Revelation (the only other instance is the periphrastic present imperative 'be watchful,' in Rev 3:2)."[52] "I became" (ἐγενόμην) is also used three other times in Revelation (1:9, 10; 2:8), and always refers to John doing something in the past i.e. "I was on the island of Patmos" (1:9), "I was in the Spirit" (1:10), and used of Christ in almost the exact construction as here (2:8). In the same way that John was on the island of Patmos at some point in time in the past, Jesus ἐγενόμην νεκρός "became dead" and according to other NT passages he dwelt in the realm of the dead (Matt 12:40; Acts 2:27, 31; Rom 10:7; Eph 4:9; 1 Pet 3:19). Jesus was then resurrected and then proclaims to John that he possesses the keys previously belonging to Death and Hades.

The primary interpretive crux of this passage is whether Death and Hades

---

[48] Christ (Rev 1:18), God the Father (4:9, 10; 7:12; 10:6; 15:7), and God the Father and Christ (5:13; 11:15). Cf. LXX Theod Dan 4:34; 6:27; 12:7; Sir 18:1; *1 En.* 5.1.

[49] See especially Rev 1:4-5; 5:12-13; 6:17; 7:10; 11:15; 22:3-4.

[50] D.E. Aune, *Revelation 17–22*, WBC, ed. D.A. Hubbard, B.M. Metzger, and G.W. Barker, vol. 52C (Nashville, TN: Thomas Nelson, 1998): 1103.

[51] G.R. Osborne, *Revelation*, BECNT, ed. M. Silva (Grand Rapids: Baker Academic, 2002): 95.

[52] Aune, *Revelation 1–5*, 102.

are places or personified entities. In other words, should the phrase τὰς κλεῖς τοῦ θανάτου καὶ τοῦ ᾅδου be grammatically understood as an objective genitive ("I have the keys *to* Death and Hades")[53] or as a possessive genitive ("I have the keys *belonging to* Death and Hades")?[54] This has great implications because if they are possessive, as many commentators quoted above have suggested, then this implies a previous battle between Christ and Death/Hades in the underworld. Commentators are just about equally divided on this question because Death and Hades are used as both places and personified beings in Revelation.[55] Some scholars take a more balanced approach that both may be in view.[56] Moreover, Beale says, "Both options may be in mind: Christ has authority over this realm, and figuratively this realm is in his possession."[57] Even though both may be in view, I believe that the possessive genitive is a little more attractive in the context especially in light of our survey of personified Death and Hades and keyholders to the underworld. A good example of this battle imagery that is implied by Christ's victory over Death and Hades would be Michael the Archangel's victorious battle over Satan and his angels (Rev 12:7-9). We are given vivid imagery of this war between Michael and Satan and how the result of this cosmic warfare threw Satan and his angels down to the earth. Even though the battle in Revelation 1:18 is not detailed, the author leaves it to our imagination of what took place when Christ took the keys previously belonging to Death and Hades.

In addition, many scholars specifically argue that the *Descensus* is in the

---

[53] Aune, *Revelation 1–5*, 103. D.E. Aune, "The Apocalypse of John and Graeco-Roman Revelatory Magic," *NTS* 33 (October 1987): 497 fn. 2. T. Holtz, *Die Christologie der Apokalypse des Johannes*, 2nd ed. (Berlin: Akademie, 1971): 86-87. S.S. Smalley, *The Revelation to John: A Commentary on the Greek Text of the Apocalypse* (Downers Grove, IL: InterVarsity Press, 2005): 155. "The idea of a descent into Hades plays no role in this writing." G.A. Krodel, *Revelation*, ACNT, ed. R.A. Harrisville, J.D. Kingsbury, and G.A. Krodel (Minneapolis, MN: Augsburg, 1989): 97.

[54] Kroll, *Gott und Hölle: Der Mythos vom Descensuskampfe*, 10-11. Bousset, *Kyrios Christos*, 65. E. Lohse, *Die Offenbarung des Johannes* (Göttingen: Vandenhoeck and Ruprecht, 1976): 11. Jeremias, "κλείς," 3:746. Charles, *A Critical and Exegetical Commentary on the Revelation of St. John*, 32. Rissi says, "the genitive can only be understood as a possessive." M. Rissi, *Time and History: A Study on the Revelation* (Richmond, VA: John Knox Press, 1965): 105. I.T. Beckwith, *The Apocalypse of John: Studies in Introduction with a Critical and Exegetical Commentary* (New York: Macmillan, 1919): 442. It is said of the god Aeacus, "Even after his death Aeacus is honoured in the abode of Pluto, and keeps the keys of Hades (τὰς κλεῖς τοῦ Ἄιδου φυλάττει)."

[55] As argued in chapter 2, Death and Hades personified continues the imagery of personified Mot and Sheol in the OT and the Greek god Hades from the Greco-Roman world.

[56] Osborne, *Revelation*, 96. Beckwith, *The Apocalypse of John*, 442.

[57] Beale, *The Book of Revelation*, 214.

background of Revelation 1:18.[58] Still others expressly deny the *Descensus* being in the background of this passage.[59] Every commentator (to this author's knowledge) believes Death and Hades are personified in some sense in Revelation 6:8, "I looked, and there before me was a pale horse! Its rider was named Death, and Hades was following close behind him." Even though "pestilence"[60] is an appropriate translation here (cf. Rev 2:23; 18:8), because of John's pairing of Death and Hades throughout Revelation, we should see

---

[58] Stroter, *Die Herrlichkeit des Leibes Christi*, 99-100. Bousset, *Kyrios Christos*, 65. Jeremias, "κλείς," 3:746-47. MacCulloch, *The Harrowing of Hell*, 49. Loofs, "Descent to Hades (Christ's)," 662. Bauckham, *The Fate of the Dead*, 39. W. Schmithals, "θάνατος," in *NIDNTT*, ed. C. Brown, vol. 1 (Grand Rapids: Zondervan, 1986), 438. Philip Schaff, *The Creeds of Christendom: With a History and Critical Notes*, vol. 2. The Greek and Latin Creeds (Grand Rapids: Baker, 2007): 46. B. Reicke, *The Disobedient Spirits and Christian Baptism* (Copenhagen: Ejnar Munksgaard, 1946): 163. N.R. Ericson, "Descent into Hell (Hades)," in *EDBT*, ed. W.A. Elwell (Grand Rapids: Baker, 1996): 167. J.S. Stone, *The Glory After the Passion: A Study of the Events in the Life of our Lord from His Descent into Hell to His Enthronement in Heaven* (New York: Longmans, Green, 1913): 34. Hans Urs von Balthasar, "The Descent into Hell," *CS* 23 (1984): 230. Plumptre, *The Spirits in Prison and Other Studies on the Life After Death*, 110-11. Beale, *The Book of Revelation*, 215. Seiss, *The Apocalypse*, 47-48, 448. Charles, *A Critical and Exegetical Commentary on the Revelation of St. John*, 32. Kroll, *Gott und Hölle*, 10-11. Barnhouse, *Revelation*, 31-32. Rissi, *Time and History*, 105. Barker, *The Revelation of Jesus Christ Which God Gave to Him to Show to His Servants What Must Soon Take Place (Revelation 1.1)*, 366. Hendricksen, *More Than Conquerors*. W.W. Mead, *The Apocalypse of Jesus Christ: An Exposition* (New York: W.W. Mead, 1909): 13-14. F.C. Ottman, *The Unfolding of the Ages in the Revelation of John* (1905; reprint, Grand Rapids: Kregel, 1967), 19-20.

[59] W. Bieder, *Die Vorstellung von der Höllenfahrt Jesu Christi: Beitrag zur Entstehungsgeschichte der Vorstellung vom sog. Descensus ad Inferos*, ATANT 19, ed. W. Eichrodt and O. Cullmann (Zürich: Zwingli-Verlag, 1949), 92-96. Aune, *Revelation 1–5*, 104. *Descensus* in this passage is "doubtful." Beasley-Murray, *The Book of Revelation*, 68. ". . . the bearing of this on the descent is at best obscure." G. W. Bromiley, "Descent into Hell (Hades)," in *ISBE*, ed. G.W. Bromiley, vol. 1 A-D (Grand Rapids: Eerdmans, 1979), 927; "The idea of a descent into Hades plays no role in this writing." Krodel, *Revelation*, 97. Leivestad says, "However, nowhere in the old accounts of the *descensus* is it said that Christ took the keys from the powers of death." Ragnar Leivestad, *Christ the Conqueror: Ideas of Conflict and Victory in the New Testament* (London: SPCK, 1954): 219. On the other hand, see *Gos. Nic.* (Lat. A) 7 in W. Schneemelcher, *New Testament Apocrypha*, trans. R. McL. Wilson, vol. 1. Gospels and Related Writings (Louisville, KY: Westminster/John Knox Press, 1991): 529-30. Even if this were true, this would be an argument from silence and it has been demonstrated that the battle imagery from Rev 1:18 has been frequently referenced in the Fathers.

[60] *Thanatos* in the LXX consistently translates *deber* which means "plague, pestilence" over thirty times. Strikingly, two of these renderings of *deber* occur in Ezek. 14:19–21 and one in Lev. 26:25, two contexts providing the model for Rev. 6:1–8. Beale, *The Book of Revelation*, 382.

personified Death wielding all these terrors on mankind, including pestilence. The other three examples are more vigorously debated.

In Revelation 20:13, Death and Hades are presented more as spatial, dwelling places because the dead "*in them*" (ἐν αὐτοῖς) are given up to stand at the Great White Throne Judgment. This is Jewish imagery for the general resurrection of the dead (the uniting of the soul and the body).[61] Bauckham says, "The basic image of resurrection is that *the place of the dead will give back the dead*"[62] In the very next verse, Death and Hades are presented as personified beings because both of them are themselves "thrown into the lake of fire" (Rev 20:14). Swete notes, "Here they appear as two voracious and insatiable monsters who have swallowed all past generations, but are now forced to disgorge their prey. The 'harrowing of Hell,' which the Gospel of Nicodemus connects with the Lord's Descent into Hades, is thus seen to belong in truth to His Return."[63] Yet, if Christ will 'harrow hell' of the wicked at his second coming (Rev 20:13-15), then why not see a similar harrowing of Death and Hades of the righteous at his first coming (Rev 1:18)?

Swete acknowledges the ambiguity in Rev 1:18 because the "conception fluctuates between two localities (xx. 13), and two personalities (vi. 8); here it is difficult to determine which view is uppermost."[64] As a result, most scholars see many different combinations here. For instance, some see Death and Hades as spatial dwellings in 1:18 and 20:13, but personified powers in 6:8 and 20:14.[65] Others see Death and Hades only personified in 6:8 and places in the rest.[66] I agree with the majority of commentators who argue that Death and Hades are personified in some sense in all four passages (1:18; 6:8; 20:13-

---

[61] See Isa 26:19; *1 En.* 51:1; *4 Ezra* 2:16; 4:41-43; 7:32; *L.A.B.* 3:10; 33:3; *2 Bar.* 21:23; 42:8; 50:2; *Apoc. Peter* 4:3-4, 10-12; Tertullian *Res.* 32.1; *Midr.* on Ps 1:20 in *The Midrash on Psalms*, trans. W.G. Braude, Yale Judaica Series, ed. L. Nemoy, vol. 13 (London: Yale University Press, 1959): 28-29. *b.* Sanh. 92a.

[62] Bauckham, *The Fate of the Dead*, 277.

[63] Swete, *Commentary on Revelation*, 273.

[64] Swete, *Commentary on Revelation*, 20.

[65] BDAG, 19; J. Sweet, *Revelation*, TPI New Testament Commentaries, ed. H.C. Kee and D. Nineham (Philadelphia: Trinity Press International, 1979): 73. Aune, *Revelation 1–5*, 66, 103-104. S.J. Friesen, *Imperial Cults and the Apocalypse of John: Reading Revelation in the Ruins* (Oxford: Oxford University Press, 2001): 156. R.L. Thomas, *Revelation 1–7: An Exegetical Commentary* (Chicago, IL: Moody Press, 1995): 112. H. Bietenhard, "Hell, Abyss, Hades, Gehenna, Lower Regions," in *NIDNTT*, ed. Colin Brown (Grand Rapids: Zondervan, 1976, 1986): 207. G.E. Ladd, *A Commentary on the Revelation of John* (Grand Rapids: Eerdmans, 1972), 274. R.H. Mounce, *The Book of Revelation*, NICNT, ed. G.D. Fee (Grand Rapids: Eerdmans, 1977): 377. Krodel, *Revelation*, 341. Smalley sees Death as a personal being, but Hades as a local place in Rev 1:18. Smalley, *The Revelation to John*, 56.

[66] Caird, *The Revelation of Saint John*, 26. J.M. Ford, *Revelation: Introduction, Translation and Commentary*, AB, ed. W.F. Albright and D.N. Freedman, vol. 38 (Garden City, NY: Doubleday, 1975): 108.

14).[67] If they are personified, the imagery in Revelation 1:18 presents Christ forcefully taking the keys that previously belonging to Death and Hades at some point in time before Christ's declaration in Revelation 1:17-18.

The question remains: When did Christ receive these keys? It seems highly unlikely that Christ would have received them before he ἐγενόμην νεκρὸς "became dead" and the evidence is not as persuasive for him receiving the keys after his resurrection (contra Stroter). That only leaves his three day interval in the realm of the dead between his death and resurrection which makes the most sense with Christ reference to Death and Hades (cf. Matt 12:40; Acts 2:27, 31; Rom 10:7; Eph 4:9; 1 Pet 3:19). "Keys" (τὰς κλεῖς) is plural because the underworld has gates that require a key for access (Rev 1:18; 9:1-2; 20:1-3 cf. Matt 16:18). The "gates of Death/Sheol/Hades" are spoken of frequently throughout the OT, NT, and Jewish and Greco-Roman background literature.[68] As we have seen from the Jewish and Greco-Roman literature, to have the keys to Death and Hades, means to have power, authority, and dominion over all they contain. It is also an exclusive claim of the God of the OT to possess the keys to the underworld. Christ is claiming the same authority that Yahweh claimed in 1 Sam 2:6, "The LORD kills and makes alive; He brings down to Sheol and raises up."[69] In addition, Wisdom 16:13 speaks of God, "For you have power over life and death; you lead mortals down to the gates of Hades and back again."[70] For Christ to claim authority over the keys is same as claiming the authority of God.

The story of Christ subduing the underworld at his descent does not end in Revelation 1:18, but is developed throughout the book of Revelation. To illustrate, in the great worship scene in the Tabernacle of Heaven, John records,

---

[67] BDAG, 442-43; J. Jeremias, "ᾅδης," in *TDNT*, ed. G. Kittel, G. Freidrich, and G. Bromiley, vol. 1 (Grand Rapids: Eerdmans, 1964–76): 1:149. Beale, *The Book of Revelation*, 214. Seiss, *The Apocalypse: Lectures on the Book of Revelation*, 47-48, 481. Charles, *A Critical and Exegetical Commentary on the Revelation of St. John*, 169. Leivestad, *Christ the Conqueror*, 219. Beasley-Murray, *The Book of Revelation*, 68, 303. W.J. Harrington, *Revelation*, vol. 16, Sacra pagina Series, ed. D.J. Harrington (Collegeville, MN: Liturgical Press, 1993): 51, 203. Osborne, *Revelation*, 96, 282. Roloff, *The Revelation of John*, 295. Hughes, *The Book of Revelation*, 87, 219. Rissi, *Time and History*, 105. Barker, *The Revelation of Jesus Christ Which God Gave to Him to Show to His Servants What Must Soon Take Place (Revelation 1.1)*, 366. Beckwith, *The Apocalypse of John*, 442. I. Boxall, *The Revelation of Saint John*, BNTC, ed. M.D. Hooker (London: Hendrickson, 2006): 111, 291.

[68] Job 38:17; Pss 9:14 (13); 23 (24):7, 9; 106 (107):16, 18; Isa 38:10; 45:1-2; Jonah 2:3, 7; Matt 16:18; Wis 16:13; *Pss. Sol.* 16:2; *3 Macc.* 5:51; 6:31; *Apoc. Zeph.* 5:1-6; *T. Isaac* 4:10; 1QH 11.16-19; 11Q11 3-4; 4Q184; *Sib. Or.* 2:225-229; 8:217-229; *Il.*, 5.646; 9.312; *Od.* 14.156; Virgil *Aen.* 6.551; Euripides *Hippol.* 56-57; *Hec.* 1; Aeschylus, *Agam.* 1291; Diogenes Laertius 8.34-35; Theocritus 2.33-34; Pseudo-Plato *[Ax.]* 371B.

[69] κύριος θανατοῖ καὶ ζωογονεῖ, κατάγει εἰς ᾅδου καὶ ἀνάγει (LXX 1 Sam 2:6).

[70] cf. Deut 32:39; 2 Kgs 5:7; Job 12:14; *4 Macc.* 18:18-19.

"Then I heard every creature in heaven and on earth *and under the earth* and on the sea, and all that is in them. . . ." (Rev 5:13; cf. 5:3; Phil 2:10) (italics mine). Friesen says, "Revelation presents at least three levels of spatial reality: heaven, earth, and the underworld (5:3)."[71] Who are these creatures under the earth? For John, Death, Hades, the Abyss, the demonic hosts, the beast, Abaddon and others all come from "under the earth."[72] The underworld must also contain the souls of people because in Revelation 20:13 they are thrust out of Death, Hades, and the sea to stand before God's great judgment. Why are they giving glory and praising God and the Lamb? Paul answers this question, "At the name of Jesus every knee should bow, in heaven and on earth *and under the earth*, and every tongue confess that Jesus Christ is Lord, to the glory of God the Father" (Phil 2:10-11). In this proleptic vision of the last judgment, all creation is praising Christ as Lord because he descended into their regions in the underworld and declared himself Lord of the Dead.

In addition, Christ is said to have ἐνίκησεν "overcome, conquered, triumphed" (Rev 3:21; 5:5) through his death and resurrection but the language implies victory won through a battle. It never says explicitly who or what the lamb has conquered.[73] The same word is used to say that the martyrs have ἐνίκησεν "conquered" Satan by the blood of the Lamb (Rev 12:11). Therefore, not only is Death and Hades conquered, but Satan, the beast, and the false prophet are also in view because they are the great enemies of God and the saints of God. It is also by the power of the keys in the hands of the Lamb that Death and Hades receive (καὶ ἐδόθη αὐτοῖς) their authority and power to kill a third of mankind (Rev 6:1, 8). In addition, Christ's power over the keys is most clearly manifest when Death/Hades and Satan are thrown into the lake of fire to burn forever (Rev 20:10, 14-15). The possessor of the keys in Revelation can open and shut the Abyss (Rev 9:1-2; 20:1-3), the New Jerusalem (Rev 2:7; 3:12; 21:12-15, 21, 25; 22:14), and Death and Hades (Rev 1:18; 20:13-14). The climax of Christ's power over the keys (1:18) is certainly Revelation 20:13-14 where Christ commands Death and Hades to release their souls to stand for judgment at the resurrection and they cannot disobey the one who holds the keys. For the Scripture says, "The sea gave up the dead that were in it, and death and Hades gave up the dead that were in them, and each person was

---

[71] Friesen, *Imperial Cults and the Apocalypse of John*, 152. A three tiered universe was the dominant view in the ancient world: Exod 20:4; Deut 5:8; Job 11:8-9; Ps 139:8-9; Phil 2:10; Ign. *Trall.* 9:1; *T. Sol.* 16:3; *T. Levi* 3:9; *Jos. As.* 12:2; PGM IV.1116-21; Corp. Herm. 16.5; 1 Clem. 28:3; *Od.* 5.184-186. "People in the ancient world generally believed in a three-tiered universe." P.S. Johnston, *Shades of Sheol: Death and Afterlife in the Old Testament* (Downer's Grove, IL: InterVarsity Press, 2002): 69.

[72] Aune associates Abyss with "under the earth" in Revelation. Aune, *Revelation 1–5*, 348.

[73] R. Bauckham, *The Theology of the Book of Revelation* (Cambridge, MA: Cambridge University Press, 1993): 74.

111

judged according to what he had done. Then death and Hades were thrown into the lake of fire. The lake of fire is the second death."[74]

It is important to remember that in the book of Revelation we are dealing with apocalyptic literature. Symbolism or metaphorical language is a fundamental characteristic of apocalyptic literature. It has been common to assume that apocalyptic symbols are mere codes whose meaning is exhausted by single referents. This is not true. The apocalyptic literature provides a rather clear example of language that is "expressive rather than referential, symbolic rather than factual."[75] A symbol in apocalyptic literature is not usually meant for one single referent, but is actually multi-dimensional. The proportion of visual symbolism in Revelation is greater than in almost any comparable apocalypse.[76] John transfers OT images and symbols from their original context to his present situation so as to enrich the communicative power of the language. This is why Death and Hades are personified, because they are frequently found together and personified in the OT. Therefore, I do not believe that these are literal keys, literal gates of Hades, and that Death and Hades are literal beings.

On the other hand, the symbolism of Christ taking the keys from Death and Hades and conquering the underworld, while metaphorical, has a true reality behind the symbols. Similarly, when it says that Christ entered heaven and sat down at the right hand of God, this too is metaphorical language, but Christ is truly ruling and reigning from a realm called heaven. Furthermore, Christ really did defeat Death and Hades because followers of Christ cannot be contained by them anymore. The NT is consistent that after Christ's death, descent, resurrection, ascension and exaltation that the souls of believers immediately enter heaven at death.[77] Even though Christ may not have literal keys on his belt, the keys represent his real authority to release those whom he wants from the realm of Hades and imprison those whom he rejects. In addition, the battle imagery throughout the NT must represent a true reality behind the symbolism and metaphor. Since Satan is a real being who is spoken of frequently in battle imagery with Christ,[78] he may indeed be behind the symbols of Death and

---

[74] Cf. *Apoc. Peter* 4:3. Alford says, "As there is a second and higher life, so there is also a second and deeper death. And as after that life there is no more death (ch. xxi.4), so after that death there is no more life." H. Alford, "Apocalypse of John," in *The Greek Testament*, vol. 4 (Chicago, IL: Moody Press, 1866): 735-36.

[75] J.J. Collins, *The Apocalyptic Imagination: An Introduction to Jewish Apocalyptic Literature*, 2nd ed. (Grand Rapids: Eerdmans, 1984, 1998), 16-17.

[76] Bauckham, *The Theology of the Book of Revelation*, 9.

[77] Acts 7:59; Rom 14:7-9; 2 Cor 5:1-9; Phil 1:21-26; Rev 6:9. Contrast this with the overwhelming evidence from Chapter 2 that the souls of the righteous descended into the underworld at death, not heaven.

[78] John 12:31; 14:30; 16:11; Eph 1:21-22; 3:10; Col 2:14-15; Heb 2:14; 1 John 3:8; Rev 12:7-12.

Hades.[79] In addition, the most significant parallel to Revelation 1:18 in the NT would be Hebrews 2:14.[80] The author of Hebrews speaks of this battle between Christ and Satan when he says, "He too shared in their humanity so that by his death he might destroy him who holds the power of death—that is, the devil" (Heb 2:14). This could just as easily read, '. . . so that by his death he might destroy him who holds *the key* of death—that is, the devil.' Chrysostom says, "Here he points out the wonder, that by what the devil prevailed, by that was he overcome, and the very thing which was his strong weapon against the world, [namely], Death, by this Christ smote him. In this he exhibits the greatness of the conqueror's power. Do you see how much good death has brought?"[81]

Similar to Revelation 1:18, the battle and victory took place at Christ's death and not his resurrection. The Greek world was filled with stories of this kind of cosmic drama where the hero descends to the underworld to conquer death through a battle and so release death's captives.[82] The most famous hero from the Greek world whose story may have even been in the background of Hebrews 2:14 was Heracles (Latin *Hercules*). Moreover, Heracles descends into the underworld and after defeating death in a wrestling match, rescues

---

[79] Gen 3:1; Wis 2:24; John 8:44; 1 Cor 5:5; Tromp says, "One might say that, in Israel, there was an evolution from a mythological conception of Death to the belief in the Enemy: Satan, the Devil." N.J. Tromp, *Primitive Conceptions of Death and the Nether World in the Old Testament* (Rome: Pontifical Biblical Institute, 1969): 100. "Christ is ultimately the one who bestows this key, since he has overcome Satan and now 'possesses the keys of death and Hades' (1:18)." Beale, *The Book of Revelation*, 493. Sweet, *Revelation*, 73. Barnhouse says Christ took the keys from Satan at his descent and that Death is symbolic for Satan. Barnhouse, *Revelation: An Expositional Commentary*, 31, 128. In *Gos. Nic.* (Lat. A) 7, Satan possesses the keys to the underworld because he is the guardian of the gates. Schneemelcher, *New Testament Apocrypha*, 529-30. Augustine *Civ.* 20.15, " In this verse, 'hell and death' stand for the devil (together with the entirety of his followers) inasmuch as he is the author of death and the torments of hell." Caesarius of Arles *Apoc.* 6.8, *Hom.* 5 says, "And they have as their rider the devil, who is death." Epiphanius Pan. 64.29.6; In Psalm 18:6, Death, Sheol, and Belial (2 Cor 6:15) are united against the saints. "The cords of death encompassed me, and the torrents of ungodliness (בְלִיַּעַל) terrified me. The cords of Sheol (שְׁאוֹל) surrounded me; the snares of death (מָוֶת) confronted me." Cf. 2 Sam 22:5; Deut 13:13; Judg 19:22; 1 Sam 1:16; 2:12; 10:27; 25:17; 2 Sam 16:7; 1 Kgs 21:13; Nah 1:15 (2:1); Ps 41:9; 2 Cor 6:15; Eph 6:12; 1 Tim 3:7; 2 Tim 2:26; *T. Levi* 19:1; 1QS 1:16-2:8.

[80] Some commentators who cite the parallel between Revelation 1:18 and Hebrews 2:14: F.F. Bruce, *The Epistle to the Hebrews*, NICNT, ed. G.D. Fee (Grand Rapids: Eerdmans, 1990): 85. P.T. O'Brien, *The Letter to the Hebrews*, PNTC, ed. D.A. Carson (Grand Rapids: Eerdmans, 2010), 115. Paul Ellingworth, *The Epistle to the Hebrews: A Commentary on the Greek Text*, NIGTC, ed. I.H. Marshall and W.W. Gasque (Grand Rapids: Eerdmans, 1993): 173.

[81] Chrysostom, *Hom. Heb.* 2:14.

[82] Euripides *Alc.* 837-1142; Diodorus Siculus *Bib.* 4.25-26; Plutarch *Thes.* 35, 46.

Alcestis.[83] Descriptions of Heracles wrestling with death and conquering may be the very kind of battle images that would have entered the mind of the original audience of Revelation and Hebrews when they first heard these Scriptures (Rev 1:18; Heb 2:14).

In chapter 3 I argued that Satan may have been the "fallen angel" holding the key to the Abyss in Revelation 9:1-2. Satan seems to have received the key/authority/power of death sometime after the fall of Adam and Eve or as a result of it.[84] Furthermore, Satan is the strong man who has "the armor" of death, sin and the law to wield in this world at his discretion. Christ has entered Satan's domain (Hades) and released those who are imprisoned there.[85] In the end, all these passages seek to describe something indescribable, "inexpressible words which man is not permitted to speak" (ἄρρητα ῥήματα ἃ οὐκ ἐξὸν ἀνθρώπῳ λαλῆσαι 2 Cor 12:4) that happened during the interval between Christ's death and resurrection. The Lion of the Tribe of Judah truly conquered Satan and nullified all his works (the Law, sin, Death, hell, the world, and the flesh)[86] forever and ever.

---

[83] Homer, *Il.* 5.394-400; Pindar *Ol.* 9.33.

[84] Gen 3:14-15; Job 1:7; 2:2; 9:24; Matt 4:8-9; 12:24; Luke 4:5-7; 10:19; 11:18; John 12:31; 14:30; 16:11; Acts 26:18; 2 Cor 4:4; Eph 2:1-2; Heb 2:14; 1 John 5:19; Jude 1:9; Rev 13:2.

[85] Origen *Comm. Rom.* 5.10.12. It should be noted that I am not saying that Satan dwells in Hades. On the contrary, the NT seems to imply with Satan's power over Death that he also has authority over the realm of Death, that is Hades. Satan has never been to Hades even though it is his house. Satan's kingdom is in the heavenlies (Eph 2:2). "Satan is not regarded as Lord of the Underworld in the Fathers, save perhaps by Origen; Death and hades are there pre-eminent, and are conquered by Christ's death and his presence in Hades." MacCulloch, *The Harrowing of Hell*, 229.

[86] See Luther's powerful comments on Hebrews 2:14 in *Luther's Works* 29, 137.

CHAPTER 7

CONCLUSION

Selwyn described Christ's descent "as the opening stage of Christ's triumph rather than as the concluding stage of His passion."[1] The doctrine of Christ's descent into the underworld between his death and resurrection was not the last step of his humiliation, but instead the first step of Christ's victorious conquest of the powers of evil. I have sought to demonstrate in this book that Revelation 1:18 not only is best understood in light of Christ's *Descensus*, but that along with a few other texts in the NT, it details the activity of Christ during this journey. I have argued that Revelation 1:18 teaches the doctrine of the *Descensus* and in each chapter I have focused on different aspect of this verse.

In the Introduction I demonstrated that many Christian writers from the early second century (writing within a generation or two of the author of Revelation) unanimously affirmed Christ's descent and spoke about it frequently in their writings. Since they are from the same cultural milieu and time period as the author of Revelation it seems that the audience and author of Revelation would have understood passages such as Revelation 1:18 and others in light of the *Descensus*. In addition, Christian writers from Ignatius to the time of the Protestant Reformation unanimously affirmed the doctrine that Christ descended into the underworld between his death and resurrection. There are three primary elements of what Christ accomplished at his descent. First, Christ released the OT saints from the underworld and transferred them to heaven (Matt 27:52-53; Eph 4:9). Second, Christ preached the Gospel to the dead in the underworld offering them salvation, but the vast majority of the Fathers limited his preaching to the righteous of the OT (1 Pet 3:18-22; 4:6). Lastly, Christ descended to the depths of the underworld to shatter the bronze and iron gates and to subdue Death, Hades, and Satan. It is this third option that most likely arose due to Revelation 1:18.

In chapter 2, I argued that it was virtually unanimous that in the OT, Greco-Roman world, and during the Intertestamental period, that all mankind descended to Sheol/Hades instead of ascending to heaven. This is important

---

[1] E.G. Selwyn, *The First Epistle of St. Peter: The Greek Text with Introduction, Notes, and Essays*, 2nd ed. (Grand Rapids: Baker, 1981): 357.

because if Christ was fully human, then he too must descend into Hades according to the 'law of the dead.' This chapter also demonstrated the consistent pairing of Death and Hades as personified beings in the ancient world. If Death and Hades are personified in Revelation 1:18, then the imagery of Christ taking their keys implies a previous battle between them that is left to our imagination (but see Rev 12:7-9). Furthermore, chapter 3 demonstrated that to possess keys in the ancient world was symbolic for possessing authority and power. Many gods, goddesses, angels, and demons possessed the keys to the gates of the underworld according to numerous sources. The audience of Revelation would have no doubt thought of these beings as being defeated by Christ when they first heard that Christ was now the true possessor of the keys.

In chapter 4, I explored the different compartments of the underworld because Revelation speaks of those "under the earth" in submission to Christ's sovereign rule (Rev 5:3, 13). Moreover, Death, Hades, Paradise, the Lake of Fire, and the Abyss are all discussed extensively throughout Revelation. These compartments of the underworld are significant to this discussion because Christ is said to have visited most of them according to many passages in the NT (Luke 23:43 (Paradise); Acts 2:27, 31 (Hades); Rom 10:7 (Abyss); 1 Pet 3:19 (Tartarus?); Rev 1:18 (Death and Hades). I believe that I presented a consistent NT theology of the afterlife and these underworld compartments. I hope this discussion of these compartments and who dwells in them brings more light on Christ's activity during his time in the underworld. In chapter 5, I exegetically discussed fundamental passages in Matthew, Luke, Paul and Peter concerning the *Descensus*. Other than 1 Peter 3:18-22; 4:6, I argued that the *Descensus* is not the *primary* teaching in any of these passages. However, I sought to demonstrate that the *Descensus* is at least in the background of all of these passages especially Matthew 12:40, Acts 2:27, 31 and Romans 10:6-7. It is agreed that these three passages say nothing about Christ's activity in the underworld, but if they assume Christ descended into Hades and the abyss, then the *Descensus* option should be given more weight in other, more controversial passages (Matt 27:52-53; Eph 4:8-10; 1 Pet 3:18-22; 4:6; Rev 1:18).

Finally, in chapter 6 I argued that Death and Hades should be seen as personified in Revelation 1:18 and not merely the 'realm of the dead.' Death and Hades are unambiguously personified beings unleashing hell on earth in Revelation 6:8 and they are thrown (like Satan) into the lake of fire at the end of the book (Rev 20:14). If they are personified in Revelation 1:18, I agree with most commentators on this passage, namely, that this would demand a previous battle taking place between them and Christ for the keys. Moreover, it is our thesis that Christ won the keys from Death and Hades in a battle at his descent into the underworld between his death and resurrection (1:18). Christ also is said to be the one who "gives" the authority to Death and Hades slay mankind (Rev 6:1, 8). Christ's power over the keys is most clearly revealed when he commands Death and Hades to release all the souls of the dead for the great resurrection at the last judgment (20:13). Lastly, Christ hurls Death and Hades into the lake of fire (20:14), symbolizing the end of Death and the realm of the dead because the saints will live forever in the New Jerusalem (Rev 21-22).

In addition, this language is metaphorical speaking about things that cannot properly be expressed in words. However, every metaphor and symbol in Revelation has a true reality behind it and I believe Satan is the reality behind Death and Hades. Satan is a real being that is said to have the "power of death" and so has power of the realm of the dead, Hades (Heb 2:14). Revelation 1:18 teaches that Satan has now lost the "keys" because Christ has stripped him of all his power and weapons forever. Along with the audience of Revelation, all who are in Christ can take great solace in the truth that Christ has the power over the keys of Death and Hades. Tertullian succinctly said it best, "Christ went to the Underworld for this very purpose,— that we might not go there."[2] Yet, no one can match the eloquence of Spurgeon:

> He died, and "It is finished!" shook the gates of hell. Down from the cross the conqueror leaped, pursued the fiend with thunder-bolts of wrath; swift to the shades of hell the fiend did fly, and swift descending went the conqueror after him; and we may conceive him exclaiming—"Traitor! this bolt shall find and pierce thee through, Though under hell's profoundest wave thou div'st, To find a sheltering grave." And seize him he did—chained him to his chariot wheel; dragged him up the steps of glory; angels shouting all the while, "He hath led captivity captive, and received gifts for men." Now, devil, thou saidst thou wouldst overcome me, when I came to die. Satan I defy thee, and laugh thee to scorn! My Master overcame thee, and I shall overcome thee yet.[3]

---

[2] Tertullian *An.* 55.

[3] From Charles Spurgeon's sermon *The Destroyer Destroyed* (1858) on Heb 2:14 (Sermon #166).

BIBLIOGRAPHY

Abbott, T.K. *A Critical and Exegetical Commentary on the Epistles to the Ephesians and to the Colossians*. ICC, ed. J.A. Emerton, C.E.B. Cranfield, and G.N. Stanton. Edinburgh: T. & T. Clark, 1897.

Achtemeier, P.J. *1 Peter: A Commentary on First Peter*. Hermeneia, ed. Harold W. Attridge, Helmut Koester, Adela Yarbro Collins, Eldon Jay Epp, and James M. Robinson. Minneapolis: Fortress Press, 1996.

Aelius Aristides: The Complete Works. Translated by Charles A. Behr. Vol. 2: Orations XVII–LIII. Leiden: Brill, 1981.

Albright, W.F., and C.S. Mann. *Matthew*. AB, ed. W.F. Albright and David N. Freedman. Garden City, NY: Doubleday, 1971.

Allo, E.B. *L'Apocalypse du Saint Jean*. Paris: Gabalda, 1933.

Apollodorus. *The Library*. Loeb Classical Library, ed. T.E. Page. Cambridge, MA: Harvard University Press, 1921.

The Apostolic Fathers. Translated by Kirsopp Lake. Loeb Classical Library, ed. G.P. Goold. Cambridge, MA: Harvard University Press, 1912.

The Apostolic Fathers. Translated by J.B. Lightfoot. Grand Rapids, MI: Baker, 1956.

Aune, D.E. *Revelation 1–5*. Vol. 52A. WBC, ed. David A. Hubbard, Glenn W. Barker, and Ralph P. Martin. Dallas, TX: Word, 1997.

—. *Revelation 6–16*. Vol. 52B. WBC, ed. David A. Hubbard, Bruce M. Metzger, and Glenn W. Barker. Nashville, TN: Thomas Nelson, 1998.

—. *Revelation 17–22*. Vol. 52C. WBC, ed. David A. Hubbard, Bruce M. Metzger, and Glenn W. Barker. Nashville, TN: Thomas Nelson, 1998.

—. "The Apocalypse of John and Graeco-Roman Revelatory Magic." *NTS* 33 (October 1987): 481-501.

Badcock, F.J. *The History of the Creeds*. New York: Macmillan, 1938.

Balthasar, Hans Urs von. "The Descent into Hell." *CS* 23 (1984): 223-36.

Barker, M. *The Revelation of Jesus Christ Which God Gave to Him to Show to His Servants What Must Soon Take Place (Revelation 1.1)*. Edinburgh: T. & T. Clark, 2000.

Barrett, C.K. *A Critical and Exegetical Commentary on the Acts of the Apostles*. Vol. 1: Preliminary Introduction and Commentary on Acts I–XIV. ICC, ed. J.A. Emerton, C.E.B. Cranfield, and G.N. Stanton. Edinburgh: T. & T. Clark, 1994.

Barth, Karl. *Credo*. New York: Charles Scribner's Sons, 1962.

Barth, M. *Ephesians: Translation and Commentary on Chapters 4–6*. Vol. 34A. AB, ed. David Noel Freedman. Garden City, NY: Doubleday, 1974.

Bauckham, R. "Descent to the Underworld." In *Anchor Bible Dictionary*, ed. D.N. Freedman, vol. 2, 145-59. New York: Doubleday, 1992.

—. "Hades, Hell." In *Anchor Bible Dictionary*, ed. D.N. Freedman. New York: Doubleday, 1992.

—. *The Climax of Prophecy: Studies on the Book of Revelation*. Edinburgh: T. & T. Clark, 1993.

—. "God who raises the Dead: The Resurrection of Jesus in relation to Early Christian Faith in God." In *The Resurrection of Jesus Christ*, ed. Paul Avis. London: Darton, Longman & Todd, 1993.

—. *The Theology of the Book of Revelation*. Cambridge, MA: Cambridge University Press, 1993.

—. *The Fate of the Dead: Studies on the Jewish and Christian Apocalypses*. Vol. XCIII. Supplements to Novum Testamentum, ed. C.K.Barret, J.K. Elliott, and M.J.J. Menken. Boston, MA: Brill, 1998.

Beale, G.K. *The Book of Revelation: A Commentary on the Greek Text*. NIGTC, ed. I. Howard Marshall and Donald A. Hagner. Grand Rapids, MI: Eerdmans, 1999.

Beare, F.W. "The Epistle to the Ephesians." *IB* 10 (1953): 597-749.

Beasley-Murray, G.R. *The Book of Revelation*. NCBC, ed. Matthew Black. Grand Rapids, MI: Eerdmans, 1981.

Beckwith, I.T. *The Apocalypse of John: Studies in Introduction with a Critical and Exegetical Commentary*. New York: Macmillan, 1919.

Behm, J. *Die Offenbarung des Johannes*. Göttingen: Vandenhoeck & Ruprecht, 1935.

Berkhof, L. *Systematic Theology*. 4th revised and enlarged ed. Grand Rapids, MI: Eerdmans, 1939, 1941.

Berkouwer, G.C. *The Work of Christ*. Grand Rapids, MI: Eerdmans, 1965.

Bertram, G. "Höllenfahrt Christi." *RGG* II (1968–70).

Best, E. *I Peter*. New Century Bible. Greenwood: Attic, 1971.

—. *A Critical and Exegetical Commentary on Ephesians*. ICC, ed. J.A. Emerton, C.E.B. Cranfield, and G.N. Stanton. Edinburgh: T. & T. Clark, 1998.

Beuken, W.A.M. "1 Samuel 28: The Prophet as 'Hammer of Witches'." *JSOT* 6: 3-17.

Bieder, W. *Die Vorstellung von der Höllenschaft Jesu Christi: Beitrag zur Entstehungsgeschichte der Vorstellung vom sogenannten Descensus ad inferos*. ATANT 19. Zürich: Zwingli-Verlag, 1949.

Bietenhard, H. "Hell, Abyss, Hades, Gehenna, Lower Regions." In *NIDNTT*, ed. Colin Brown. Grand Rapids, MI: Zondervan, 1976, 1986.

Bigg, C. *A Critical and Exegetical Commentary on the Epistles of St. Peter and St. Jude* ICC, ed. J.A. Emerton, C.E.B. Cranfield, and G.N. Stanton. Edinburgh: T. & T. Clark, 1956.

Blaiklock, E.M. *The Seven Churches: An Exposition of Revelation, Chapters two and three*. London: Marshall, Morgan & Scott, 19__.

Blass, F., and A. Debrunner. *A Greek Grammar of the New Testament and Other Early Christian Literature*. Translated by Robert W. Funk. Chicago: The University of Chicago Press, 1961.

Bloesch, D.G. "Descent into Hell (Hades)." In *Evangelical Dictionary of Theology*, ed. Walter A. Elwell, second ed., 338-340. Grand Rapids, MI: Baker Academic, 2001.

Blomberg, Craig L. *Matthew*. NAC, ed. David S. Dockery. Nashville, TN: Broadman Press, 1992.

Böcher, O. *Die Johannesapokalyse*. 2nd ed. Darmstadt: Wissenschaftliche Buchgesellschaft, 1980.

Bock, D.L. *Luke 9:51–24:53*. Vol. 3B. BECNT, ed. Moisés Silva. Grand Rapids, MI: Baker, 1996.

—. *Acts*. BECNT, ed. Robert W. Yarbrough and Robert H. Stein. Grand Rapids, MI: Baker Academic Press, 2007.

Bonner, Campbell, ed. *The Homily on the Passion by Melito Bishop of Sardis with Some Fragments of the Apocryphal Ezekiel*, vol. XII. Studies and Documents, ed. Kirsopp Lake and Silva Lake. Philadelphia: University of Pennsylvania Press, 1940.

Boring, M.E. *Revelation*. Interpretation: A Bible Commentary for Teaching and Preaching, ed. James L. Mays. Louisville, KY: John Knox Press, 1989.

Bornkamm, Günther. *Jesus of Nazareth*. New York: Harper, 1960.

Bouman, C.A. "He Descended into Hell." *Worship* 33 (1959): 194-203.

Bousset, W. *Kyrios Christos: A History of the Belief in Christ from the Beginnings of Christianity to Irenaeus*. Translated by John E. Steely. Nashville, TN: Abingdon Press, 1970.

Boxall, I. *The Revelation of Saint John*. Black's New Testament Commentaries, ed. Morna D. Hooker. London: Hendrickson, 2006.

Bradshaw, Paul F., Maxwell E. Johnson, and L. Edward Phillips. *The Apostolic Tradition: A Commentary*. Hermeneia, ed. Helmut Koester and Harold W. Attridge. Minneapolis, MN: Fortress Press, 2002.

Bremmer, Jan N. *The Rise and Fall of the Afterlife: The 1995 Read-Tuckwell Lectures at the University of Bristol*. New York: Routledge, 2002.

Brockwell, W.C. *Bishop Reginald Pecock and the Lancastrian Church: Securing the Foundations of Cultural Authority*. Vol. 25. Texts and Studies in Religion. Queenston, Ontario: Edwin Mellen, 1985.

Bromiley, G.W. "Descent into Hell (Hades)." In *The International Standard Bible Encyclopedia*, ed. Geoffrey W. Bromiley, vol. 1 A-D, 926-27. Grand Rapids, MI: Eerdmans.

Brooks, O.S. "1 Peter 3.21—The clue to the Literary Structure of the Epistle." *Nov. Test.* 16 (1974): 290-305.

Bröse, E. "Der Descensus ad inferos Eph. 4, 8-10." *NKZ* 9 (1898): 447-55.

Brown, Colin. "The Gates of Hell and the Church." In *Church, Word, and Spirit*, ed. James E. Bradley and Richard A. Muller, 15-43. Grand Rapids, MI: Eerdmans, 1987.

Brown, M.L. "רְפָאִים." In *NIDOTT*, ed. Willem A. VanGemeren, vol. 3, 1173-80. Grand Rapids, MI: Zondervan, 1997.

Brown, R.E. *The Death of the Messiah, from Gethsemane to the Grave: A Commentary on the Passion Narratives in the Four Gospels.* AB, ed. David Noel Freedman. New York: Doubleday, 1994.

———. "Eschatological Events Accompanying the Death of Jesus, Especially the Raising of the Holy Ones from Their Tombs (Matt 27:51–53)." In *Faith and the Future: Studies in Christian Eschatology,*, ed. John P. Galvin, 43-73. New York: Paulist, 1994.

———. with Karl P. Donfried, and John Reumann, eds. *Peter in the New Testament: A Collaborative Assessment by Protestant and Roman Catholic Scholars.* New York: Geoffrey Chapman, 1973.

Bruce, F.F. *The Acts of the Apostles: The Greek Text with Introduction and Commentary.* 3rd ed. Grand Rapids, MI: Eerdmans, 1990.

Büchsel, F. "κατωτερος." In *TDNT*, ed. G. Kittel and G. Friedrich, vol. 3, 640-42. Grand Rapids, MI: Eerdmans, 1964-1976.

Bultmann, R. "θάνατος." In *TDNT*, ed. G. Kittel and G. Friedrich, vol. 3, 8-25. Grand Rapids, MI: Eerdmans, 1964–1976.

———. *νεκρός.* Vol. 4. TDNT, ed. G. Kittel and G. Friedrich. Grand Rapids, MI: Eerdmans, 1964–1976.

Burgess, J. *A History of the Exegesis of Matthew 16:17-19 from 1781 to 1965.* Basel: Theological Dissertation, 1965.

Burkert, Walter. *Greek Religion.* Translated by John Raffan. Cambridge, MA: Harvard University Press, 1985.

Burn, A.E. *An Introduction to the Creeds.* London: Methuen, 1899.

Burns, J.B. "The Mythology of Death in the Old Testament." *Scottish Journal of Theology* 26 (1973): 327-40.

Cabaniss, A. "The Harrowing of Hell, Psalm 24 and Pliny the Younger: A Note." *Vigilae Christianae* 7 (1953): 65-74.

Caird, G.B. *A Commentary on the Revelation of St. John the Divine.* New York: Harper and Row, 1966.

———. *The Revelation of Saint John.* BNTC, ed. Henry Chadwick. Peabody, MA: Hendrickson, 1966.

Calvin, J. *Institutes of the Christian Religion.* Vol. 20-21. Library of Christian Classics, ed. John T. McNeill. Philadelphia: Westminster Press, 1960.

Casey, Robert P., ed. *The Excerpta Ex Theodoto of Clement of Alexandria.* Studies and Documents, ed. Kirsopp Lake and Silva Lake. Cambridge, MA: Harvard University Press, 1934.

Cassuto, U. *Biblical and Oriental Studies.* Translated by Israel Abrahams. Vol. II. Bible and Ancient Oriental Texts. Jerusalem: The Magnes Press, 1975.

Chaine, J. "La Descente du Christ aux Enfers." *DBSup* 2 (1934): 395-430.

Charles, R.H. *A Critical and Exegetical Commentary on the Revelation of St. John.* 2 vols. ICC, ed. J.A. Emerton, C.E.B. Cranfield, and G.N. Stanton. Edinburgh: T. & T. Clark, 1966.

Chilton, Bruce. "Shebna, Eliakim, and the Promise to Peter." In *The Social World of Formative Christianity and Judaism*, ed. Jacob Neusner, Ernest S. Frerichs, Peder Borgen, and Richard Horsley, 311-26. Philadelphia: Fortress Press, 1988.

Collins, Raymond F. "Keys of the Kingdom of Heaven." In *ABD*, ed. D.N. Freedman. New York: Doubleday, 1992.

Connell, Martin F. "*Descensus Christi ad inferos*: Christ's Descent to the Dead". *TS* 62 (2001): 262-82.

Conybeare, F.C. *The Apology and Acts of Apollonius and other Monuments of Early Christianity*. New York: Macmillan, 1894.

Cooper, A. "Ps 24:7-10: Mythology and Exegesis." *JBL* 102 (1983): 37-60.

Cooper, John W. *Body, Soul, and Life Everlasting: Biblical Anthropology and the Monism-Dualism Debate*. Grand Rapids, MI: Eerdmans, 1989.

Cullmann, Oscar. *Peter: Disciple, Apostle, Martyr*. Translated by Floyd V. Filson. Philadelphia: Westminster Press, 1953.

Dalton, W.J. *Christ's Proclamation to the Spirits: A Study of 1 Peter 3:18–4:6*. Rome: Pontifical Biblical Institute, 1965.

Danielou, J. *The Theology of Jewish Christianity*. Translated by J.A. Baker. Philadelphia: Westminster Press, 1964.

Davies, J.G. *He Ascended into Heaven: A Study in the History of Doctrine*. London: Lutterworth Press, 1958.

Davies, W.D., and Dale C. Allison Jr. *A Critical and Exegetical Commentary on the Gospel According to Saint Matthew*. Vol. 2: Commentary on Matthew VIII–XVIII. ICC, ed. J.A. Emerton, C.E.B. Cranfield, and G.N. Stanton. Edinburgh: T. &T. Clark, 1991.

Day, John. *Yahweh and the Gods and Goddesses of Canaan*. Journal for the Study of the Old Testament Supplement Series 265. Sheffield: Sheffield Academic Press, 2000.

"Descent." In *Dictionary of Biblical Imagery*, ed. Leland Ryken, James C. Wilhoit, and Tremper Longman III, 204-5. Downers Grove, IL: InterVarsity Press, 1998.

Deuteronomy. Translated by J. Rabbinowitz. Midrash Rabbah, ed. H. Freedman and Maurice Simon. New York: Soncino Press, 1983.

Doehler, Gottihilf. "The Descent into Hell." *The Springfielder* 39 (June 1975): 2-19.

Dublin, John. "The Descent into Hades and Christian Baptism (A Study of 1 Peter III.19 ff.)." *The Expositor* 8, 88 (April 1916): 241-74.

—. "The Gates of Hades." *The Expositor* 8, 88 (April 1916): 401-409.

Erickson, Millard J. *Christian Theology*. second ed. Grand Rapids, MI: Baker, 1998.

Ericson, Norman R. "Descent into Hell (Hades)." In *Evangelical Dictionary of Biblical Theology*, ed. Walter A. Elwell, 166-67. Grand Rapids, MI: Baker, 1996.

Exodus. Translated by S.M. Lehrman. Midrash Rabbah, ed. H. Freedman and Maurice Simon. New York: Soncino Press, 1983.

Fabry, H.-J. "מָוֶת." In *Theological Dictionary of the Old Testament*, vol. 8, 185-209. Grand Rapids, MI: Eerdmans, 1997.

Fiorenza, S. *The Book of Revelation: Justice and Judgment*. 2nd ed. Minneapolis: Fortress Press, 1998.

Ford, J.M. *Revelation: Introduction, Translation and Commentary*. Anchor Bible, ed. W.F. Albright and David N. Freedman. Garden City, NY: Doubleday, 1975.

France, R.T. *The Gospel of Matthew*. NICNT, ed. Ned B. Stonehouse, F.F. Bruce, and Gordon D. Fee. Grand Rapids, MI: Eerdmans Publishing, 2007.

Friedman, J. "Christ's Descent into hell and Redemption through Evil: A Radical Reformation Perspective." *Archiv für Reformations-geschichte* 76 (1985): 217-30.

Friesen, S. J. *Imperial Cults and the Apocalypse of John: Reading Revelation in the Ruins*. Oxford: Oxford University Press, 2001.

Galot, Jean. "Christ's Descent into Hell." *Theology Digest* 13 (1965): 89-94.

Gatch, M.M. "The Harrowing of Hell: A Liberation Motif in Medieval Theology and Devotional Literature." *Union Seminary Quarterly Review* 36 (1981): 75-88.

Gero, S. "The Gates and the Bars of Hades? A Note on Matthew 16:18." *NTS* 27 (April 1981): 411-14.

The Greek Magical Papyri in Translation. ed. Hans Dieter Betz. London: University of Chicago Press, 1986.

Grether, H.G. "Abyss." In *ABD*, ed. D.N. Freedman, vol. 1. New York: Doubleday, 1992.

Grillmeier, Aloys. *Christ in Christian Tradition: From the Apostolic Age to Chalcedon (451)*. Translated by John Bowden. Vol. I. Atlanta: John Knox Press, 1975.

Grudem, W.A. "He did not Descend into Hell: A Plea for Following Scripture Instead of the Apostles' Creed." *JETS* 34 (March 1991): 103-113.

Gschwind, Karl. *Die Niederfahrt Christi in der Unterwelt: Ein Beitrag zum Exegese des Neuen Testaments und zum Geschichte der Taufsymbols* Münster: Aschendorff, 1911.

Gundry, R.H. *Matthew: A Commentary on His Handbook for a Mixed Church under Persecution*. 2nd ed. Grand Rapids, MI: Eerdmans Publishing, 1994.

Hagner, D.A. *Matthew 14–28*. Vol. 33B. WBC, ed. David A. Hubbard, Ralph P. Martin, and John D.W. Watts. Dallas, TX: Word, 1995.

Hamilton, V.P. "שָׁחַת." In *TWOT*, ed. R. Laird Harris, Gleason L. Archer, and Bruce K. Waltke. Chicago: Moody Press, 1980.

Hanson, A.T. *The New Testament Interpretation of Scripture*. London: SPCK, 1980.

Harris, Hall W. III. *The Descent of Christ: Ephesians 4:7-11 and Traditional Hebrew Imagery*. Grand Rapids, MI: Baker, 1998.

Harris, R. "שְׁאוֹל." In *TWOT*, ed. Gleason L. Archer and Bruce K. Waltke. Chicago: Moody Press, 1999.

Harris, R.L. "Why Hebrew Sheol was Translated "Grave"." In *The NIV: The Making of a Contemporary Translation*, ed. Kenneth L. Barker. Grand Rapids, MI: Zondervan, 1986.

Heidel, A. *The Gilgamesh Epic and OT Parallels*. 2nd ed. Chicago: University of Chicago, 1949.

Heine, Ronald E., ed. *The Commentaries of Origen and Jerome on St Paul's Epistle to the Ephesians*. Oxford: Oxford University Press, 2002.

Heintz, J.-G. "חֵשַׁ." In *Theological Dictionary of the Old Testament*, vol. 1, 463-66. Grand Rapids, MI: Eerdmans, 1974.

Hemer, Colin J. *The Letters to the Seven Churches of Asia in Their Local Setting*. Journal for the Study of the New Testament Supplement Series 11, ed. David Hill. Sheffield: JSOT Press, 1986.

Hendricksen, W. *More Than Conquerors: An Interpretation of the Book of Revelation*. Grand Rapids, MI: Baker Academic, 1967.

Heppe, Heinrich. *Reformed Dogmatics: Set Out and Illustrated from the Sources*, ed. Ernst Bizer. Grand Rapids, MI: Baker, 1950.

Hesiod. *Theogony*. Translated by Apostolos N. Athanassakis. London: Johns Hopkins University Press, 1983.

Hiers, Richard H. "'Binding' and 'Loosing': The Matthean Authorizations." *JBL* 104 (1985): 233-50.

Himmelfarb, M. *Tours of Hell: An Apocalyptic Form in Jewish and Christian Literature*. Philadelphia: University of Pennsylvania Press, 1983.

Hodge, Charles. *Systematic Theology: Anthropology*. Vol. II. Peabody, MA: Hendrickson, 2008.

Horsley, G.H.R. *New Documents Illustrating Early Christianity:A Review of the Greek Inscriptions and Papyri Published in 1976*. Vol. I. North Ryde, N.S.W: The Ancient History Documentary Research Center, Macquarie University, 1981.

Horsley, Samuel. *Biblical Criticism of the First Fourteen Historical Books of the Old Testament; Also, on the First Nine Prophetical Books*. Vol. II. London: Longman, Brown, Green, & Longmans, 1844.

Ilarion, Hieromonk. *Christ the Conqueror of Hell: the Descent into Hades from an Orthodox Perspective*. Crestwood, NY: St. Vladimir's Seminary Press, 2009.

The Isaiah Targum. The Aramaic Bible, ed. Kevin Cathcart, Michael Maher, and Martin McNamara. Wilmington, DA: Michael Glazier, Inc., 1987.

Jeremias, J. "ἄβυσσος." In *TDNT*, ed. G. Kittel and G. Freidrich, vol. 1, 9. Grand Rapids, MI: Eerdmans, 1964–76.

—. "ᾅδης." In *TDNT*, ed. G. Kittel and G. Freidrich, vol. 1, 146-49. Grand Rapids, MI: Eerdmans, 1964–76.

—. "γεννα." In *TDNT*, ed. G. Kittel and G. Freidrich, vol. 1, 657-58. Grand Rapids, MI: Eerdmans, 1964–76.

—. "Παραδεισω." In *TDNT*, ed. G. Kittel and G. Freidrich, vol. 5, 765-73. Grand Rapids, MI: Eerdmans, 1964–76.

—. "πύλη." In *TDNT*, ed. G. Kittel and G. Friedrich, vol. 6, 921-28. Grand Rapids, MI: Eerdmans, 1964–76.

—. "κλείς." In *TDNT*, ed. G. Kittel and G. Freidrich, vol. 3, 743-53. Grand Rapids, MI: Eerdmans, 1964–1976.

Johnston, P.S. *Shades of Sheol: Death and Afterlife in the Old Testament*. Downer's Grove, IL: InterVarsity Press, 2002.

Keener, C.S. *Revelation*. NIVAC, ed. Terry Muck. Grand Rapids, MI: Zondervan, 2000.

Kelly, J.N.D. *Early Christian Creeds*. 3rd ed. London: Longman, 1972.

Kraft, H. *Die Offenbarung des Johannes*. Tübingen: Mohr-Siebeck, 1974.

Kroll, J. *Gott und Hölle: Der Mythos vom Descensuskampfe* Studien der Bibliothek Warburg 20. Leipzig-Berlin: B.G. Teubner, 1932.

Lachenschmid, Robert. "Christ's Descent into Hell." In *Sacra Mundi: An Encyclopedia of Theology*, ed. Karl Rahner, vol. 3 Habits to Materialism, 9-10, 1969.

Ladd, G.E. *A Commentary on the Revelation of John*. Grand Rapids, MI: Eerdmans, 1972.

Lewis, Jack P. "The Gates of Hell Shall Not Prevail against it" (Matt 16:18): A Study of the History of Interpretation." *JETS* 38 (1995): 349-67.

Lightner, Robert P. "Excursus: The Spirits in Prison in 1 Peter 3." In *Understanding Christian Theology*, ed. Charles R. Swindoll and Roy B. Zuck, 592-93. Nashville, TN: Thomas Nelson, 2003.

Lohse, E. *Die Offenbarung des Johannes*. Göttingen: Vandenhoeck & Ruprecht, 1976.

Loofs, F. "Descent to Hades (Christ's)." In *ERE*, ed. J. Hastings, vol. IV. Edinburgh: T. & T. Clark, 1908–1921.

Lucian. *Dialogues of the Dead*. Translated by M.D. Macleod. Vol. 7. Loeb Classical Library, ed. T.E. Page. Cambridge, MA: Harvard University Press, 1961.

MacCulloch, J.A. *The Harrowing of Hell: A Comparative Study of an Early Christian Doctrine*. Edinburgh: T. & T. Clark, 1930.

Marcus, J. "The Gates of Hades and the Keys of the Kingdom (Matt 16:18–19)." *CBQ* 50 (1988): 443-55.

Martínez, F. García, ed. *The Dead Sea Scrolls Translated: The Qumran Texts in English*. Translated by Wilfred G. E. Watson, 2nd ed. Grand Rapids, MA: Eerdmans, 1996.

McGiffert, A.C. *The Apostles' Creed: Its Origin, Its Purpose, and Its Historical Interpretation*. New York: Charles Scribner's Sons, 1902.

McLay, T.R. *The Use of the Septuagint in New Testament Research*. Grand Rapids, MI: Eerdmans, 2003.

Menard, J. "Le '*Descensus ad inferos*'." In *Ex Orbe Religionum: Studia Geo Widengren*, ed. C.J. Bleeker, S.G.F. Brandon, M. Simon, J. Bergman, K. Drynjeff, and H. Ringgren, vol. 2. Leiden: Brill, 1972.

Merrill, E. H. "מָוֶת." In *New International Dictionary of Old Testament Theology & Exegesis*, ed. Willem A. VanGemeren, vol. 2, 886-888. Grand Rapids, MI: Zondervan, 1997.

—. "שְׁאוֹל." In *NIDOTTE*, ed. Willem A. VanGemeren, vol. 4, 6-7. Grand Rapids, MI: Zondervan, 1997.

—. "שַׁחַת." In *NIDOTTE*, ed. Willem A. VanGemeren, vol. 4, 93-94. Grand Rapids, MI: Zondervan, 1997.

—. *Everlasting Dominion: A Theology of the Old Testament*. Nashville, TN: Broadman & Holman, 2006.

Metzger, B.M. *A Textual Commentary on the Greek New Testament*. New York: United Bible Societies, 1971.

Michaels, R.J. *Revelation*. IVP New Testament Commentary Series, ed. Grant R. Osborne. Downers Grove: InterVarsity Press, 1997.

The Midrash on Psalms. Translated by William G. Braude. Vol. 13. Yale Judaica Series, ed. Leon Nemoy. London: Yale University Press, 1959.

Morris, L. *The Book of Revelation: An Introduction and Commentary*. Tyndale New Testament Commentaries, ed. L. Morris. Grand Rapids, MI: Eerdmans, 1987.

Moulton, J.H., and G. Milligan. *The Vocabulary of the Greek Testament: Illustrated from the Papyri and Other Non-Literary Sources*. Grand Rapids, MI: Eerdmans, 1980.

Mounce, R.H. *The Book of Revelation*. NICNT, ed. Gordon D. Fee. Grand Rapids, MI: Eerdmans, 1977.

Muenscher, Joseph. "The Descent of Christ into Hell." *Bib Sac* 16 (1859): 309-353.

Murray, Robert. *Symbols of Church and Kingdom*. New Jersey: Gorgias Press, 2004.

Nicholas of Lyra's Apocalypse Commentary. Translated by Philip D.W. Krey. Kalamazoo, MI: Medieval Institute Publications, 1997.

Nolland, J. *The Gospel of Matthew*. NTGTC, ed. I. Howard Marshall and Donald A. Hagner. Grand Rapids, MI: Eerdmans, 2005.

The Old Testament Pseudepigrapha. vol. 1, ed. J.H. Charlesworth. Garden City, NY: Doubleday, 1983–85.

Oosterzee, J.J. Van. *Christian Dogmatics*. Translated by John Watson Watson and Maurice J. Evans. Vol. 2. New York: Charles Scribner's Sons, 1882.

The Orphic Hymns. Translated by Apostolos N. Athanassakis. Society of Biblical Literature Texts and Translations Graeco-Roman Religion Series, ed. Hans Dieter Betz and Edward N. O'Neil. Atlanta, GA: Scholars Press, 1977.

Osborne, G.R. *Revelation*. BECNT, ed. Moisés Silva. Grand Rapids, MI: Baker Academic, 2002.

Otto, R.E. "*Descendit in Inferna*: A Reformed Review of a Doctrinal Conundrum." *WTJ* 52 (1990): 143-50.

Pannenberg, Wolfhart. *The Apostle's Creed: In the Light of Today's Questions*. Philadelphia: Westminster Press, 1972.

—. *Jesus–God and Man*. Translated by Lewis L. Wilkins and Duane A. Priebe. 2nd ed. Philadelphia: Westminster Press, 1977.

Pearson, J. *An Exposition of the Creed*. Oxford: Oxford University Press, 1857.

Pindar. *The Odes of Pindar*. Loeb Classical Library, ed. T.E. Page. Cambridge, MA: Harvard University Press, 1915.

Pitstick, Alyssa Lyra. *Light in Darkness: Hans Urs von Balthasar and the Catholic Doctrine of Christ's Descent into Hell*. Grand Rapids, MI: Eerdmans, 2007.

Plummer, A. *An Exegetical Commentary on the Gospel according to St. Matthew*. Grand Rapids, MI: Baker, 1982.

Plumptre, E.H. *The Spirits in Prison: and Other Studies on the Life After Death.* New York: Thomas Wittaker, 1889.

Rad, G. von. *Old Testament Theology: The Theology of Israel's Prophetic Traditions.* Translated by D.M.G. Stalker. Vol. 2. London: Westminster John Knox Press, 1960,1965.

Rahner, Karl. *On the Theology of Death.* New York: Herder and Herder, 1961.

Rakow, Mary. "Christ's Descent into Hell: Calvin's Interpretation." *RL* 43 (1974): 218-226.

Ramsay, W.M. *The Letters to the Seven Churches,* ed. Mark W. Wilson. Peabody, MA: Hendrickson, 1994.

Reicke, Bo. *The Disobedient Spirits and Christian Baptism.* Copenhagen: Ejnar Munksgaard, 1946.

—. "Descent into Hell." In *The Oxford Companion to the Bible,* ed. Bruce M. Metzger and Michael D. Coogan, 163. Oxford: Oxford University Press, 1993.

Rohling, J.H. "Descent of Christ into Hell." In *NCE,* ed. Berard L. Marthaler, vol. 4 Com-Dyn, second ed., 683-686. Washington, D.C.: Thomson & Gale, 2003.

Rosenberg, R. *The Concept of Biblica Sheol within the Context of ANE Beliefs.* Ph.D. diss. Cambridge, MA: Harvard University Press, 1980.

Scaer, D.P. "He Did Descend into Hell: In Defense of the Apostles' Creed." *JETS* 35 (1992): 91-99.

Schaff, Philip. *The Creeds of Christendom: With a History and Critical Notes.* Vol. II The Greek and Latin Creeds. Grand Rapids: MI: Baker. Reprint, 2007.

Schuyler, E. "Did Christ Descend into Hades?". *Our Hope* 9 (1945): 599-604.

Seiss, J.A. *The Apocalypse: Lectures on the Book of Revelation.* Zondervan Commentary Series. Grand Rapids, MI: Zondervan, 1950.

Selwyn, E.G. *The First Epistle of St. Peter: The Greek Text with Introduction, Notes, and Essays.* 2nd ed. Grand Rapids, MI: Baker, 1981.

Shedd, W.G.T. *Dogmatic Theology.* Vol. II. New York: Charles Scribner's Sons, 1888.

Smalley, S.S. *The Revelation to John: A Commentary on the Greek Text of the Apocalypse.* Downers Grove: InterVarsity Press, 2005.

Smelik, K.A.D. "The Witch at Endor: 1 Samuel 28 in Rabbinic and Christian Exegesis till 800 A.D.". *VC* 33 (1979): 160-79.

Smith, Constance I. "*Descendit Ad Inferos*–Again." *JHI* 28 (1967): 87-88.

Smith, Henry P. *The Books of Samuel.* International Critical Commentary. Edinburgh: T. & T. Clark, 1969.

Smyth, E.C. "Is the 'Descensus' in the Apostles' Creed an 'Interpolation' and Superfluous?". *AR* II (1889): 414-24.

St. Maximus the Confessor's Questions and Doubts. Translated by Despina D. Prassas. Dekalb, IL: Northern Illinois University Press, 2010.

Stone, J.S. *The Glory After the Passion: A Study of the Events in the Life of our Lord from His Descent into Hell to His Enthronement in Heaven.* New York: Longmans, Green and Co., 1913.

Sullivan, L.E. "The Gates of Hell (Mt. 16:18)." *TS* 10 (1949): 62-64.

Suriano, Matthew J. "Underworld, Descent into the." In *The New Interpreter's Dictionary of the Bible*, ed. Katharine Doob Sakenfeld, vol. 5 S-Z, 710-12. Nashville, TN: Abingdon Press, 2009.

Sweet, J. *Revelation*. TPI New Testament Commentaries, ed. Howard Clark Kee and Dennis Nineham. Philadelphia: Trinity Press International, 1979.

Swete, H. B. *The Apostle's Creed: It's Relation to Primitive Christianity*. London: University Press, 1908.

—. *Commentary on Revelation*. Grand Rapids, MI: Kregel Publications, 1977.

Targum Neofiti I: Genesis. The Aramaic Bible, ed. Kevin Cathhart, Micheal Maher, and Martin McNamara. Collegeville, MN: Liturgical Press, 1992.

Targum Pseudo-Jonathan: Deuteronomy. The Aramaic Bible, ed. Kevin Cathcart, Michael Maher, and Martin McNamara. Collegeville, MN: Liturgical Press, 1998.

Thomas, R.L. *Revelation 1–8: An Exegetical Commentary*. Chicago: Moody Press, 1995.

—. *Revelation 8–22 an Exegetical Commentary*. Chicago: Moody Press, 1995.

"Tractate Sanhedrin." In *Hebrew-English Edition of the Babylonian Talmud*, ed. I. Epstein, trans. Jacob Shachter and H. Freedman. New York: Soncino Press, 1969.

"Tractate Shabbath." In *Hebrew-English Edition of the Babylonian Talmud*, ed. I. Epstein. New York: Soncino Press, 1972.

"Tractate Taanith." In *Hebrew-English Edition of the Babylonian Talmud*, ed. I. Epstein. New York: Soncino Press, 1969.

Tromp, N. J. *Primitive Conceptions of Death and the Nether World in the Old Testament*. Rome: Pontifical Biblical Institute, 1969.

Tsumura, David T. *The First Book of Samuel*. New International Commentary on the Old Testament, ed. R.K. Harrison and Robert L. Hubbard. Grand Rapids, MI: Eerdmans, 2007.

Turner, R. V. "'Descendit ad Inferos: Medieval Views on Christ's Descent into Hell and the Salvation of the Ancient Just." *JHI* 27 (1966): 173-94.

Ussher, J. "Limbus Patrum and Christ's Descent into Hell." In *Ussher's Works*, vol. 3, 278-419. London, 1847.

Wächter, L. "שׁאוֹל." In *Theological Dictionary of the Old Testament*, vol. 14, 239-48. Grand Rapids, MI: Eerdmans, 2004.

Wallace, Dewey D. "Puritan and Anglican: The Interpretation of Christ's Descent into Hell in Elizabethan Theology." *Achiv für Reformationsgeschichte* 69 (1978): 248-87.

Walvoord, J.F. *The Revelation of Jesus Christ*. Chicago: Moody Press, 1966.

Watts, J.D.W. *Isaiah 1–33*. Vol. 24. WBC, ed. David A. Hubbard, Glenn W. Barker, and J. D.W. Watts. New York: Word, 1985.

Wilcock, M. *I Saw Heaven Opened: The Message of Revelation*. BST, ed. John R.W. Stott. Illinois, TN: InterVarsity Press, 1975.

Williams, George H. *The Radical Reformation*. Philadelphia: Westminster Press, 1962.

Witsius, Herman. *Sacred Dissertations on What is Commonly Called the Apostles' Creed.* Translated by Donald Fraser. Vol. II. London: Khull, Blackie & Co., 1823. Reprint, 1993.

Wright, N.T. *The Resurrection of the Son of God.* Vol. 3 of Christian Origins and the Question of God. Minneapolis: Fortress Press, 2003.

Wright, Stephen Neill and Tom. *The Interpretation of the New Testament 1861–1986.* Second ed. Oxford: Oxford University Press, 2003.

Yates, J. "'He Descended into Hell': Creed, Article and Scripture." *Churchman* 102 (1988): 240-50, 303-15.

Young, Edward J. *The Book of Isaiah.* New International Commentary on the Old Testament, ed. R.K. Harrison. Grand Rapids, MI: Eerdmans, 1969.

INDEX OF AUTHORS

SCRIPTURE INDEX

133

117:19   27 n.43
117:20   27 n.43
118   15 n.59
118:18   26 n.37
118:19   27 n.43
118:20   27 n.43
134:6   60 n.57
135:6   60 n.57
138   15 n.59
138:8   27, 27 n.41, 87 n.87
138:15   85 n.80
139:8   27, 27 n.41, 78 n.60, 87 n.87
139:8-9   118 n.71
139:15   85 n.80
141:7   68
142:7   26 n.35, 68
143:7   26 n.35
146:4   50 n.10
147:7   60 n.57
148:7   60 n.57
152:2   29 n.48, 60 n.59
152:6   29 n.48, 60 n.59
153:3   29 n.48, 60 n.59

Proverbs
1:12   27 n.42
2:18   25 n.33; 26 n.37; 27 n.42, n.44
2:18-19   27
3:20   60 n.57
5:5   26 n.37; 27; 27 n.42, n.44
7:27   26 n.37; 27; 27 n.42, n.44; 49 n.4; 67 n.5
8:24   60 n.57
8:36   26 n.37
9:18   25 n.33, 27, 27 n.42, 87 n.87
10:2   26 n.37
11   26 n.37
11:19   26 n.37
12:28   26 n.37
13:14   26
14:12   27 n.42
14:19   27 n.43
14:27   26

15:11   27, 27 n.42, 28
15:24   27, 27 n.42
16:14   26
16:25   27 n.42
18:6   26
18:21   26 n.37
21:6   26
21:16   25, 25 n.33, 27
23:4   26 n.37
23:14   23 n.13
24:8   26
27:20   27, 28
29:4   27 n.42
30:16   27 n.42, 61

Ecclesiastes
2:5   51 n.13, 52, 53 n.21
7:3   56 n.40
7:14   56 n.40
9:3   31 n.59
9:5   31 n.59
9:10   23 n.18, 27 n.41, 31 n.59
12:7   50 n.10

Song of Solomon
4:13   51 n.13, 52, 53 n.21
8:6   26, 27, 27 n.44

Isaiah
1:22   69
1:30   51 n.13, 53 n.21
1:31   63, 63 n.70
3:3   69
4:14   69
5:13   27
7:11   23 n.13, 87 n.87
8:17   69
9:1   26 n.37
9:6-7   44 n.54
9:7   26
12:17   69
14:2   89 n.99
14:9   25 n.33, 27
14:9-11   25, 68
14:11   27 n.41, 67 n.5, 87 n.87
14:12   46 n.60

136

137

138

141

142

144

145

SUBJECT INDEX

passion of, 95, 115; preaching of, 2, 3, 7n.32, 9, 9n.36, 10, 11, 12, 12n.48, 13, 14, 15, 16n.72, 18, 56, 57, 58, 64, 85, 86, 87, 89, 91, 92-94, 94n.147, 95, 101, 115; pre-existence of, 87; resurrection of, 2, 3, 3n.11, 7, 7n.32, 16, 22n.17, 29, 45, 55, 64, 65, 67, 69, 70n.48, 73n.57, 74, 75, 77, 81, 84, 87, 88, 89, 89n.119, 91n.134, 93, 95, 97, 98, 100, 101, 103, 104, 106, 110, 111, 112, 113, 114, 115, 116; soul of, 2, 6, 13, 29, 55, 70, 70n.48, 73n.57, 73n.59, 87n.110, 97; suffering of, 94; triumph (victory) of, 3, 8n.34, 11, 14, 15, 17, 18, 27, 28, 37, 64, 65, 71, 77, 81, 83n.95, 83n.98, 85, 87n.110, 92, 93, 94, 95, 97, 98, 100, 101, 102n.31, 102n.35, 103, 103n.37, 104, 107, 111, 112, 112n.79, 113, 114n.85, 115, 117;

Chrysostom, John, 15, 16, 82, 83, 113

church, 28, 37, 38, 39n.44, 40, 44, 84, 100

Clement of Alexandria, 11-12, 11n.46, 13, 18, 71, 85, 91

community, (new, eschatological), 37, 38, 39, 40, 67, 68, 70

Council of Constantinople, 6n.24

Council of Niké, 6n.24

Council of Toledo, 6n.24, 12n.47

Cyprian, 13, 66, 71

Cyril of Alexandria, 15

Cyril of Jerusalem, 15

Dante, 16

Death, 2, 3, 3n.11, 5, 11, 13, 14, 15, 18, 21-30, 35, 37, 38n.35, 39, 40, 44, 45, 84, 98, 99, 100, 101, 102, 103, 104, 106, 107,

108, 109, 110, 111, 111n.74, 112, 112n.79, 113, 114, 114n.85, 115, 116, 117

Descensus, 1, 2, 2n.9, 3, 3n.11, 4, 5, 6, 7, 8, 8n.34, 9n.38, 11, 11n.46, 12, 13, 15, 16, 16n.72, 17, 18, 38, 39, 39n.43, 47, 66, 66n.29, 68, 74, 75, 80, 81, 84, 85, 96, 97, 100, 102, 103, 107-108, 108n.59, 115

descent myths, 62-63, 64

Edwards, Jonathan, 99

Ephram the Syrian, 14

Epiphanius, 97

Erasmus, 17

Epistle of the Apostles, the, 10

eschatology, 42, 49, 50, 94

faith, 95

forgiveness, 10

Formula of Concord, the, 17

Fortunatus, Venantius, 16

Fourth Lateran Council, the, 16

Gehenna, 4, 5n.21, 17n.88, 45, 45n.1, 58-61, 76

God's anger, 26

gospel, the, 12, 13, 67, 85-86, 92, 94, 94n.146, 95, 98, 101, 115

Gospel of Nicodemus, the, 14

Gospel of Peter, the, 9

Greco-Roman world, the, 3, 22, 30, 31, 32, 57, 80, 92, 115

Gregory of Nazianzus, 15

Gregory the Great, 16

Hades, 2, 3, 3n.11, 5, 5n.21, 6, 6n.26, 7, 8, 8n.34, 9, 9n.38, 10, 11, 12, 13, 14, 15, 16, 18, 20-21, 22-30, 27n.49, 34, 35, 36, 37, 39, 40, 41, 44, 46, 64, 65n.23, 66n.30, 68, 70, 71, 72, 74, 87n.110, 97, 98, 99, 100, 102, 103, 104, 106, 107, 108, 109,

Made in the USA
Columbia, SC
02 April 2024

33942868R00091